EXPECTING TO DIE

Center Point
Large Print

Also by Lisa Jackson and available from
Center Point Large Print:

Wicked Ways
Sinister
After She's Gone
Never Die Alone
Deserves to Die

**This Large Print Book carries the
Seal of Approval of N.A.V.H.**

LISA JACKSON

EXPECTING TO DIE

CENTER POINT LARGE PRINT
THORNDIKE, MAINE

Library of Congress Cataloging-in-Publication Data

Names: Jackson, Lisa, author.
Title: Expecting to die / Lisa Jackson.
Description: Center Point Large Print edition. | Thorndike, Maine : Center Point Large Print, 2017.
Identifiers: LCCN 2016059548 | ISBN 9781683243304 (hardcover : alk. paper)
Subjects: LCSH: Large type books. | GSAFD: Mystery fiction.
Classification: LCC PS3560.A223 E96 2017 | DDC 813/.54—dc23
LC record available at https://lccn.loc.gov/2016059548

ACKNOWLEDGMENTS

Special thanks to Bre Casey of Texas
who submitted the winning name
for Regan Pescoli and Nate Santana's baby,
who arrives in this book!

CHAPTER 1

She was a dead woman.

He would kill her. *Kill* her.

She glanced down at the wand from the pregnancy test kit and saw once again that yes, she was pregnant. Then she looked into the mirror over the sink of the public bathroom at the local Walgreens and stared at her reflection. Wide, scared blue eyes peered back at her beneath a fringe of pale bangs.

You. A mother. At seventeen . . . well, eighteen by the time the baby gets here.

Her throat grew thick and she blinked back tears. She couldn't cry, not now. There was plenty of time for that later. She slapped the tears away, sniffed, then stuffed the wand into her purse and stuffed the packaging deep into the trash bin beneath a wad of paper towels. Not that it mattered, she told herself. No one knew her here. She'd driven to Missoula for the test, taken it here in the restroom, and now had to drive home.

What was she going to do?

Oh. Dear. God.

Cheeks flaming, feeling as if everyone in the aisles of the store knew her secret, she hurried to the front door and nearly tripped over a boy stocking shelves with cans of hair spray and sticks of deodorant in an overflowing metal cart.

"Hey!" he said sharply, and she mumbled a hasty, "Sorry," on her way past the counter, where pharmacists in lab coats were filling prescriptions and two people waited near the register to pick up their meds.

Through the glass doors and into the August sunshine she flew, then found her way to the car, her mother's ancient Ford Taurus, and hopped into the sweltering interior. She switched on the ignition, threw the car into reverse, and as she hit the gas, she heard a sharp beep and stood on the brakes, just in time before she nearly clipped the fender of a Honda cutting through the lot. The driver, a brunette woman in sunglasses and a baseball cap, flipped up her middle finger as she swept by.

Destiny didn't care.

Let the girl flip her off.

She had more important issues to deal with.

Pregnant. You're pregnant.

Oh. No.

A baby? She couldn't handle a baby. No way, and it's not as if the father would be any help. Oh, Lord . . . the father. He would be pissed.

She took three deep breaths, rolled down the window as the for-crap air conditioner wasn't working, eased out of the parking space more carefully, managed not to scrape a fender or crumple a bumper, and wended the old Taurus out of the crowded lot.

Maybe she wouldn't tell him. Just have the baby by herself . . . but how? She couldn't tell Mom and Dad, and she couldn't just wish the baby away.

The thought of abortion skated on sharp wheels through her mind, cutting deep. But only for a brief moment and she banished it. No—her cousin had an abortion once and never forgave herself. And then there was Mom. How many times had she admitted that Destiny was not only a happy surprise, but a "miracle baby," whom she'd christened with her name for that very reason? It had been the only instance Helene Montclaire had ever gotten pregnant in some twenty-odd years of marriage. Despite the fact that she and Destiny's father, Glenn, had hoped and prayed for a sibling for their only daughter, it had never happened. Helene had even broken down once, tears of anguish filling her eyes with the frustration of not being able to bear another child.

So the thought of terminating this tiny little life was out of the question. There had to be a better option, she decided, as she hit the gas and made it through an amber light, then started south on the highway out of town.

She could give it up for adoption, she thought, squinting against the glare. She fished in the glove box for a pair of sunglasses with one hand while she drove, sliding the Ray-Bans onto her nose. She came up too fast on a hay truck, so she eased off the accelerator.

That's what she would do, right? Go to a lawyer and set up a . . . oh, crap, that's what would happen after she had the baby. What about before? When she was hugely pregnant? She wouldn't be able to hide it for too many months. She was slim and a baby bump would be noticeable and . . .

And there was the baby's father to deal with.

"Damn it." *He* would be a problem.

Or . . . would he? There was a chance . . . oh, dear Lord, no . . . She swallowed back a new fear. Wouldn't let her mind travel down that dark, insidious path.

If only this were a dream. A really bad nightmare.

After turning on the radio, she played with the stations, heard bits of songs she didn't recognize, then clicked it off, all the while staring through the bug-splattered windshield, wondering what the hell she was going to do.

She glanced at her worried eyes in the rearview, but wasn't sure. Shouldn't she keep it? What was it the reverend had always told her in one of their counseling sessions? When she had a problem? To think about it. Yes. And pray. Talk it over with God.

"You're stronger than you know, Destiny," he'd said in his smooth voice, then gently touched her hair, letting his fingers slide down to the back of her neck before withdrawing his hand quickly. As if she'd burned him. Or as if he'd had a sudden attack of conscience. Or as if someone was coming up the stairs to this, his private office, located under the sharply pitched roof near the bell tower. And the stairs had squeaked, announcing the arrival of his wife.

As if she'd known.

Destiny took a breath. She would take his advice, talk things over with God and then decide how to handle the problem. No, not a problem. A baby wasn't a problem. This was just a situation. A "mere stumbling block in the road of life" was how the reverend would put it.

The fifty miles or so to Grizzly Falls went by in a blur of western Montana farmland, fences, grazing cattle and horses. She drove straight down the valley, turned toward the mountains, and didn't even remember crossing the bridge that spanned the Grizzly River.

She managed to make it home and avoid too many questions from her mother, who was canning peaches in the kitchen, before holing up in her bedroom. The house was hot and smelled of sugar, and Destiny flopped on her bed and tuned in to her private thoughts, talking with God a bit but still coming up with no answer.

She did arrive at a plan of action, however, so after a dinner of cold ham and potato salad, fresh peaches and cream, she told her folks she was going for a walk.

Her mother seemed worried, but didn't argue, just fanned herself with a leaflet the Jehovah's

Witnesses had dropped by earlier in the week and sat in "her" recliner. Destiny's father was already tuned in to the television, the footrest of his La-Z-Boy already elevated, his reading glasses on the tip of his nose, newspapers spread on the table next to his chair and spilling onto the sculpted carpet Mom had picked out a year or so after Destiny had been born.

Another typical night at the Montclaire home.

Except that their only daughter was, as near as she could figure, about eight weeks pregnant. She wondered if there was some kind of app on her phone that would tell her precisely when she'd gotten pregnant.

That would help a lot.

By the time she set out, her parents barely looked up. The house was surrounded by the fields of neighboring spreads, and she set out across the Joneses' south pasture. Until a few weeks earlier, the fenced acres had been covered with lush hay, green stalks that had shimmered silver in the breeze, but the crop had been harvested. Now, she trod across the sun-bleached stubble that remained.

At the far side of the field, she slipped through the sagging barbed wire, then headed into the woods. Familiar woods, a place she'd always thought of as a sanctuary. In the shade, the temperature dropped a bit, but the air was still warm. Dry. Smelling of pine and dust.

Out of sight of the windows of her parents' home, she studied the screen on her cell phone, sent out three texts, and called Donny.

As she waited for him to pick up, she listened to the sounds of the forest, the whisper of pine branches overhead, the flutter of birds amidst the trees, the soft chortles and chirps they emitted a balm to her fevered thoughts.

No answer. She didn't leave a voice message. Couldn't.

She glanced at the face of her phone and saw no quick responses to her texts.

Of course *he* was mad at her.

He was always mad lately.

She texted Donny next and told him she was heading to "their" spot up near the reservoir. She asked him to meet her or text her, then headed up the hiking trail that led over the hill. The trail was steep, a rigorous climb that took over twenty minutes, and she was sweating by the time she wound up the switchbacks to the ridge. From there, it was a quick climb down. She paused. Caught her breath. Gathered her courage. Noticed how dark the woods had become.

The sun had settled over the western mountains, and long shadows were fingering through the stands of pine, hemlock, and aspen. The birds had quieted, and there were a few bats swooping overhead. The silence was strange and . . .

Snap!

She turned at the sound of a twig breaking.

The hairs on the back of her nape lifted.

Nothing. It's nothing!

She squinted, her gaze racing from one thicket to the next, but nothing moved, no animal showed itself. Not even a rabbit or racoon stirred in the thickening umbra, at least none she could see.

Just your imagination.

You're freaked, that's it.

And yet suddenly she felt something wasn't quite right in this all-too-still forest, this place where she'd come for solace.

She bit her lip as she remembered every damned zombie, werewolf, and vampire movie on TV she'd ever watched about a girl alone in the wilderness.

Stop it!

Making one last sweep of the area and seeing nothing out of place, she continued, but goose bumps raised on the back of her arms, and she felt as if hidden eyes were following her every move.

It's nothing.

She kept telling herself that over and over, but her willing mind went to images of snarling cougars and black bears, maybe wolves, too. Hadn't they been reintroduced or something? Hadn't she heard about that in school or something? And what about bobcats and . . . oh, God, snakes. *Rattlers.* Hadn't her father told her they hunted at night? Or was she wrong?

Oh. Shit.

Relax. You know this place. You've never *encountered anything scarier than a porcupine waddling through the brush, right?*

Nerves tight as bowstrings, she kept moving, deeper into the woods, her ears straining, her pulse pounding. She heard nothing more, no footfalls, no rustling through the undergrowth, no heavy breathing, but still she *felt* those eyes upon her.

As darkness encroached, she chanced the flashlight app on her cell phone to make certain she was sticking to the trail. Of course she was almost out of battery life, and she didn't want anyone or any*thing* to see her anyway, so she used the light sparingly as she made her way to the canyon floor.

She heard and smelled the creek before she saw it, a dark ribbon slicing through the woods. The path she was following downhill bled into a dusty trail that ran along the banks of the creek, which serpentined through this part of the canyon floor. When she reached the intersection, she turned upstream, walking quickly, hearing the water gurgle and splash over stones before it eddied in deeper pools, imagining the sound of footsteps following behind, though every time she stopped suddenly, she heard nothing.

She let out her breath.

You're an idiot. An idiot who has psyched herself out. This is all just because you're nervous, you know. No one is following you. No bloodthirsty creature is hunting you. No zombies are walking stiff-legged over this rough terrain. No, Destiny, the only freak out here tonight is you . . . pregnant, stupid you.

So much for a mental pep talk, she thought as she continued. Through sparse pine and hemlock thickets, she made her way to the spot he'd agreed to meet her, where the trees gave way to a parking area, rarely used any longer, the gravel that had once covered the lot now choked with dry weeds.

Could she tell him?

Swallowing hard, she gathered her courage.

She wouldn't just blurt out that she was pregnant. No. She would measure how angry he was first and take it slow. Besides . . . who could tell what he would do? And then there was her little lie . . . well, make it a *big* lie. She licked her lips and almost turned around and ran, abandoning the meeting. Because of his lightning-quick temper . . . maybe this wasn't the best plan.

Before she could decide, she heard the rumble of a large engine. Too late. Turning toward the access road, she saw the beams of headlights splashing against the trunks of the surrounding trees. Her heart went into overdrive. No, this was a bad idea. A really bad idea. He would go ballistic.

She should never have contacted him.

She wasn't ready to confess the truth. Reflexively, one hand went to her flat abdomen.

That was the problem; she often reacted before thinking things through. Wasn't that what Mom was always telling her?

This was wrong. All wrong. Meeting him up here alone with the coming night. No one knowing where they were. And it wasn't as if she could text or call as her cell needed charging. Stupid! It would have been smarter to risk a public scene, maybe give him the news at a coffee shop, or a park full of people or somewhere that was public, so he wouldn't . . .

Oh, Destiny, what have you done? Do not tell him. Not tonight. Be nice, don't cause a fight. Remember, you broke up with him. You've got the upper hand. And he's majorly pissed off.

Maybe she could just take off, before he saw her.

The Jeep rolled to a stop and she was caught in the headlights.

She steeled herself and stepped out of the beams.

He let the Jeep idle, headlights illuminating a conical area in front of the rig as he stepped out. She saw him in the thin glow cast by the interior light, an alarm dinging to remind him that he hadn't turned out the headlights. No doubt about it. He was a big man. Muscular. Strong. A college athlete.

But he wouldn't be carrying a weapon, would

he? He wouldn't bring a gun or a knife or . . .

Every muscle in her body tightened as he slammed the door.

"Des?" he called, his voice a harsh whisper.

"Right here."

He saw her then and approached, dwarfing her. "What did you want?"

She couldn't do it; she couldn't tell him. Not about the baby. Not here. Not tonight. "I, um, thought we should talk."

"About what?" He was still angry, his words clipped.

"You know."

"About you breaking up with me in a text? About that?" he guessed and yeah, he was pissed.

She shrank inwardly as he went on. "You know what? When it happened? When I got the text? I thought it was a joke, that someone had gotten your phone and fuckin' pranked me. Like it was real funny. Ha-ha-ha."

"I know."

"It was a chicken-shit thing to do, Des," he charged, his voice a little higher as his anger increased. "By fucking text? Really? Fuck me!"

"I should have talked to you."

"Hell, yeah, you should have. But you didn't. Just fired off a chicken-shit text and ended it." He spat in the ground. "So what's this about, Des? Tonight? Why did you want to meet up here?"

She heard the derision in his voice, felt his fury radiating from him.

"Are you . . . are you like trying to get back with me or something? Because no way. No damn way. It's over! Hear me?" He took a step toward her and she stood her ground, even though she was shrinking inside. She wasn't going to let him see that he frightened her.

"I just want to know why," she lied, knowing now she couldn't, wouldn't, dare tell him about the baby. Not here. Not alone. "Why you cheated, huh? With that girl at college, Veronica *bitch* or whatever?"

"I told you she meant nothing to me." But he was a little shocked at the turn in the conversation.

"Yeah, well, I heard you were staying over at her apartment, like, all the time." Her turn to be angry. "That you practically lived at her place."

"You want to go there, Des? Really? About seeing other people?" He was close now, looming over her.

Looking up, she could see his eyes for the first time, burning bright in his sockets, catching the light from the Jeep's headlights. "Because we both know that you've been slutting around."

"What? No! Who told you that?"

"I have friends down here," he snarled. "Don't you think they keep me informed, let me know what's what?" His jaw was tight, his teeth flashing white as he spoke.

19

She remembered seeing him so mad once he'd kicked a dent into the side of Emmett Tufts's Honda. Another time, he'd physically beat the crap out of Bryant Tophman for hitting on her at a party.

"Your friends lie."

"Not about this!" He pointed an accusing finger at her, wagged it toward himself and back at her. "Not about us! You want to know why?" Before she could answer, he said, "Because, you know what, Des? It was important to me." A muscle worked in his jaw. "A helluva lot more important to me than it was to you." He leaned down, his face a little closer to hers, and she smelled the beer on his breath, the sweat on his skin. "Now that it's all out in the open, you lying little bitch, it's over for good. Now you don't have to sneak around anymore. You can fuck anyone you want to—"

Smack!

She reacted. Just hauled off and slapped him so hard across the jaw that she felt the bristles of his beard shadow.

Oh, crap. Why had she—?

He froze. His eyes blinked, disbelieving. Then his fists balled and she didn't wait. Spinning, she took off the way she'd come, back down the path that ran by the creek, her feet flying in the dust.

He was a foot taller than she was, his stride immense and fast as lightning, but she was quick and agile and knew these woods like the back of her hand. She sprinted, adrenaline firing her blood, sending her feet pounding on the trail.

Run, run, run!

She heard him behind her, yelling at her, chasing her down.

"I'll fucking kill you!" he roared and she believed him. With every breath in her, she believed that if he caught her when he was this furious, he'd murder her with his bare hands, the very hands that had touched her and caressed her and turned her inside out with wanting.

Don't even go there! Just freakin' run!

Ducking branches, she cut around a tree, a few seconds later heard a thud, then a cry of pain. Probably a limb smacking him in the face, maybe the eyes. If only! That's what she needed, pine needles piercing his eyes, half-blinding him and stopping him.

She sped on, thought she might have lost him at the juncture where the trail split, one spur heading uphill. But she was wrong.

Footsteps pounded, shaking the earth and sounding as if he were right behind her.

Noooo!

She turned up the hill, took two steps, and felt a huge hand on her shoulder, fingers tight.

Stumbling, she tried to scramble away, to get her footing, but it was too late. He had her. He spun her around and in the darkness, she tried to see his face, to plead with him, to tell him she was sorry, but she couldn't see him at all.

Hands closed over her throat as she tried to scream.

All that came out were gurgling, sputtering sounds and she couldn't breathe. He was squeezing so hard. She fought, tearing at the hands on her throat, trying to dislodge the steely fingers that cut off her air, realizing belatedly that he was wearing gloves. That he'd planned this!

Her lungs felt as if they'd explode. She needed air!

Oh, God, please, stop! Please don't. . . .

Frantically she kicked and flailed, unable to land any solid blows, wishing she could thrust a foot or knee into his groin.

The bastard was really going to kill her. Strangle her!

Her lungs were on fire, the pain excruciating, the night-dark trees swimming in her vision.

Panicked, she clawed at his gloved hands. If she could bite him, kick him, scratch the hell out of him . . . All she could think about was drawing in a breath, just one. But there was nothing.

She was desperate for air, her lungs screaming, her brain pulsing against the skull.

Dear God, please, please help me. Save me. Save my baby.

Her eyes felt as if they would pop out of her

head and her arms became useless, swinging without any force as the blackness began to swallow her. She struggled, but it was useless, she could do nothing, her arms and legs still, the pain receding as she began to lose consciousness.

No . . . No . . . My baby . . . My precious . . .

Then she was gone.

CHAPTER 2

This was a stupid idea.

Make that a *really* stupid idea.

Bianca Pescoli ran through the darkened forest with only a weak shaft of moonlight as her guide. She'd been a fool to agree to come here, in the middle of the night, lying to her parents, for what? Some sick kind of game in the woods? Frowning, she slapped away a mosquito as the heat of the summer simmered through the Bitterroots and the sound of crickets was a low hum. Faintly, from a distance, she thought she heard the sound of voices, but then there was silence. Just the crickets. She decided to stick as closely to the trail as possible, that way she wouldn't get lost.

At least she hoped not.

Up, up, up, she loped, the path dusty, rocks poking through the dry soil, a canopy of pine branches nearly destroying what there was of the moonlight. Why had she agreed to this? she wondered for about the millionth time as her legs began to ache.

The idea had been Maddie's. Make that Madison Leona Averill, Bianca's heretofore best friend. Well, after tonight, maybe she'd change all that. Maddie's status was about to go down. Big time.

A branch slapped her in the face and she let out a yelp, then bit back any more noise as she didn't want to be heard. That was the whole point of the game, an idiotic teenage version of hide-and-seek, up here at Reservoir Point. Again, it was dumb. She rubbed her cheek where the pine limb had hit her and swore under her breath. Her calves ached and her lungs had started to burn with her run up the hill.

She should never have come, she knew that now, but it was too late to back out. A group of kids from school had come up with the brainstorm of meeting at midnight at the lower parking lot of the wilderness that abutted the Long property, where Bianca's stepfather worked as a manager. That was another problem. If Nate Santana ever got wind of the fact that Bianca was one of the kids who trespassed across the Long property to get to this spot, he would have a fit and probably ground her for life or something—that was, if her mother didn't kill her first.

She was reaching the highest point on the trail, where the path jogged around several massive

24

trees, and she slowed a bit, catching her breath, glancing over her shoulder to the darkness below. For a second, she was certain someone was following her, chasing her up this ridge, and her nerves pulled tight. Even though that was the whole point, that a random boy would "catch" her, it was scary. She didn't know who was behind her. Or what. Her pursuer could be a moron of a teenager or it could be a deer or an elk. Maybe a mountain lion, even a bear. Right now, an innocent rabbit hopping through the underbrush was enough to scare her to death. Anything larger would give her a heart attack.

Get over yourself.

She swallowed hard and slowed, taking in deep breaths, feeling the forest close in on her. Cautiously, she looked over her shoulder, her gaze piercing the blackness. Was that a pair of eyes staring at her from beneath a nearby tree, or just her imagination?

Her insides went cold. She stopped breathing.

Don't panic. Remember: this is just a game. You grew up in these woods.

The eyes disappeared as if swallowed in the malevolent darkness.

Oh. God.

A twig snapped in the summer night.

What?

A musky smell wafted toward her. She peered into the gloom, squinted at the shadows and heard a low warning growl that caused the hairs on her nape to rise.

What the hell is that?

She didn't take the time to find out.

Bianca bolted.

Fear propelled her. Up the hillside, the sensation that she was being followed by something malevolent driving her upward. Her feet slipped a little and she pitched forward, caught her balance, and kept moving. Ahead, the trail would crest on the ridge, then wind its way down the backside of the mountain. She'd end up in Desperation Flats, which wasn't a lot better.

Did she hear footsteps? Heavy breathing? More growling. In the distance, she heard the howl of a coyote and her blood froze in her veins.

Run! Faster!

She sprinted wildly, crazily, one foot in front of the other, panic gripping her, her breath coming in short gasps, her legs cramping, her damned lungs burning.

Go! Go! Go! Don't stop.

Upward she raced, driving forward until her lungs felt as if they might explode, and she came to a narrow spot where the trail twisted between two huge boulders. She flung herself against one. Gasped for air. Was certain a bloodthirsty demon, the kind she'd been reading about in her latest horror novel, was on her tail and ready to leap out at her to rip her face off.

She looked back over her shoulder, ready to square off with the otherworldly creature or lunatic or creep of a teenager, only to find nothing but the engulfing black night, the forest of towering pines and scrub brush, the heat of August settling like a shroud.

No footsteps pounded up the path, no labored breathing echoed through the night, no guttural sounds of a beast's warning reached her ears.

She saw and heard nothing. No bat wings. No frantic footsteps of kids in the forest. No breath of wind moving the branches. Even the coyote had stopped its lonely cry.

Which was weird. Less than an hour ago, there had been at least fifteen kids when they started the stupid game, maybe closer to twenty. Who counted? All she knew was that she was with a group of teenagers who had collected in the scrubby area that had once been a parking area for some of the Long family's lumber business. Cars and trucks had been parked haphazardly over the sparsely strewn, weed-choked gravel, music pulsing from the speakers of Austin Reece's car, a BMW, the only one in the mix of beaters, pickups, and ancient SUVs. Kids had been hanging out in clusters, some drinking, more smoking, some toking it up, she guessed from the skunk-like odor of weed mingling with the more acrid scent of cigarettes. A low murmur of conversation, punctu-ated by laughter, had rumbled across the open area while silhouettes moved across the smoky beams of headlights from some of the vehicles. Red tips of cigarettes and the glow of cell phone screens indicated where others had been gathering.

Bianca knew some of the girls. Red-haired Simone Delaney had been in her English class and Seneca Martinez, who had been on the track team, lived just down the road from the little cottage in the woods where Bianca had grown up. They'd ridden the bus together all through grade school. But they weren't close now. And Lindsay Cronin? She was okay but always followed along with the crowd. You just didn't know where you stood with her. One minute she was your best friend, the next your enemy. So weird.

Maddie had come to one of these parties before, and her reason was simple: she hoped to hook up with Teej O'Hara. As if she had a chance.

Come on, Maddie. Get real. Everyone knows that Teej is half in love with Lara Haas. And even he has to stand in line.

Lara was definitely the "it" girl of Bianca's class. And Teej, with his quick, killer smile, athletic body, and sharp wit, was out of Maddie's league, at least in his inflated opinion of himself. Bianca suspected Maddie knew she was being used, but didn't care, or thought it was a way to make TJ fall in love with her.

Oh, sure.

While they'd hung out before the game had started, Maddie had barely shown interest in what Bianca had been saying, and it wasn't just because even then Bianca had second-guessed the idea of the party.

"I really should get back," she'd said. "This doesn't look good."

"Stop being such a wuss." Maddie's fingers had still clutched her phone, her head moving slightly, her eyes squinting as she surveyed the group that had gathered.

"He's over there. By Reece," Bianca whispered back, hitching her chin to a clutch of boys passing around what appeared to be a bottle on the far side of Reece's Beemer. With its parking lights giving off an unearthly golden light, a throbbing beat coming from its speakers, the silver car was the hub of the party. "He's with Castillo and Devlin," Bianca added. "Big surprise." Those two were always hanging around Teej, hoping some of his popularity would rub off on them.

Finally, Maddie caught sight of Teej, and the faintest of smiles had slid across her jaw.

"You know the idea is to run from him, right?" Bianca reminded.

"Run, but not too fast." Arching a brow, Maddie slid Bianca a knowing glance, and from that point on, Bianca had realized she was on her own. The minute the girls took off into the woods at Reece's "Go!" she'd lost sight of Maddie. It was as if her friend, who'd begged her to sneak out and join the others, had planned to ditch Bianca from the get-go.

Even now, Maddie was probably trying to hook up with Teej—that was, if she wasn't with him already.

But that didn't explain why there were no others nearby. In the parking lot, the "rules" of the game had been explained by Kywin Bell, a nineteen-year-old with a near-shaved head of blond hair and intense blue eyes. A couple of important inches shy of six feet, Kywin had one claim to fame. As a senior this past football season, he'd scored the winning touchdown in the big game against their archrivals by intercepting a pass and snaking his way to the end zone with two opposing players clinging to him but unable to bring him down.

That had been nearly a year ago. Kywin had since graduated, and now worked in a local feed store and still hung out with the younger kids. He kept saying he was going to college like his older, larger, and more athletic brother, but was waiting for the "right" offer to play ball, which was all BS, as most of the colleges Bianca knew about had already started practicing for the coming season. It was the end of August, for God's sake.

Obviously Kywin was either a liar or self-deluded or both. Somehow he'd placed himself and Austin Reece in charge of the phones so that everyone was "cool" with the cells and keys being confiscated. Then, while the burning tip of a cigarette had bobbed from the corner of his mouth, Kywin had told everyone that the girls were supposed to go "hide" and the boys would "seek." That produced a snort of laughter from Austin. The object, Austin had interjected, was for the girls to elude their hunters by running or hiding or using any trick they could. The two boys, tall, broad-shouldered Austin and all-bunched-muscle Kywin, had shared a knowing look that should have sent alarm bells ringing through Bianca's brain. Reece had explained that the last girl who didn't get caught was the big winner, though Bianca didn't know exactly what that girl might win. Kywin, the bohunk, hadn't explained. Nor had any of the other idiot boys, most of whom she'd known since preschool, including Teej, who had, she hated to admit, turned out to be a real hottie with a hard soccer body.

Big deal. He was also one of the biggest ego-maniacs in the school and his two sidekicks, Rod Devlin and Joaquin Castillo, weren't much better.

A minute or so after the girls had taken to the woods, the boys were let loose. She'd heard the boys hollering, big feet thundering as they gave chase. It had been unnerving and energizing and scary as hell. For the first time in her life, she'd felt like prey being stalked. Adrenaline had fueled her as she'd picked her way through a copse of saplings. All she'd known was that she didn't want to get caught. As careful and silent as she'd moved, it had worked. For a while. Then she'd cautiously stepped around a clump of brush.

A meaty hand, slick with sweat, had reached out of the umbra and clamped over her shoulder. She'd shrieked and jumped before she'd recognized Kywin Bell, the jerk-wad.

"Got you, you little cop-kid-bitch! Now, you're gonna git it!" There had been an evil, almost sexual, tone to his deep voice, and she, quick as a cat, had managed to slip out of his thick-fingered grasp.

Heart drumming, she'd yanked back her arm and spun away from him, then taken off, cutting up the north-face path that she'd hiked as a kid with her father.

"Hey! Wait. I *got* you!"

She'd ignored his outrage.

She was fast and sly and had quickly eluded him, but if that jackass caught up with her and tried to scare her again, she planned to nail him good by kicking him hard, right in the nuts. She only wished she had a pair of steel-toed boots to make it worth her while instead of her pink Nike running shoes. Shoes with a reflective strip near the soles. Shoes that would give her away if anyone shined the tiniest bit of light in her direction.

Gulping in lungfuls of air, she forced her heart rate to slow as she listened for any sounds from the others. No voices. No excited screeches of a girl being found. No laughter. No running footsteps. Not one damned sound other than her own breathing.

Weird.

And wrong. Very wrong.

Aside from the hoot of an owl or the occasional riffle of air as a bat passed, the woods were silent. And dark.

What the hell was going on?

She considered the fact that this whole "game" might have been a setup. That *she* was being pranked, or hazed or whatever, that while she was running and trying to elude the boys, everyone had let her go off in the woods alone and now were partying somewhere else.

Great.

Despite the heat rising from the forest floor, a chill slid down her spine.

Don't let your own paranoia get the better of you. Maddie would never set you up like this. Right? And you're a nobody, not anyone that the others would target. More likely, aside from Maddie, they don't even know you're out here.

Truth to tell, she wasn't sure what to believe.

A darker voice inside her mind reminded her that she could be a target, that as a cop's daughter she was looked upon with suspicion. Hadn't her mother arrested Kywin's old man just a few months ago for some kind of domestic violence?

It would be just like that jerk-wad to turn this on her. Hadn't he called her a "cop-kid-bitch"? Damn. And Reece, he was just bad news, the only son of a rich lawyer. Smart, surly, and smug all rolled into one Princeton-bound golden boy. Ugh.

Of course there were others, too. Donald Justison, the son of the town's mayor, back from college. He was a douche bag if there ever was one. And Bryant Tophman? The preacher's son who was all innocent and godly to his family? What a two-face! Far from the angel he portrayed himself to be, he might be the worst of the lot, what her mother called "a devil in disguise." Tophman wasn't the ring leader—that honor was reserved for Austin Reece—but Toph was an instigator.

Once again, she decided, she should never have come. Why had she listened to Maddie?

Because you're an idiot!

Even though she was sweating from her exertion and the heat, Bianca shivered, rubbed her arms, and considered heading back down the hill. What was she afraid of? They were just boys, after all. Boys she knew. So she didn't like them. Big deal. She'd almost convinced herself to turn back when she heard it. A rustling sound, like dry leaves turning in the wind, or a snake slithering through summer-bleached grass.

Her heart jerked.

Everything went quiet.

Eerily so.

Goose bumps rose on her flesh.

She eyed the undergrowth, the surrounding trees knifing upward into the dark sky.

Nothing.

Not even a breath of wind.

So what had the noise been?

She heard it again.

Closer.

And not a rustle, but more of a shuddering of branches.

A muffled sound. Steady.

Footsteps? Someone or something heading her way through the brush?

Well, that would make sense, considering the game. Right?

A twig snapping?

Again, that would be a normal sound.

And yet . . .

From the corner of her eye, she caught movement, a shadow darting. Then the rustle of dry leaves, sounding like the warning from a coiled rattler ready to strike.

Her skin prickled.

The wind?

Not on this still, hot night.

Without another thought, she took off, willing herself up the final point of the hill, hearing the big, snorting beast following after.

What the hell was it?

She wasn't going to slow down to find out. As she crested the ridge, the trees parted and moonlight filtered from the sky. Breathing hard, she hazarded a quick glance over her shoulder and saw the immense creature, whatever it was, still running, lumbering on hind legs, one eye catching the weak light and seeming to glow. Man? Beast? God, the hairy thing had to be seven feet tall! A low growl emanated from the brute. Oh, no!

She let out a terrified scream and kept running.

It's a prank. It has to be.

But she wasn't listening to the rational side of her mind, not when her heart was pounding double-time! All her instincts screamed at her to run, get away, put as much distance as she could between her and the . . . the monster. Downward she sprinted, trying to be careful, not twist an ankle, as branches and cobwebs clawed at her. She slipped and slid on the trail, running blind but trying to see the path. Behind her, the . . . the *thing* crashed through the underbrush. No longer was it being stealthy, content to surprise her. No. Now it raced in full, noisy pursuit.

Again she heard its growl. A thunderous peal.

Oh, God, oh, God, oh, God!

Down, down, down!

Faster, faster . . . oh, Jesus. She stumbled. The toe of her sneaker caught beneath an exposed root. She pitched forward into the darkness. Her foot caught, her leg twisting painfully.

"Aaaooow." Her arms flew out. Her knee wrenched as her foot became untangled and she hit the ground. Hard. *Bam!* Her chin bounced on the unforgiving ground, and she felt the skin split.

"Oof!" All the wind in her lungs came out in a rush.

Get up, get up! No time for this. Get onto your feet, Bianca.

Hot pain pulsed in her shoulder. Too bad. She couldn't stop moving. She had to get away.

Move!

The forest seemed to shrink around her.

More loudly, the earth trembling beneath it, the monster rushed at her.

"Damn it," she muttered, forcing herself to her feet, to find traction. Her ankle throbbed. Oh, crap, it hurt, but she gritted her teeth and moved more slowly, not by design, but because the pain prevented her from running all out. Limping slightly, she hurried along the path. Batting away branches, listening hard, she slipped and slid ever downward.

Get off the trail. It's too easy to track you if you stick to the worn path.

She eyed the surrounding trees, the shadowy hillside, the unknown. Could she risk it? Biting her lip, she strained to hear. Was the thing closer? Had it given up? Was it even now waiting farther down the hill, ready to ambush her?

If only she had her damned phone! She could

call or text, use her GPS to find out where she was or get hold of *some*one to help her, even if she had to call her older brother and listen to him read her the riot act. It didn't matter.

Damn it, *why* had she listened to stupid Maddie and come up here?

Frustrated and sucking in her breath, she stuck to the path. She figured she was more than half-way down the hillside, and it was easier to slide down than climb up. Besides, the last time she'd seen the creature, it had been higher up. Once she reached the bottom, she would follow the creek, knowing that it would lead back to the Long property. From there, given enough moon-light, she could make her way home and hopefully sneak back into the house.

And tell no one? You're scraped and bruised and probably have a sprained ankle or worse. Mom will find out. And what about that thing, the massive creature that chased you? Are you just going to forget about that, too? Get real, Bianca.

Battling tears, she kept on.

Another growl.

So close!

She jumped, scrambling faster, losing her footing on the gravel again.

"Shit!"

Down she went, her feet sliding out from under her as she began to roll down the hillside, the world dark and spinning. Scrabbling to grab hold of anything solid, she tumbled over rocks and twigs and pine cones that scraped and cut her bare arms and legs. She couldn't help the cry that escaped her as she wildly grasped for grass or roots or shrubbery, something that would slow her plummet to the bottom of the ravine. Her heart was thudding, her mind spinning, her fingers bleeding, nails splitting as she clawed into the dry earth.

Oh, God, please help me!

Clunk! Her wrist banged into a scraggly sapling. "Yeeooow!" she cried, barreling downward, bouncing and spinning until suddenly she stopped, her body landing at the bottom of the chasm, dust and pine cones flying as she skidded over a bank and into a shallow creek. Cool water slid beneath her.

"Oooh." The sound came from her own parched throat. She tried to lift her head, to get her bearings, but the world was spinning, starlit sky moving wildly, her vision swimming, her balance off.

Don't stop! Get up. It's still out there.

Dizzy, she attempted to focus. Her hair was wet, curls moving with the slow current. Pain wracked her body, and she coughed and snorted dust.

On your feet, Bianca!

Her mind was screaming at her, but she was woozy, her entire body aching. Bruises, she felt, were forming as she gazed upward to the stars far, far away, winking in the heavens. A thin veil of clouds scudded across the moon. The vision of the heavens was surreal, a balm over her pain.

For the love of God, you can't just lie here! Move!

It's coming!

Her mind was screaming at her, yelling at her to get her battered body moving again. Water splashed against her legs and torso. With what she considered a monumental effort, she lifted her head, pain searing through her brain. Oh, God, was she seriously hurt? And where was the beast, that horrid monster with its bad breath, gold eye, and hairy arms? She squinted into the surrounding scrub brush and trees as she moved her arms and legs.

She saw nothing. No huge, towering Neanderthal. Heard not a whisper over the gurgle of the creek, water sliding over stones.

Thank God.

But he's out there. Get up! Get out of here! Follow the creek back to the old Long logging camp. From there, you can get home.

But the others? Maddie . . .

Forget them. Forget her. Get the hell out. NOW!

She listened again, her ears straining, all her senses on alert. She noticed a weird, rotting smell. *A skunk spray? The creature's breath. Oh, dear God—*

Something slimy slid over her leg.

Move, Bianca!

Struggling, she rolled over, found a rock or limb or whatever to push herself upright when she felt that branch give a little. She gripped harder and realized that she wasn't holding on to a limb at all. It was too soft. Almost mushy with a hard core. And . . . oh, God, as her mind cleared, she realized the stink was something awful, not a skunk smell at all, more like the odor of something dead.

She recoiled. Backed up. Scrambling and sliding away from whatever it was, the trickle of water cold on her buttocks, she stared at the form —was it human?—lying across the creek bed.

She barely breathed.

No . . . no . . . but . . .

What the hell?

The thin wisps of clouds moved, moonlight shining along the silvery stream. Bianca's head cleared and she realized she was staring at a corpse. Decomposing, flesh rotting, bones exposed to the scant moonlight, the dead woman—a young one—lay face up in the ravine. Pale hair floated around a decomposing head in the slowly moving water. Teeth were exposed, with no lips to hide them, and black holes were drilled deep into her skull where once her eyes had been.

Oh. Jesus. No!

Bianca threw herself to her feet. Running, stumbling along the creek, she let out a scream loud enough to wake the dead in all of Pinewood County.

CHAPTER 3

Regan Pescoli's eyes flew open at the buzzing sound. The room was dark. Santana was snoring softly in the bed beside her, the digital clock blinking a blue 2:32, her cell phone vibrating and skittering on the nightstand.

Great, she thought sarcastically. This was the problem with being a detective with the Pinewood County Sheriff's Department. There was always the chance of what Deputy Pete Watershed called "Sleepus-Interruptus." Watershed was a dick, of course, but even dicks could be funny once in a while.

With one hand, she reached for her cell, missing it and knocking it onto the floor. *Stupid.* With an effort, she slid to the edge of the bed. Leaning over the edge, she swiped the damned phone from the floor before pressing it to her ear.

"Pescoli," she answered around a yawn and blinked as she pushed herself to a sitting position. The last thing she wanted to do in her current state was climb out of bed, squeeze into her usual work clothes, and head down to a crime scene. Pushing her hair from her face with her free hand, she tried to shake away the remnants of a nightmare that had been chasing through her brain.

"It's Rule," a male voice said. Kayan Rule was

a deputy with the department, an African-American who looked like he would be more at home as a power forward on a basketball court than he did in a Pinewood County Sheriff's Department uniform. He was a good cop and a hunk with a killer smile. "I think you might want to come up to the old lumber camp owned by the Long family."

"You think wrong," she said, then, regretting her tone, added, "What's up?"

Beside her, Santana stirred, his near black hair visible on the pillow in the darkened room. With a groan, her husband roused and levered himself up on an elbow to stare at her.

She ignored him.

"I've got your daughter here with me," Kayan said.

"My daughter?" she repeated, suddenly wide awake, her heart clutching. "Bianca?" As if she had another.

"Yes."

"What's she doing there? What's she done?" Pescoli asked, images of Bianca being caught with a boy, or alcohol, or weed, or all three, running through her tired mind. *Perfect.* Now that Jeremy, her eldest, was finally starting to get his act together and had become a semi-valuable member of society, his younger sister was taking up the Pescoli Torch of Rebellion. Just what she needed.

"She stumbled on a dead body. At least that's the way she's told it."

"*What?* Bianca came across a corpse?" This wasn't computing. Bianca was supposed to be spending the night with a friend.

And this surprises you, that your daughter lied about what her plans were? Come on, Regan, you remember what it was like to be seventeen.

"Bianca's at Reservoir Point with a dead body," Pescoli said.

"Right."

Pescoli tried to wrap her mind around what she was being told, to think more like a cop, less like a mother. "Who's the victim?"

"Unconfirmed. Female. Teen from the looks of her. Maybe fifteen, or sixteen, around there. No ID. But, there was a girl who was reported missing about a week ago. Friday of last week, to be exact. Destiny Rose Montclaire. We're checking it out."

A teen. Little more than a child, a girl. Pescoli's heart nosedived. "Does Bianca know her?"

"She says she knows of her, but they weren't friends. That's the general consensus of the kids up here, but we're still checking it out."

"Who's up there with Bianca?"

"Quite a few teenagers. A party. They claim they were playing some kind of game. War or tag or hide-and-seek, something. Boys chasing girls."

44

Pescoli's heart dropped like a stone. This was getting worse by the second.

"Your daughter was being chased when she stumbled upon the body. We're sorting it all out, but it'll take a little time. Like I said, you probably want to come up here."

"I do. But first I need to talk to Bianca."

"Right here."

Why was Bianca up there? Whom was she with? Why had she lied? Dozens of questions echoed through her brain.

"Mom?" Bianca's voice was weak, almost trembling. Scared. Not like her usually bull-headed, opinionated daughter.

Pescoli's anger seeped away. "Yeah, honey, I'm here," she said. She was already rolling out of bed, her ungainly body making it difficult. She nearly tripped on her slippers and kicked them out of the way. Cisco, her mottled terrier mix, was on his feet and chasing after her, acting more a puppy than a dog well into his teens.

Bianca whispered, "Come get me."

"I will." Avoiding the exuberant dog, Pescoli made her way into the adjoining bath and asked, "What happened? What're you doing up at the reservoir? I thought you were spending the night with Maddie."

"I am. I mean, I was. Crap, I—I don't know. A bunch of kids came up here to play a stupid game. Look . . . I'll . . . I'll explain when you get here." Her voice had risen an octave, and she was defensive, sounding more like the girl Pescoli had raised. Good.

"The body you discovered? You recognized her?"

"Not at first. It was dark and . . ." She cleared her throat, obviously attempting to pull herself together. "Then they ran a flashlight beam over her face and I think . . . I think it's a girl from school. I don't know her, but she was in my English class when we were sophomores. Destiny Something. Didn't he just tell you that? Geez, Mom! I don't want to talk about it."

"You'll have to—"

"I know, but please, *please* just get up here!"

"Okay, okay. Stay with the deputy. He's a good guy. I'll be there in . . . as soon as I can."

"Hurry!"

"Okay."

Pescoli clicked off her cell and hit the bathroom light. Wincing against the brightness, she caught her image in the mirror mounted over the sink. Oh. Dear. God. Not that she could worry about it now, but she looked immense. At thirty-five weeks pregnant, she appeared more than at term, her stomach protruding as she stripped away her pajamas and stepped into her maternity jeans, top, and jacket. It wasn't the pregnancy bump that was the problem, it was her bloated face, her lackluster hair, and the dark circles under her eyes that caused her to cringe. She was tall and athletic—

well, usually—but she'd never been a woman who "glowed" during the months of carrying a child, not when she was pregnant with Jeremy when she was around twenty and certainly not now when she was nearly twice that age. Her hair was a reddish blond, loosely curled, and right now, a tangle.

But it didn't matter, she thought, as she returned to the bedroom and sat on a bench at the end of their bed. Cisco, whining, had returned to his bed, where Sturgis, her recently inherited black lab, lay curled next to Nikita, Santana's husky. Sturgis's long nose rested on the pillowed edge of his dog bed, while his dark eyes followed every move Pescoli made as she walked through the room. Pescoli's heart twisted a little as she considered his previous owner, Sheriff Dan Grayson. She missed him. Grayson had run the department with a firm hand and a cool head. Unlike Cooper Blackwater, the current gung-ho yahoo who commanded the offices of the Pinewood County Sheriff's Department as if it were a military base in enemy territory.

Santana asked, "What's up?"

"Bianca." Pescoli managed to slip on a shoe. "She's up at the reservoir with a bunch of other kids and there's a dead girl, one she doesn't know. I don't have the details yet." Forcing her foot into the second shoe, she grimaced. How could a person gain weight in her damned feet?

47

She walked back to the closet, then unlocked the safe where she kept her sidearm. "So I might not be back for a while."

"You sure you're okay with this?" he asked, now wide awake.

"I'm never 'okay' with anything like this. What kind of question is that? A girl is dead," she said testily as she made sure the weapon was loaded, then slid it into her shoulder holster. "Besides, my kid found her."

"Even if she didn't, if Bianca wasn't up there, you'd go."

"It's my job," she reminded him.

"Yeah, I know." He swung his bare legs over the side of the bed. Santana made a habit of sleeping in the nude. Which she usually liked. Now, she didn't need the distraction. "You should be on maternity leave."

"Yes, Mom," she said and noticed him raise a dark eyebrow at her snarky tone. "I'll remember that."

"Do." His lips twisted into that cocky smile that had always won her over. He reached up behind him, snagged one of the pillows, and threw it at her backside as she hurried out of their master bedroom.

"You missed by a mile!"

"Meant to," came the lazy response that trailed her down the stairs.

"Just warning you: I'm armed," she yelled back

at him, though she really wasn't in the mood for any horseplay. Usually she got a kick out of the mischief that Santana sometimes exhibited, but not when her daughter was involved in . . . in what? She didn't know. But it scared the liver out of her.

"I'm coming with you!" Santana shouted.

She heard his feet land on the floor.

"Nope. Official police business."

"Involving my pregnant wife's daughter."

"I've got this!" Why were they even having this conversation? Santana knew how she felt about her job. She headed across the kitchen and located her keys and purse on a table near the garage door, just as she heard his boot heels hit the floorboards overhead. Well, fine, he could damned well come if he wanted, just not with her.

She went through the door to the garage and slapped the button for the garage door opener, engaging the interior and exterior lights. Seconds later, she was reversing into the driveway and then turning around. As she pressed the remote to close the garage door, she spied Santana's silhouette in the connecting doorway. From the corner of her eye, she saw him make his way to his truck. She didn't wait, just threw the Jeep into drive and gunned it down the long drive leading to the county road.

Their house was fairly new, built on a piece of land Santana had inherited from Brady Long, his boss. Santana had worked as a horse trainer and ranch manager for the wealthy Long family for years, though now that Brady Long was gone, he worked for himself. Originally into mining, the Longs had branched out into lumber, ranching, and you name it. They even owned the property up near the reservoir, where even now Bianca was waiting.

Pescoli hit the gas.

Bianca noticed that her mom was the first to arrive. Less than fifteen minutes from the time the black dude had called her, Regan Pescoli's Jeep roared into view. Never in her life had Bianca been so glad to see her mother, even though it was really embarrassing, not just that her mom was a cop but that she was pregnant. Nearly forty and going to have a baby; damned near ancient in Bianca's opinion. None of her friends' mothers was having a baby and none of them was a cop—homicide detective. These were Bianca's personal crosses to bear.

Still, Bianca almost crumbled when she spied her mom climbing out of the Jeep and striding over to her.

"Hey. How're you doin'?" Her mother's arms surrounded her, and something inside Bianca broke.

"Horrible." Bianca's tears started to flow. She knew she should rein in her emotions, that she was probably going to sound like the drama queen her brother, Jeremy, continually accused her of being, but she didn't care. She was scared. And mad. And beyond freaked out by what she'd seen: the dead girl, the monster, that awful Kywin Bell.

"You'll be fine."

Bianca shook her head. She would never be "fine" or "okay" or even "kinda sorta fine." Not after what she'd seen, what she'd felt.

"Tell me what happened," her mother said softly, glancing up at the deputy. "Give us a minute. Okay? We'll be in my Jeep."

At that second, another vehicle rolled up and a deputy stopped the pickup. Bianca's heart sank. Santana's truck. Great. Her mother's new husband had arrived. *Stepdaddy. Ugh.* He wasn't a bad guy really, but who needed him?

Not Bianca.

Not right now.

He must've figured that out because he didn't come busting over to the car with a dozen questions. Well, he wouldn't. It wasn't his style, and Mom probably told him to wait until she'd talked to Bianca. Regan Pescoli—ever the cop.

The whole situation was already surreal with police cars parked everywhere, their light bars flashing blue and red, strobing the parking lot where they'd trapped everyone who'd come to party. When she'd seen the dead body and screamed, disentangling herself and splashing out of the creek, racing along the bank, she'd nearly run into Rod Devlin, Teej's friend. Tall and lanky, he'd emerged from a copse of pines and put on the brakes, skidding to a stop to avoid running into her.

"What was that scream about?" he'd asked.

"She's dead!" Bianca had shouted at him.

"What? Who?"

"I don't know!"

He'd looked over her shoulder then, and his gaze had landed on the grotesque corpse lying in the creek. "Holy shit! Is that what I think it is? A body?" He'd turned the color of death himself, his eyes rounding. "A fuckin' body? Is that what it is?"

"That's what it is." She'd been shaking as he backed away. Wet and shivering, Bianca had tried to grab hold of his arm. "And there's something out there—I don't know what, but it's really huge. And *hairy!* And it chased me all the way here! It's . . . it's a monster!"

Still backpedaling, his eyes searched the darkness as other voices began to ring closer. "You're fuckin' nuts, Bianca!" he'd declared, but he'd looked ready to bolt.

"I'm not kidding! It was chasing me and it was like . . . *Big Foot.* Smelled rotten! Oh, God." By that time, she'd nearly been hyperventilating. "We have to get help!"

He'd shot one more horrified glance at the

creek, backing up, nearly tripping over her own feet. "Too late."

"I know, but we have to call someone. You . . . you have a phone, right?" she'd begged desperately "Right, Rod? You've got your cell on you. Call nine-one-one!"

"What?" He'd shaken his head, his brown hair flying around his face. "No way! I mean—a body? Big Foot? Are you *serious?* No. No way! I'm not callin' no cops!"

"Just call the emergency line. For an ambulance."

"She's way past needing EMTs."

She'd caught a glimpse of his phone in his hand. "Just do it, Rod!"

"Forget it!" His eyes had been wild, and she'd realized he might be on something. "We're in enough trouble as it is. Holy shit! We—I—gotta get outta here!"

"Oh, for the love of God!" She'd jumped up then and taken a swipe at his outstretched hand, ripping the phone from his fingers. Before he could sputter another word, she'd punched 911 into his phone.

"Hey! Stop!" He'd snatched at his phone, but she'd feinted and ducked under some low branches, scaring some bird. Within seconds the dispatcher had answered.

"Nine-one-one, what's your emergency?"

With Rod going ape-shit in the background,

Bianca had given her name and location, reporting the body as rapidly as possible. "Send someone quick," she'd cried. "An ambulance!"

"I told you, it's too late for that!" Rod had screamed at her. "An ambulance? What good is that gonna do? That girl, whoever she is . . . she's . . . dead! *Already rotting.* No fuckin' EMT in the world is gonna revive her. Come on! We have to leave. Now! End the call. You . . . you can tell your mom when you get home."

"And call Detective Pescoli. . . . I'm her daughter!" Bianca had yelled into the phone, trying to ignore Rod as he scrambled for his phone.

"You're fuckin' crazy!" he'd spat, getting his hands on the cell and ripping it away from her. "What the hell's wrong with you? Now the cops have my number! We're all gonna be in trouble. You're an idiot, Pescoli. A fuckin' hysterical idiot!"

"A girl is dead!"

But he had already been gone, running along the trail into the general area of the parking area. She'd heard him start yelling at the top of his lungs, warning the others. "Cops! The cops are coming!"

"What?" a girl had shouted from a ridge above. "No!"

"Wait!" another voice had cried over the sudden thunder of running footsteps as kids ran

54

pell-mell crashing through the forest. No one trying to be stealthy any longer. Nope. They were all running to save their own skins.

"Hey! What's going on?" Maddie's voice had suddenly added to the din.

"Are you sure, dude?" another boy had demanded, his voice carrying down the canyon. "Oh, shit!"

"Help me get Maddie out of here!" another one had hollered. "She's drunk."

Someone else had started crying. "Ow! Watch out!" Heavy breathing, snapping branches, dust rising.

In the distance, sirens had begun to wail.

There had been screaming, cursing, and general pandemonium as everyone tried to make it to their cars or flee on foot into the dark woods. The sirens had wailed more loudly. Flashlights and lights from cell phones had dotted the dark hills.

But few had escaped.

By the time Bianca had arrived at the parking area, limping and breathing hard, cop cars had sealed off the gravel lane. The night had been illuminated by the red and blue flashes from the vehicles from the sheriff's department. Two deputies with flashlights and weapons drawn had begun running along the path Bianca had indicated, the dusty trail that wound along the banks of the creek to where the body lay partially submerged.

Bianca crumpled against the front of an old pickup that belonged to Joaquin Castillo, then realized the bumper was covered in dirt and dead insects. She jerked herself upright as some of the other kids trickled out of the woods to be confronted by the cops. Those who were still hiding, the idiots who thought they could escape on foot, would certainly be identified through the vehicles that had been abandoned and the statements of their friends, assuming everyone came clean.

Had it really been Destiny? The quiet girl who had sat in the back of the English class she'd shared with Bianca? A girl who had barely spoken? A girl with big eyes and a shy smile? A girl no one had really noticed?

Now the events of the night caught up to her and she thought she might be sick, right here, in the front seat of her mom's car. She fought the urge to puke and instead told her detective mother what had happened. Bianca didn't hold back. Usually she kept a lot of secrets from her mother. She had to. Not only did Mom think she should run Bianca's life, but there was just a lot of stuff that was private, things she'd rather not let her mom know about. It was *her* life after all, not her cop mom's. But tonight, after being scared as hell, she spilled everything. She'd already pointed out the way to the body, but then she'd led Deputy Rule along the trail herself. She knew, deep in her heart, not to hold back, and she'd made herself watch as they'd shined lights on the girl in the creek. They'd asked if she recognized her. Could the body be that of Destiny Rose Montclaire? The near-white hair was right. But the rest?

She thought so and had simply nodded.

Now, considering it, she shivered again.

"I'm sorry," she said to her mother, but for once Regan Pescoli didn't go ballistic, nor read her the riot act, nor even mention that Bianca had been a Cretin to be a part of the party. She didn't point out that Bianca had lied to her, or that there was a curfew or anything. She didn't even ask if Bianca had smoked any weed or drunk as much as a swallow of beer. No. All Regan had been concerned with was that Bianca was okay. Which she wasn't.

Bianca still shuddered at the thought of that pallid body, eye sockets empty and dark, water causing her pale hair to float around what was left of her face.

"It . . . it was horrible," she said now, and looked out the open window of the Jeep. No more music now, no rumbling engines, just the sound of cops asking questions, low voices and boots or shoes or flip-flops on the bare, sparse gravel. She wondered if she could ever get the image of the dead girl out of her mind. She doubted it.

"But you recognized her?"

"I don't know, Mom. Maybe she's Destiny. Her hair was right, I think . . . she could be." She shuddered, again trying to eradicate the horrid, deeply etched image from her brain.

"We'll figure that out. How's your ankle?"

"Awful." That wasn't a lie—it was throbbing like crazy.

"Let's have the EMTs look at it."

"No! I just want to go home." Never had her new bedroom sounded so good.

"That's not happening," her mother said, and Bianca noticed she shifted uncomfortably behind the wheel. "Santana will take you to the hospital. For X-rays. I've got to stay here for a while."

"Mom, no!"

"It'll be okay. If you want, I'll have your father meet you there." For once, her mother's lips didn't tighten at the mention of her ex, Bianca's dad, Luke Pescoli. Everyone called him "Lucky" and everyone liked him. Everyone, that was, but Regan Pescoli. While all of Bianca's friends thought Lucky was fun and kind of cool, even sexy for an old guy, her mom seemed to hate him, or at least be irritated by him all of the time. Worse yet, Mom didn't like his wife, Michelle, even though Bianca thought her stepmother was pretty cool. Yeah, Michelle was only a few years older than Jeremy, but she was fun. Mom wasn't. Bianca guessed her mother hated Michelle because she was thin, blond, and fashion conscious, always wore high heels, and looked great in a bikini. Bianca had heard her mother called Michelle a "Barbie doll," so it stood to reason she was jealous.

Whatever. It didn't really matter. At least not tonight.

"Dad doesn't need to come," she said, then hesitated, wavering, thinking about her run down that mountain.

Regan Pescoli's parent radar went up. Or maybe her detective radar. "There's something else." It wasn't a question.

Bianca nodded. Swallowed hard.

"What?" Her mother's voice was soft. Not demanding.

"It sounds stupid."

"Nothing's stupid."

Bianca blew out a long breath of air. "Well, this is. I mean . . . I told you about being chased through the woods."

"Umm."

"Well, it was more than just the boys, you know, chasing the girls. I think there was something else."

Her mother tensed. "Like what?"

"I—I'm not really sure." Bianca lifted a shoulder. Felt dumb. "Maybe a wild animal— some kind of creature chasing me."

"What kind of creature?"

Bianca felt her mother's gaze boring into her.

"I don't know. Something big and smelly. A huge thing. I mean, this is crazy, I know. But . . . I think it was a monster, you know."

"No, I don't know." Her mother stared hard at her.

How could she explain when it seemed weird, stupid, even made-up? "A beast, I guess." Saying it out loud made her cringe inside.

"What kind of beast?"

"Just big and kind of *animal*. Horrible. Not human." She shuddered remembering the immensity of the thing, how it had reeked, its glowing eye. God, it did seem surreal now. "I just had the feeling that, whatever it was, it was . . . like pure evil."

"Evil?"

"Yeah, like really, really bad. I had the feeling it wanted to kill me!"

"This was before you saw the dead girl?"

"God—yes! I told you it chased me! Right down to the creek!" Bianca remembered the creature's loud footsteps, its hulking size, and she felt that mind-numbing fear all over again. "I already told you. Can we just stop now?"

"We will . . . yes. But first. Just answer this," her mother said calmly while Bianca was on the brink of hysteria. "This 'monster,' could it have been someone dressed up in a costume, you know, one of the boys playing a joke on—"

"*A joke?* Are you serious? This *thing* was like a

mountain, so big, so scary . . . oh, crap, you don't believe me."

"No, no. I'm just trying to figure out what it is."

"I told you what!" Bianca wrapped her arms around herself. Her mother didn't believe her.

"Then try again. Calmly."

"Okay. It was huge."

"We've established that."

"And hairy and smelled like . . . wet dog, only a hundred times worse, like if Sturgis took a bath in a lake filled with raw sewage, that *bad.* And it had an eye that kind of glowed gold. Like topaz or something. You know, like the stone in that necklace Michelle wears sometimes. It was like that."

"One eye?"

"I only saw one." It sounded weird. All of it sounded weird, not just the eye. Bianca knew that.

"Could it have been a cougar? A mountain lion was spotted not far from here."

"No! Mom! This thing was *huge.* Massive. Like way taller than me and it . . . I mean, I couldn't tell, but it was on two legs. Or rearing up. I don't know. It was dark. It all happened so fast, but it scared me. It scared the hell out of me." Oh, God, she was saying this all wrong.

"But could it have been human? Just bear with me and think about it. Someone dressed up to really scare you?"

"No! Yes? I don't know! But it would have had to have been a giant. A hairy, stinky giant!" She let out her breath and tried to calm a bit. "It was . . . awful. And then . . . and then it chased me down to the creek where . . . where *she* was." The more Bianca thought about it, the crazier it sounded. Tears welled in her eyes. "Can we just go home?"

"You can. After you go to the hospital. I'll be a little longer. I have things I have to deal with here."

"But—"

"I know." Struggling with her massive girth, Mom turned in her seat and hugged Bianca. "I'll be home as soon as I can. Promise."

Bianca nodded as she stared out the windshield to the eerie gloom. Knots of kids, now with parents or cops beside them, were huddled in the play of light from flashlights and headlights, everyone telling his or her side of the story. She spied Austin Reece, blond head held at a lofty angle, looking down his nose at a short woman cop. Maddie was standing next to Teej, leaning on him. She was probably drunk. Not good.

But then nothing was. Groups of other kids, some with their parents, formed a wide, uneven circle as they talked to the cops. Rod Devlin was dealing with the same deputy with whom Bianca had first spoken, Kayan Rule. The party mood had dissipated, and most of her friends looked grim or scared or both.

"Okay, I need to talk to some of the others," her mother said. "Find out if anyone else got a look at the body."

Bianca's stomach turned over as she thought of the corpse still lying in the creek. She swallowed hard and didn't let her mind wander too far to what had happened to the girl.

Her mother urged, "Let's go."

"Fine." Reluctantly, Bianca climbed out of the Jeep and saw that Santana was out of his truck in an instant, as if he'd gotten the high sign from Mom, or more likely been watching like a hawk. He acted as if he was going to do something stupid like try to help her, so she shouted, "I'm okay!" before he touched her, then hobbled her way over to Santana's pickup, wincing with each step. Still, she made it and was able to climb into the passenger seat and roll down the window unaided.

"Really, how ya doin'?" Santana asked as he stood next to the cab.

"How do ya think?" she tossed back, not bothering to hide her sarcasm. "Just super."

He lifted one dark eyebrow and she felt immediate remorse. "I just want to get out of here. To go home," she muttered.

"Okay. I'll be right back. Just want to get a couple of things straight with your mom."

"Perfect." She waited in the passenger seat of her stepfather's battered pickup and listened to the sounds of the night.

Over the drone of insects and a frog croaking somewhere she heard the voices of kids being interviewed, the rumble of engines and crunch of tires as more parents or guardians arrived. Bianca also caught pieces of the conversation between Santana and her mother as they stood in front of the pickup's grill. Regan was filling him in and giving instructions. "Bianca . . . body . . . unconfirmed but working on it . . . a girl reported missing . . . some kind of one-eyed monster . . . I know . . . crazy . . . shock probably . . . check it out at the hospital with the ankle. Yeah, it'll be a while. Take her home . . . I know. I'll call him."

Dad, she thought from the tone of her mother's voice. The only other "him" they could be talking about, she thought, was her brother, Jeremy, but her mom didn't talk about him the same way. Surprisingly, she wished Jeremy were here. As much as he'd bugged her while they were growing up, now she missed him.

Bianca closed her eyes, felt the heat of the summer night against her skin, and wondered what the hell she'd seen in the woods. A wild animal? A kid dressed up like a monster—but who? And how? And why? Or something else? The skin on the back of her arms prickled as she considered the options. Possibly something otherworldly. Lately she'd been reading a lot of books with paranormal themes, about ghosts and ESP, and vampires. She'd even gone through a zombie phase and the truth was, she did believe in an alternate universe, one few could see. But she probably shouldn't mention ghosts or wraiths because it would only freak out her seeing-is-believing mother.

Again, the image of the dead girl came to mind, and she tried like crazy to think of anything else.

But it was no use. As the old driver's-side door opened with a creak and Santana climbed behind the steering wheel, her mind wandered back to that moment when she'd touched what she'd thought was a stick but had turned out to be a bone with rotting flesh still attached.

Acid climbed up her throat. "Wait!" she yelled and she shoved open the door and heaved, vomiting over the gravel and part of the truck's door frame. Her stomach turned inside out, bile rising, the stench burning through her nostrils as she hurled again. When it was over, she spat, wished she could wash her mouth of the sour taste that lingered, then yanked the door shut and leaned against the back of the seat. Tears were hot in her eyes.

"You done?" Santana asked and reached into the glove box to pull out a box of Kleenex.

She didn't know. "Yeah." She plucked several

tissues from the box and cleaned herself. "Let's just go." Though her eyes were closed, she couldn't shake the image. Deeply embedded in her brain was the mental photograph of the dead girl's mangled face, pale floating hair, and deep, empty eye sockets.

CHAPTER 4

Blackwater arrived at the scene.

"Bad news travels fast," Pescoli said under her breath as she watched the acting sheriff's Tahoe roar along the access road, headlights cutting through the darkness, dust rising in a plume behind the rear wheels. She just didn't like the guy. Laid-back wasn't in his vocabulary, and he was very big on agendas, meetings, and finding ways to "pump up" enthusiasm in everyone on the force. Pescoli didn't need it. He also seemed to preen for the cameras, but Alvarez had told her she was overreacting, that Blackwater was just trying to use the press to the department's advantage to solve cases.

Well, maybe.

But she still didn't trust him.

He parked his SUV near a couple of cruisers, crossed under the crime-scene tape, and strode up to Pescoli. Just under six feet, with a compact, athletic body, short black hair, and intense hawkish eyes, he appeared as if he were still an active member of the Marine Corps, though he was dressed down for him in pressed jeans and an open-throated polo shirt, his usually clean-shaven jaw showing night stubble.

"What've we got?" he asked.

"Dead female. Possibly a girl reported missing since sometime last week, Friday, I think," Pescoli said and gave him the rundown. As she spoke, he didn't interrupt, but his eyes scanned the area. She figured he didn't miss much.

"You interviewed everyone?"

"Almost done," Pescoli said. She was still sweating, even in the coolest wee hours of the morning. "A couple of deputies are wrapping things up. Then we're sending the kids home with their parents."

"Any caught with alcohol?"

"Not in their hands. A couple of coolers, though," Pescoli said.

"Drugs?"

"None found," Pescoli said. "I checked with the deputies, who searched the cars. But I smelled marijuana."

"Probably ditched in the undergrowth." His eyes scanned the scrub brush and thickets surrounding the parking area, his head shaking slightly. "They all need to be cited."

"You think that will help?" Pescoli asked.

"It's against the law." His lips were flat. "I'm the sheriff."

"Zero tolerance."

"You got it. And don't let any of them drive." He pointed a finger at her for emphasis. "If they don't have an adult, I mean a sober adult, to drive them, then we haul them back to the station. At least while we deal with the bigger situation."

Pescoli's gut tightened. She knew he was right, but she'd been down that route before, on both sides of the law. Not only had she arrested kids, but her own son had done some time in juvie.

"Maybe if they're scared enough, they'll talk," he said. "What do we know about the victim?"

"Seems like the girl's been dead a few days. Body bloating, decaying."

"Not a part of this." He motioned a finger to include the vehicles and kids still cluttering the area.

"Whatever happened to her occurred before these kids met up tonight."

"But they might know something." Blackwater's brow furrowed as he eyed the crowd. "The girl went to the local high school, right?"

"Yes."

"Same with most of these kids," he guessed.

Pescoli couldn't argue and decided to come clean. "My daughter was here, too. She called it in to nine-one-one on another kid's phone. She was injured so I sent her to the hospital."

In the blue and red flashes of light, she saw

the muscles in the back of his neck tighten. "Cite her," he said. "I can't play favorites."

"I wasn't asking you to."

"Good."

At that moment, a fresh set of headlights pierced the night as the first television van arrived.

Pescoli inwardly groaned. The press. Already.

"I'll speak to them," he said, as the lumbering white vehicle parked on the far side of the police barrier.

I bet you will.

"Make sure we get statements from everyone up here." He glanced pointedly at Pescoli. "Including anyone who's already left. I want a list of every person who was here."

Pescoli ground her back teeth together.

Without another word, he crossed the lot, rounding the rear bumper of a BMW as the passenger door of the van opened, and a reporter Pescoli recognized from the local news stepped out. Petite. Blonde. In a dress and jacket in the middle of the night, like she'd been sitting by the phone waiting for the call.

"He treats us like newbies," she said as Rhonda Clemmons, a road deputy who had been one of the first on the scene, approached.

"Who? Blackwater?" Clemmons waved away the comment as if it were a bothersome fly. "Just his style."

"Bullshit. And the TV crew. Oh, yeah, that's just what we need."

"At least he'll deal with them," Clemmons said. "That way we don't have to."

"Tonight."

"One day at a time. And maybe they'll help us."

"Yeah, yeah." But Pescoli couldn't really argue. The press had come to the department's aid in finding suspects in the past. Didn't mean some of the members, including that worm Manny Douglas of the *Mountain Reporter*, didn't bug the crap out of her. It wasn't so much what Manny wrote, but how he handled himself, as if he were somehow more virtuous than the cops in the department, as if the Pinewood County Sheriff's Department might be dirty.

Scumbag. But so far, he hadn't appeared. As Clemmons headed to her vehicle, Pescoli dug into her pocket for her cell phone to call Santana and saw that he'd left a text: At the ER. Waiting. Not seen yet. Bianca in some pain, but holding up.

She wrote back: Ok. Still at the scene. Keep me posted. Home ASAP.

She didn't mention that Bianca would be cited. After all, she had to leave some of the fun stuff for later, right? Once the whole family was back home and the trauma of the hospital was behind her, then Pescoli could lower the hammer. Oh, joy.

She clicked off and caught sight of Alvarez climbing out of her Subaru.

"Sorry I'm late," Alvarez said. "Out of town."

"I thought you were on vacation."

Alvarez had been spending time with her biological son, Gabe, a teenager who lived with his adoptive parents.

"Got back a few hours ago," she said. "The trip got cut short."

"Why?"

"Addie," she replied, mentioning Gabe's adoptive mother. "I don't want to talk about it."

"Okay."

Alvarez's dark hair was slicked back into a ponytail. Like Pescoli, she hadn't bothered with makeup, but somehow looked fresher, ready to go. "Let's see what we've got."

"The victim is up that trail."

They headed out, Pescoli struggling to keep up with Alvarez, who was walking briskly, the beam of her flashlight bobbing along the trail ahead.

"Bianca was here?" she said. "Part of the party?"

"Yeah," Pescoli admitted, still wondering about that. "She found the body, called it in, so the road deputies in the area got here before the kids had a chance to scatter." There was a lot more to it than that, of course, but she'd fill in Alvarez later.

"Good."

Selena Alvarez had been Pescoli's partner for years, and they got along. It had been a little rocky at first, as their backgrounds, educations, and viewpoints on life, as well as how they handled their jobs, were at odds, but they'd sorted most of that crap out. Alvarez came from a large family in Oregon somewhere, had gone to school, excelled, and worked by the book, a scientist who valued evidence far more than any gut instinct. Pescoli, on the other hand, was known to fly by the seat of her pants and relied on her own perceptions.

Even so, Pescoli had grudgingly come to respect the younger woman's skills.

Straightforward, usually calm, Alvarez was relentless when it came to collecting evidence, checking and rechecking facts, and working a case by the book. Hers was never a forty- or even sixty-hour work week. Alvarez was a student of all things in life and she could think outside the box. She was also far more adept at today's technology, was an Internet/social media whiz, and kept abreast of the most recent theories in psychology. However, she never wanted to bend the rules, which, in Pescoli's mind, were meant to be pushed to the breaking point if need be. And, she found, "need be" turned out to be pretty often.

While Alvarez was calm under pressure, a cool head, Pescoli's emotions often got the better of her.

"What've we got?" Alvarez asked as they walked along the dusty trail that wound along the creek.

Breathing hard, Pescoli filled her in on as much as she knew, which was, at that point, mostly what she'd learned from Bianca.

By the time they reached the spot where the victim lay in the shallows of the creek, Pescoli was sweating. Lights had been set up so they could view the scene, and insects were hovering above the stream, where a girl's body was tangled in roots and stones. She was rapidly decomposing, her face disfigured and, in Pescoli's estimation, unrecognizable. Techs were already combing the area around the creek while the EMTs, after confirming what was obvious, that she was deceased, were waiting for someone from the coroner's office to arrive.

Pescoli's stomach turned at the sight. Still, she crouched near the creek bed, shined the beam of her flashlight over the body.

The girl looked under twenty. Maybe around Bianca's age and the age of most of the kids who were up here tonight. Had her death been an accident? Had she tripped and fallen here? Sustained head trauma? Had she been all alone in the forest or with someone? Had that someone killed her? Or harmed her and left her here to die? Could she have come out here to be alone in nature to take her own young life? If so, why?

Every aspect about it was disturbing.

Straightening with effort, she squinted into the shadowy undergrowth rising with the walls of this canyon. Yes, this part of the wilderness was somewhat remote and certainly not a tourist attraction, but in summer there were outdoor enthusiasts who hiked or mountain-biked, fished or picnicked, birdwatched, picked huckleberries, or generally communed with nature. So not as remote as it might seem.

"Detective. Please?" one of the crime scene techs said as she aimed her flashlight's beam over the tufts of dry grass not far from Pescoli's shoes. "Do you mind?" The tech was a thin woman with angular features, a pinched mouth, and thick, oversized glasses.

Pescoli backed up and took a broader look at the area. The path that was being examined cut down from the surrounding cliff to angle along the shores of what, during the spring thaw, was a sizeable, fast-moving stream. Now, in August, the water was shallow and sluggish, the pool in which the body lay the deepest part of the creek.

Alvarez, who'd been okayed by the same tech, was crouching over the body, carefully studying the victim's face and hairline before using the illumination cast by her own flashlight to explore the shallows. Water riffled over shiny stones as it flowed slowly over the girl's face, distorting the macabre features even more. From there, the creek moved around her torso to run past her legs and bare feet. The skirt of her short dress billowed around her thighs.

Pescoli had seen enough.

Another tech, Lex Farnsby, was searching the hillside, and Pescoli followed him along the steep trail, the dusty path—she was certain, from Bianca's description—on which her daughter had recently fled. "Footprints?" she asked, breathing hard, beads of sweat collecting near her hairline.

"Mmm. A few, hard to tell exactly how fresh," he said as he kept at his job, sweeping the beam of his flashlight over the dust. The climb was taxing but slow, and Pescoli stopped several times, looking over the canyon, trying to imagine if the victim had come down this path. Had she been followed? Chased like Bianca? Seen "a monster"? Had someone caught up with her, attacked her, and either killed her or injured her and left her for dead? If so, had she known him? Had her attacker been a male? Or had she died in some freak accident?

"Holy . . ." Farnsby said from about ten feet above Pescoli on the trail. A short, compact man with a receding hairline and a perpetual scowl, he was studying the ground intently. "What the hell is this?"

"What?" Breathing hard, Pescoli followed him to a narrow space between two boulders that loomed over her. He'd angled his flashlight to run its beam on the ground between the huge stones to a spot in the trail where several footprints, with what appeared to be the tread of a running shoe, had left an imprint. Next to them was another massive print, clearly defined and shoeless, as if it had been made by an immense man.

Pescoli froze. Studied the print. "Big guy?"

"Bigger than anyone I've ever seen." He crouched next to the impression, then placed a folding scale next to the print and snapped a photo. The flash further illuminated the footprint.

It was pretty damned big.

Using a slim tape measure, he took measurements of the length and width of the print. "Wow," he whispered, rocking back on his heels and frowning, his features visible in the light from Pescoli's flashlight. "Don't move," he ordered and swung his beam around the area in an obvious attempt to find another print. "What the hell made that?"

Though he was probably talking to himself, she ventured a guess. "Grizzly bear?"

"You see any claws?" he snapped, as if she were an idiot.

"A mountain man?"

"With size-twenty or more shoes?"

"Basketball player?"

Farnsby glanced up at her. He didn't bother to hide his contempt. "I don't think Shaq or Yao Ming has been to Grizzly Falls lately."

"So what're you saying?"

"I don't know."

But she thought he had an idea, one she wouldn't like. She saw the spark in his eyes, the bit of wonder in his features in the half-light from their flashlights. "Don't say it, Farnsby," she said, guessing what he was thinking. "Don't even go there."

His gaze locked with hers. "Gotta be."

"Sasquatch?" She shook her head. "Don't tell me you're a Big Foot guy."

"Well, this here"—he pointed at the print with one finger—"came from a helluva big foot. Okay? I'm not saying it was made by a Sasquatch—"

"Big Foot's a myth. That's it. Nothing more." But just as the words were rolling over her tongue, she, for a second, remembered what Bianca had said: *This . . . this thing was huge. Massive. Like way taller than me and it . . . I mean, I couldn't tell, but it was on two legs. Rearing up. And it smelled. Bad. . . . maybe a really big human. Massive. And hairy.*

"I'm just sayin'—" Farnsby said, but Pescoli had heard enough.

She held up a hand to stop any further argument. "Yeah, I know. Just collect the evidence, bring it in, and . . . let's not go anywhere near the whole Sasquatch thing. Okay? We just need to ID the victim, find out what happened to her, prove it, and if foul play was involved, nail the bastard who did it to her. That's our job. End of story."

What the investigation didn't need was anything

that would turn a tragedy into a media circus. Like some tech, a supposed man of science, bringing Sasquatch into the mix. If it was anything, it was some kind of hoax.

"Big Foot," she muttered under her breath and wondered why those two words sounded like an omen.

Pescoli headed downhill and met up with her partner; then, seeing that Alvarez was dealing with the coroner, she made her way back into the graveled area where the kids were being detained. By now, parents were at their children's sides.

Wiping the perspiration from her forehead, she observed the little groups of parents, kids, and cops standing between the parked cars of the teenagers. The interviews were progressing.

The thing of it was, Pescoli knew most of the teens, as well as a good many of the adults. She'd met several sets of parents, or the single parents, over the years that Bianca had been in school, some of them as far back as preschool, over a dozen years earlier.

Interviewing them would be a trip down memory lane—make that a bad trip, considering the situation.

Reading their faces in the strobing lights from the department-issued cruisers, she noted that a good percentage of the parents were horrified, as would be expected, a few seemed angry and nervous, and a few others refused to have their children talk to the cops at all, as if the kids, or maybe the parents themselves, had something to hide, or because they'd been down this road before and decided to say nothing until they lawyered up.

Too bad. The way Pescoli figured it, every last one of them, including herself, should be relieved that it wasn't their child being hauled out of the woods in a body bag sometime this morning.

The interviews weren't going to be fun. That much was certain. She headed to a clutch of women she recognized, all of whom had aged in the dozen or so years that had passed since she'd seen them every morning as she'd dropped off or picked up Bianca from preschool. At this time of night—make that morning—being pulled out of sleep to come and get their kids at a wild-ass party where a body had been found—yeah, it didn't look good on anyone. Except maybe for Mary-Beth Delaney, who was as trim as ever, her auburn hair without any gray, no lines marring a face with high cheekbones, pointed chin, and wide eyes. She was dressed in a jogging suit, her hair drawn up in a messy bun, hooped earrings glinting in the harsh lights from the cruisers, not a smudge of makeup out of place.

She smiled at Regan, though her gaze did flick down Pescoli's body for a quick, judgmental second.

Never had Pescoli felt so hugely pregnant.

"This is so awful. *So* awful. Can we just get

out of here?" Mary-Beth asked anxiously, as if she and Pescoli were tight, had been friends for years, though they hadn't seen each other for a decade. Pescoli remembered Mary-Beth as being a pushy mom in preschool, already insisting her little Simone excel at letters and numbers or whatever it was the kids did then. While Bianca was coloring butterflies outside the lines and drawing some additional free-form insects on the page, Simone had been encouraged to keep her work neat, the coloring shaded, the hues blended, each stroke of the crayon smooth. Like the little toddler was going to become some female twenty-first-century Michelangelo or something.

And yet both of their daughters had ended up here, in the forest, in the dark of the night, where a classmate had apparently died.

"You can go soon. I just have a few more questions for Simone," Pescoli said, turning toward Mary-Beth's daughter. She forced a smile as Mary-Beth flicked another glance at her protruding waistline.

"Bianca left," Simone asserted. Challenging. Defiant.

"Yes, she did," Pescoli agreed.

"I don't see why she got to leave, and I have to stay." She flipped her hair off her face, her eyes narrowed, her lips in a flat angry line.

"It's not fair," Lindsay Cronin chimed in petulantly. In a quicksilver moment, Pescoli

80

remembered Lindsay as a preschooler, chubby arms crossed over her chest, chin pointed out, lips turned down, spouting the same words, "It's not fair," over some minor infraction at the school. Then, as apparently now, Lindsay felt the need to point out when things didn't go as she liked.

"She gave her statement. I already spoke with her," Pescoli said.

That was too much for Mary-Beth. "They let you interrogate your own daughter?" One manicured hand flipped skyward in an expression of disbelief. "Isn't that like a major conflict of interest?"

Well, yeah. "Not interrogate. We're interviewing. Asking a few questions. That's all. Someone else from the department will talk with Bianca again. Of course."

Mary-Beth silently accused her of lying.

"It's so unfair!" Simone crossed her arms over her chest. Her pouting was nearly palpable.

A step behind her daughter, Mary-Beth was nodding.

Pescoli agreed. "You're right. It's not. Fair, that is. But then nothing is." She eyed the girl, who was wearing enough makeup to look like she was trying out for a reality show. Simone's eyeliner and mascara were applied nearly as thickly as her haughty expression.

"And I heard Bianca thinks she saw a monster, some kind of big hairy ape thing in the woods." Simone's chin inched up a fraction.

"You heard that?" Pescoli really wanted to downplay any talk of a monster. Finding the dead girl up here would create enough of a media frenzy as it was.

"Everybody heard it. Rod Devlin said she was raving like a lunatic. Emmett Tufts says he was walking back to base camp, and Bianca came racing down the hill and nearly knocked him over, she was so out of it."

Pescoli caught a glimpse of Emmett and his brother, Preston, standing next to a pickup with a king cab. Between them was their mother, Terri. The boys had gotten their height from their mother, as she nearly looked eye-to-eye with her sons, both of whom were over six feet and had played basketball for the high school. Terri, she'd heard, had played college ball. As had she. Terri had been a center, Pescoli a guard.

"Everyone knows about the Big Foot," Simone said, and Lindsay nodded vehemently.

Pescoli thought of the huge footprint Farnsby, the supercilious Sasquatch-believing tech, had discovered and even now was probably casting. It wouldn't be long before the story got out.

Pulling her small recorder from her pocket before the girl could protest again, she said, "Let's get started, so we can get you home." She hoped she sounded affable, but she wasn't quite able to hide the sarcasm in her words. Too bad. "So, Simone, why don't you tell me what you were doing up here at around two in the morning?"

Her mother winced.

Good.

"Just hanging out. With friends," the girl said, some of her attitude dissipating.

"What time did you get here?"

"I dunno. Maybe a little after midnight?" she said slowly, eyeing her mother for her reaction. Mary-Beth's tight mouth seemed to pinch even tighter.

"Were you alone, or did you come with someone?"

"With Lindsay," she admitted, blowing air through her nose as if disgusted with herself.

"Lindsay?"

"Lindsay Cronin."

"The girls are best friends," Mary-Beth cut in. "Good girls. Simone even volunteers at the hospital." She placed her hands over Simone's shoulders, her fingertips clenched in the girl's T-shirt, as if she were trying to silently and subtly warn her daughter to tread carefully.

Of what?

A cop they'd known forever? Pescoli remembered a time when Simone, all of four, had been on a playdate with Bianca after preschool, where Simone had played dress-up and tried to master Candy Land. Even then, Pescoli had caught the little girl cheating, if she'd even understood what she was doing, which Pescoli hadn't believed.

83

Now, in the middle of the hot August night over a decade later, she considered that maybe she had.

The rest of the interview didn't go well, no surprise, nor did any of the others.

As it was: Nobody knew nothin'.

At least that's what all the teenagers who'd been rounded up wanted the cops to believe. But Pescoli wasn't so sure. She figured they were more interested in covering their asses than finding out the truth. Most of them smelled like a brewery, and talking to any of them to get any relevant information was like pulling teeth from a cement jaw.

Madison Averill, who'd probably been instrumental in getting Bianca to come up here in the first place, had been sullen and clinging to TJ O'Hara, "Teej" to the kids. TJ had tried to shrug Madison off, but she'd wrapped her fingers tightly around his arm and looked at him with doe-soft eyes.

Teenage angst on display. At a tragedy. Pescoli had trouble dealing with it.

TJ had been polite enough, but had kept his answers short and had avoided eye contact with Pescoli. In fact, he'd kept tossing looks across the parking lot to a spot where Lara Haas was engaged in a whispered conversation with both of her parents. She was hard to miss with blond hair, and a tight, white T-shirt and shorts, not exactly the kind of outfit one would wear trying to hide in the game of hide-and-seek that Bianca had described.

The girl was a knockout with a body the stuff of teenage boys' wet dreams; a porn movie producer's opinion of a "real woman." Huge breasts, nipped-in waist, and a rounded butt above legs that wouldn't quit.

No wonder TJ was throwing surreptitious glances in her direction. Most of the boys were, including the Bell kid, who had been belligerent, almost defiant, just like his old man and older brother, Kip. In the Bell brothers' case, the bad apples certainly hadn't fallen far from the rotten tree.

Some of the girls had been crying and couldn't or wouldn't tell them anything,

Lindsay Cronin's histrionics had apparently taken over her ability to speak coherently as she'd looked up at the sky and sobbed, only to be comforted by TJ's brother, Alex. Older than TJ by a couple of years, Alex O'Hara was also taller and heavier, a football-lineman type. He had his arm around the wailing Lindsay while Simone Delaney, standing a few steps away and still with her mother, took in the scene and scowled darkly. Something was definitely going on there, Pescoli thought and made a mental note.

It didn't look like those "besties" were all that close, at least not as tight as Mary-Beth Delaney wanted Pescoli to believe.

The worst of the lot, Pescoli thought, was Austin Reece. He was smart and privileged and wasn't about to be intimidated by the authorities.

"I don't have to talk to you without my lawyer present," he first told Detective Sage Zoller, a bit of a thing with a tight, gymnast's body, springy curls and a bad-ass attitude. Now he was giving Pescoli the same song and dance all served up with a smug, frat-boy smile. "I know my rights."

"We're just trying to find out what was going on." She was attempting to hold on to her patience, but it was growing thin . . . fish-line thin.

He arched an imperious eyebrow. "I've called my dad. He's on his way."

Perfect. Not that the kids didn't need their parents. Hell, hadn't Bianca? But this one? Not so much. Reece's imperious attitude rankled. Big time. Pescoli was hot, tired, and not interested in playing nice. What she'd like was a cool bath, a cigarette, and a Coors Light, not necessarily in that order, but she'd given up nicotine—well, kinda—years before, drinking anything alcoholic was out while she was pregnant, and a cool bath, well, that would have to wait.

"My father's with Reece, Connors and Galbraith," Austin reminded her. "Actually, he's the 'Reece,' in the firm's name. You know, as in senior partner."

Pescoli regarded him with a cool eye. He really

had a bad case of the I'm-better-than-you flu. A lot of it going around these days. "I know who your daddy is. And I don't care. But when he gets here, I've got a few more questions for you."

She was rewarded with a bored "oh-sure" expression that was mostly a smirk, but she held on to her fast-escaping cool for all she was worth.

Now was not the time to get in a wrangle with a teen.

CHAPTER 5

At her desk, Alvarez glanced at her watch. Barely 6 a.m. And she'd been up all night. From the crime scene, she'd driven to the morgue, then here, to the office. Her muscles ached, and a slow, steady headache was building at the base of her skull as her stomach rumbled to remind her that her last meal had been half a cheese sandwich she'd grabbed the previous afternoon. She'd been up for over twenty-four hours, and it would be a few more before she could go home and tumble into bed. A nap, that's what she needed, then a hot shower, a cup of tea, and a bowl of fruit, yogurt, and granola. Better yet, a long yoga session to stretch her tense muscles. As it was, she'd have to settle for the tea.

Maybe.

Stretching her arms over her head and twisting

her neck, she eyed her computer monitor, where pictures of the crime scene were displayed, the screen cut into four images with different angles of the victim visible.

The girl in the photos was definitely Destiny Rose Montclaire. Not only had she been reported missing, but distinguishing marks had helped the department ID her. The victim's stature, her coloring, her tattoos, and a scar, which was still visible on her ankle from a surgery she'd endured as a four-year-old, had matched those described on the missing persons report.

Two deputies had been dispatched to her home in the wee hours.

At 4 AM, her ashen-faced parents had walked into the viewing room of the morgue, where, in abject horror and denial, they had identified the unknown girl's remains and promptly broken down.

It was the worst part of her job, Alvarez thought now as she reflected on the scene. She'd been little comfort to the father, whose lip had trembled as he'd held his wife as she collapsed against him. Alvarez had warned them about the condition of the body, but, of course, both had insisted on viewing their daughter despite her disturbing and grotesque appearance. Helene Montclaire, a heavyset woman with filmy blond hair and drizzling blue eyes, had keened and crumpled in that tiled room, her knees giving way and buckling as she took a long look at the corpse that had once been her child.

"No, no, no!" she'd cried, needing to deny what her eyes had confirmed as she'd clung, fingernails twisting in his T-shirt, to her white-faced husband. He'd appeared haunted, his eyes shining with unshed tears, his hands shaking despite his efforts to stay strong.

"You'll get whoever did this," Glenn Montclaire had stated through lips that had barely moved. It wasn't a question.

"If it does prove that Destiny was the victim of homicide— "

"What else could it be?" he'd cut in, pained dark eyes cutting into her. "What? An accident?"

"We'll know more after the autopsy," she'd replied, not wanting to go into the possibility of suicide. "We will do our best. I'll see to it personally."

"Make sure your best is good enough." He had held her gaze as a tear slid from the corner of his eye and his wife, Helene, buried her face in his shirt. Her shoulders had been shaking, her muffled sobs echoing against the tile walls and floor of the sterile room.

"And once you confirm that . . . that this wasn't an accident, check out Donald Justison," he'd added as his wife's sobs increased, her shoulders shaking in the cold room with its tile walls.

"Justison?" Alvarez had repeated, making a mental note.

"Yeah. Don Junior, the mayor's son."

The mayor being Carolina Justison.

"Donny's her ex-boyfriend. A pissant loser if there ever was one. And a stalker! He couldn't leave her alone after she broke up with him."

"Is that right?"

"You bet it's right. He's been calling her. Harassing her!" His once-ashen face showed color again.

"Do you know if they'd been together recently?"

"Probably."

"When was the last time you saw your daughter?"

He'd looked at his wife. "A week ago last Friday. Around eight o'clock. I already put all this in the report I gave to the missing persons officer."

"I know. Just refresh my memory."

"It wasn't anything unusual. Not at the onset. She'd come back from volunteering at the hospital. Northern General. She's worked there for nearly a year. First in the cafeteria and lately in the children's ward. You know, played with the kids, read them stories and such . . . and . . . that was, I don't know, maybe around six, I guess, because she said she stopped off and saw a friend before driving home, so she was later than usual. Her shift is over at five. Then, after dinner, she went out for a walk. Never came back."

"With anyone?"

"Alone." Glenn had shaken his balding head. "Someone called and no, she didn't say who, but I heard her phone ring and then she took off, said she'd be back in an hour or so. We didn't think anything of it. It was still light, probably seven, seven-thirty. She did it all the time. Loved being outside in the summertime. Ever since she was a kid." His voice had cracked. "Oh, Jesus . . ."

"Had she done this before?"

Destiny's mother had given off a soft mewling sound.

"A couple of times. That's why we didn't report it until . . . until well into the next day, after we'd checked with some of her friends. No one had seen her or talked to her or texted or nothin'."

"Did you talk to Donny?"

"He wouldn't answer the phone," Glenn had said bitterly. "So we filed a report."

"My baby, my baby, my baby," Helene had whispered brokenly, and her husband had held her for several minutes, whispering into her hair to comfort her when he, himself, was blinking back tears.

"We're going home now," he'd said, shepherding his wife out of the viewing room. "Come on, Helene," he'd whispered. "It'll be all right." Then he'd thrown Alvarez a final dark look that said what they both knew: It would *never* be all right. Not ever.

Alvarez had barely been able to control her own emotions, which was unusual. She prided herself on staying calm and keeping her expression unreadable. She'd trained herself, practiced remaining emotionless for years, ever since high school, when she'd had to rein in her feelings, her anger and shame and hatred after her girlhood had been stripped from her.

She could usually pull it off—the heartless ice-princess image—but grieving parents got to her. Always had. Her heart had bled for the Montclaires.

Now, despite her lack of sleep and the fact that her eyelids felt like sandpaper scraping against her eyes, she was bound and determined to do whatever it took to find out what had happened to Destiny Rose.

Officially, the jury was still out on whether Destiny had met with foul play or suffered a fatal accident.

But Alvarez was betting on option one.

Nonetheless, she'd withhold judgment until all the facts were in. Cause of death determined. Alvarez had requested a rush on the autopsy.

She pushed her desk chair back and made her way past Blackwater's office on her route to the lunchroom. The acting sheriff hadn't yet arrived, but then few had at this early hour. She hesitated for a second at the closed door, one that had always been left ajar when Dan Grayson was sheriff. Her heart twisting, she remembered how she'd looked up to Grayson, even fancied herself in love with him at one time, how comforting it had been to see him at his desk, his Stetson hung on a peg, Sturgis, his black lab, curled on the dog bed near his desk. Grayson had had an easy smile and there had been kindness and intelligence lurking in the depths of his firm, uncompromising stare.

She still missed him.

And though she was now deeply involved with Dylan O'Keefe and was considering marriage to the private investigator, she would never forget Dan Grayson. She couldn't. He still came to her in her dreams, even once when she was locked in O'Keefe's embrace. A bit of guilt ran through her at the thought, but Grayson had been her mentor and so much more. There had never been a physical relationship between them, but there had been a connection, an unspoken meeting of the minds or souls or whatever you wanted to call it. Though rationally she couldn't explain it, she felt that link still existed.

Which was ridiculous, of course.

And against everything she held true.

She'd always been a realist, trusted the facts, relied on science. Anything considered remotely paranormal was dismissed as just plain bunk. Reaching out to the dead or communing with spirits in a twilight world of afterlife was folly.

Dreams were just dreams, misfires of neurons in her subconscious. Nothing more.

For a nanosecond, she considered Grace Perchant, a loner of a woman who lived outside of town with two hybrid dogs, each part wolf, and believed she communed with the dead and was a conduit from this world to the next, could even see the future.

Alvarez hadn't bought any of it, though the ghostly woman with white-blond hair and pale eyes had made some predictions that had come eerily close to the truth and it had put this niggling, persistent doubt in her brain.

Was it possible that she, Selena Alvarez, could somehow communicate with Grayson?

No. Not a chance. She *knew* better. Dan Grayson did not "visit" her in her dreams. It was just her subconscious working its way through her grief and guilt. Nothing more.

Yet, as she stood outside his old office, she placed her hand, fingers splayed, on the solid wood frame, and whispered, "I miss you." Then, squaring her shoulders, she forced herself to shake off her case of nostalgia and continued down the hall toward the lunchroom. Time to bury her ancient fantasies. She was now with the man who was certainly the love of her life, and the dreams she was having of Grayson were all because of her own guilt that she'd survived when an assassin had taken him down. It was still so unbelievable that no one in the department, including herself, had been able to protect the man who had helmed this office with such a fair and even hand.

In the break room, which smelled faintly of coffee and some pine-scented cleaner, she glanced through dust-streaked windows mounted high overhead. The sun was rising, thin shafts of light oozing through the dirty panes as the sky started to lighten, dusty lavender turning to a hazy blue. She eyed the half-empty pot that had been warming for hours over a hot plate, but decided today was not the time to start a coffee habit. Instead, she heated water in the microwave while scrounging through the basket of tea bags and settling on the last packet of chai green.

Dunking the bag in her cup, she returned to her office. At her desk, she rotated her neck, stretched her arms over her head, and tried to release some of the tension from her muscles. Then she sipped from the hot brew and once again looked over the information that had been gathered from the crime scene, the pictures and video now on her computer. She'd already read all of the statements from the kids they'd found at the reservoir. She skimmed them again, hoping she'd missed something important the first time through, but they didn't hold much information. Everyone interviewed said he or she had come to the area to "hang out" or "party" or "play a game." Each had been reluctant to name their peers and had denied any use of alcohol or drugs. Most importantly, to a one, they'd sworn they didn't know about the victim, who, it seemed, had been in the creek for over a week. Unless the body had been moved, but so far there was no indication that it had been.

Alvarez frowned. She hated that the kids were holding back, but she had to agree that the victim had been dead long before the party with its bizarre game of hide-and-seek had begun. That, of course, didn't mean any of the kids didn't know more about the girl or who might have been with her at Reservoir Point.

The teenagers and their code of silence irked her, but she understood it. While in high school, she'd kept secrets that should have seen the light of day, secrets that could have changed her life and the lives of her own set of friends, her own family.

Her lips flattened as she considered that old black cloud of her own past, then steadfastly pushed it aside. For now, she had to concentrate on the job at hand. She thought of the kids gathered up at the Point last night, Bianca Pescoli included.

"Teenagers," she muttered.

Boot heels rang down the hallway, and from the sound of the purposeful stride, she guessed the acting sheriff had arrived.

Though she missed Dan Grayson's easy manner and quick smile, she didn't really mind Cooper Blackwater as a boss. If she took her feelings for Grayson out of the equation, she knew that Cooper Blackwater was a good cop, thorough and determined. His attitude meshed well with hers: all business. He was very "gung-ho," as Pescoli said, and his style was crisp, almost military, but it worked for him. Though he was more inclined to use the media to his advantage, get his face on camera while the department was working a case, he didn't seem overly conceited or self-aggrandizing, not to Alvarez anyway. His cocky attitude was different from his self-deprecating predecessor, but still effective. Detractors had faulted Grayson for being "too laid-back" or "not hands-on enough" or "too folksy, everyone's best friend." For Blackwater it was just the opposite, "too cold" or "too ready for a photo op" or "more interested in power and climbing his way to the top than in helping the people of Pinewood County."

It seemed here, in Grizzly Falls, you were definitely damned if you did and damned if you didn't.

"How's it going?" Blackwater asked as he paused in the open doorway to her office. His black hair was military-clipped, his jaw freshly shaven, his dark eyes interested and piercing. His coloring and bladed features probably harked back to a Native American ancestor, presumably the same one who had handed down his surname. "I saw our victim is definitely the Montclaire girl," he said, his eyes showing a little bit of empathy. "Anything new on what happened? Don't suppose the autopsy's been done yet? Probably not started."

"I put a rush on it."

As if her request weren't good enough, he said, "I'll make a call."

"Good." She wouldn't let herself be irritated that he pulled rank, using his influence as sheriff. Whatever worked. " 'Til we get the results, we're not sure what we're dealing with."

"Which is?"

She gave him a quick, brief update on what they'd discovered, most of which he probably already knew. She finished with, "I've got a list of family, friends, and acquaintances that I've added to current and ex-boyfriends. We're checking phone records and trying to confirm who was the last person to see her and when that was, double-checking it with the missing persons report and cross-referencing any names to those kids who were up there last night, but that, so far, seems to be just a coincidence."

"No such thing."

"Maybe."

"What's with Pescoli's kid being up there?"

"Part of the group. All friends, or at least they all knew each other, ran with the same crowd."

"And the Montclaire girl?"

"No. At least she wasn't tight with any of them. Most of the kids said they knew her or had seen her in school, but no one admitted to being her friend."

He leaned against the doorframe and rubbed his jaw thoughtfully. "I hear Pescoli's kid thought she saw a monster or Big Foot or something." Dark eyes pierced hers. Questioning.

"She doesn't know what she saw. But something was chasing her." Alvarez felt her muscles tense a bit. She was ready to defend Bianca, if necessary.

But Blackwater's attention had turned to her computer monitor, where the picture of Destiny Rose Montclaire's body was visible. "You think she was murdered?" he asked, nodding to the screen's disturbing image.

"It's definitely a possibility. Trying to figure it out."

His eyes narrowed. "I'm betting homicide, but don't quote me on that." He flashed a rare smile. "I'm not a betting man." With a couple of slaps to her doorframe, he said, "Keep me in the loop," then charged down the hallway toward his office.

"Will do," she said, though it was to herself. And she wasn't going to take his bet. She, too, believed that someone had killed Destiny Rose Montclaire. She didn't have the proof yet, but she'd lay odds that when she received the autopsy report, she'd find that the victim had been murdered.

She turned her attention back to the names of friends, neighbors, family, and anyone considered an enemy or adversary. The ex-boyfriend whom Glenn Montclaire had mentioned, Donald Justison Junior, was at the top of her list. She'd done a preliminary check on him and found out that Justison, barely nineteen, had already had a couple of run-ins with the law, little brushes that hadn't come to much, but she wondered if Mommy Mayor had stepped in for him, cleaned things up.

Now you're starting to think like Pescoli.

She sipped her rapidly cooling tea, the sweet scent of chai filtering up her nose, the warm liquid soothing.

There was nothing in the files to suggest that Carolina had used her municipal influence to save her kid's reputation.

Anyway, Alvarez was definitely getting the cart before the horse. First, the department had to have a confirmation that a homicide had been committed.

She flipped through the computer images, pictures of the rotting body in the creek, pale hair floating around a decomposing face, then an earlier yearbook shot of a blonde girl with wide, ingenuous blue eyes, a turned-up nose, and a timid smile.

What happened to you? Alvarez thought, setting her cup aside to study the image of the girl who appeared so innocent. So far, she didn't have a profile on the girl, didn't understand her relationship with her parents, family, or friends. She'd just begun to scratch the surface of Destiny Rose Montclaire's life.

Why, she wondered, would anyone want this nearly angelic-looking girl dead?

CHAPTER 6

Pescoli opened a bleary eye and saw that it was ten o'clock and sunlight was streaming through the cracks in the blinds to stripe the foot of her bed. Santana wasn't with her; he'd probably gone to the Long ranch to oversee the daily routine and, it seemed, he'd taken the dogs with him or at least moved them from the room. There were now three canines, a pack in Pescoli's groggy mind. She envied her husband's energy; he'd been up as late as she, filling her in on the trip to the hospital before he'd fallen asleep. Fortunately, Bianca's injuries were minor, and she was only supposed to wear a splint to stabilize her foot for a week or two to make sure she didn't tweak it again.

She threw back the covers but continued to lie in bed. The bedroom was warm despite the fan moving the air slowly overhead and the summer breeze that wafted into the room from the open sliding door that led to the deck.

She closed her eyes for what she thought was less than five minutes, but as her gaze focused on the bedside clock she realized it was now nearly eleven. Great. Every muscle in her body ached from lack of sleep, and she felt as if she could just grab a few more minutes. . . . She closed her eyes again.

Get up!

She'd never been a morning person, but today was worse than ever. She was so tired, and a headache from lack of sleep had started to bang at her temples. At that moment, the baby kicked. Hard. "Okay, okay," she grumbled. "You don't have to nag me, too." The kicking continued and she sighed. So it was going to be that kind of day.

Terrific.

With an effort she pushed herself up, waddled to the bathroom, used the toilet, and turned on the shower. She peeled off her nightgown and stepped under the spray as it began to warm, her skin goose-pimpling at the shock. Any remnants of sleep were chased away as the water heated, pulsing jets throbbing over her body, steam rising. That was more like it.

As she lathered, she thought about the night before, the party, the dead girl, Bianca's weird story about being chased by a hairy monster.

Big Foot, my ass.

Just kids messing with each other.

Except that a girl is dead. Most likely murdered.

As the warm water flowed over her, she brushed her teeth in the shower, a trick she'd learned from Santana, rinsed quickly then turned off the faucet and grabbed a towel from its hook. Her headache had lessened, but now she was ravenously hungry. Eying the scales across the room as she towel-dried, she frowned, cast a look in the mirror, and decided to forgo the morning routine of depressing herself by checking her current weight.

In less than ten minutes, she was fully dressed in gawd-awful maternity slacks, a T-shirt, and a light jacket, her hair twisted into a loose, wet ponytail, what little makeup she bothered with, lipstick and a brush of mascara, applied.

"Ready for the day," she muttered as she pulled on lightweight boots that were getting tight. Just like everything else.

Pushing open the door of the master bedroom, she started down the hallway, then heard Bianca's voice through the nearly closed door of her room. Pescoli rapped softly, then pushed on the door to find her daughter in a pool of pink blankets, cell phone pressed to her ear as she sat, cross-legged on her bed, a purple splint visible over her ankle.

As in Pescoli and Santana's bedroom, bright Montana sunlight was piercing through the curtains, illuminating Bianca's room with its stark white walls, accented by every shade of pink imaginable. The light fixture was a small chandelier, the carpet a silvery gray, curtains, bedding and art bright splotches ranging from bubble-gum pink to almost lavender, nothing Pescoli would have ever chosen.

Santana and Pescoli had built this cabin in the last year and had decided to allow Bianca to decorate her room to her taste, create her own space. They'd thought it would help her adjust to the fact that her mother had remarried, Bianca now had a stepfather, and yes, on top of all that, she, nearly finished with high school, was soon to become an older sister.

So far, the plan had worked—even if all the girly touches were the antithesis of everything Pescoli had ever believed in and, unfortunately, an homage to Michelle, Bianca's ever-irritating high-maintenance stepmother. Pescoli had grown up a tomboy and athlete and had never had any interest in princesses, castles, fingernail polish, or jewelry. Not so her daughter.

"Yeah . . . I know . . . I'm okay . . . I *know! Really* scary. Freaked me out . . . umhmm," Bianca was saying into her cell. She glanced up at her mother, and even from across the room, Pescoli noticed the two tiny stitches that held the skin beneath her chin together. "Yeah, that would be nice. Tell Michelle thanks," Bianca was saying. "I'm just glad I don't have to go to school. I look *awful.* Like something out of *The Walking Dead* . . . oh, yeah. *Seriously* freaked me out . . . What? Sure . . . of course. I will . . . Love you, too. Bye, Daddy." She hit a button, disconnecting the call, then started immediately texting someone.

"Hey," Pescoli said. The room smelled faintly of fingernail polish. Clothes were strewn over the floor, desk chair, makeup table, and window seat.

"Hey." Bianca didn't look up, her fingers flying expertly over the phone's smooth surface.

"How're you feeling?"

"Not great."

"How not great?"

"I dunno. I kinda hurt all over. My arm and shoulder and leg, but this"—she pointed to her chin—"it's sooo *awful*. I mean, I might have to have plastic surgery."

"I doubt it."

"You don't know. Mom, I *can't* have a scar, not on my face!" Bianca was nothing if not a drama queen.

"Let's not go off the deep end, okay. Wait until it heals. It could add character to your face. You know, like Harrison Ford."

"He's a man, Mom. An *old* man.*"

"That 'old man' is still a bona fide heartthrob, let me tell you."

Bianca rolled her eyes. "It's going to take forever to look okay, if it ever does!" She was texting again.

"How's the ankle?"

"It hurts! Bad!" But Bianca hadn't really mentioned it until her mother brought up the subject. A good sign.

"Take care of it, okay? I have to go to work."

"You know, Mom, I'm pretty sure that girl was Destiny." Her lips folded over themselves as she tossed the idea through her brain. "I mean, I can't be a hundred percent, but I thought about it last night—I couldn't *stop* thinking about it— and I saw her face, the way it was in the water all, you know, rotting, the flesh falling apart."

She shuddered, finally dropping the phone into her lap as she met Pescoli's eyes. "And I think it must be her . . ."

Pescoli navigated her way over a river of strewn clothes to take a seat on the end of the bed. "You're right. About the girl being Destiny, I mean. Alvarez texted me earlier this morning. The ID was confirmed by her parents."

Bianca blanched. It was one thing to conjecture, another to learn the truth and have reality hit. "Oh, God." She blinked, then bit her lip. "So . . . what happened to her? Was it—? Did someone kill her?"

"Don't know yet. That's what we're going to find out."

Absently rubbing one forearm with her fingers, she asked, "Do you . . . do you think it was one of the kids, the ones that were there?"

"Have no idea. But we do know that whatever

happened to her didn't occur last night. Time of death's all wrong. It was sometime before, but we haven't really pinned it down yet. Long before your party got started anyway. Whose idea was it to meet up at Reservoir Point?"

She lifted a shoulder. Eyed her phone as a soft ding alerted her to the fact that another text was arriving. "One of the boys. I don't know. Probably Austin. He's kind of in charge."

The ring leader. "What about the Bell kid?"

"Kywin?" She shook her head as her phone dinged again and she glanced at the screen. "He does what the others want. Goes along, you know. Never has an original thought."

"TJ?"

"Oh, geez. I don't know, Mom," she snapped, then a little more contritely. "What . . . what if she wasn't killed by a human?"

"We're not certain her death is a homicide."

Bianca sent her a look that said, *Yeah, right.* "But what if it was something else that murdered her?"

The monster again. They were back to that. "Like?"

"You know, whatever it was that chased me."

"We still haven't figured out who that was."

"Not 'who,' Mom, but 'what'?"

"Okay."

Anger flashed in her wide eyes. "You don't believe me. You never believe me!"

"I do believe you. I know you saw *some*thing

and it chased you down to the creek and scared the hell out of you. Of course. But, I don't know what it was or why. That's all I'm saying." Bianca looked about to explode again, and Pescoli said, "I'm just thankful you're okay." To prove it, she hugged her daughter, and for once Bianca didn't tense up at the gesture.

"Just scarred for life," she grumbled as Pescoli released her. A finger with a now-broken nail tenderly touched her chin. "Jeremy came by my room a while ago. You were still sleeping, and . . . well, so was I, but he came in anyway and woke me up, said he heard about what happened up at the reservoir."

"How?" Pescoli asked, as neither she nor Santana had woken him last night.

"On his iPad, I guess."

"It's out there? On social media?"

Of course.

Bianca stared at her mother as if she'd grown up during the time of Conestoga wagons. "Geez, Mom. What d'ya think?"

Kids. Cell phones. Instant messaging. Texting. Tweets. Her heart sank. These days, information passed in a nanosecond. One text, tweet, or post and the info, bad or good, was sent into cyber-space, passed along exponentially at the speed of light. Not good. Not good at all.

"Jeremy believes me. About Big Foot. He told me a lot of people around here believe in it.

There's even a group that meets and discusses Sasquatch in the old lodge building, the one that originally housed the Sons of Grizzly Falls, I think."

"Yeah, I know." There were nutcases who were a part of the group. Ivor Hicks, a man who believed he'd been abducted by lizard-like aliens for testing purposes, was one. Fred Nesmith, an anti-government nut, another. For that matter Lex Farnsby was probably a charter member.

"Alex O'Hara. He's a part of it."

"What about TJ?"

"He's never said. Probably. But some of Jeremy's friends are members and he says they put together these elaborate searches every year and go looking for them. Families of 'em or loners."

"Have they found any?"

"I don't know . . . maybe . . . well, maybe not. It would be really big news, if they had."

Regan had made her point and wasn't going to press it. Besides, she was already running late. Really late.

Cisco, toenails clicking on the hardwood of the hallway, appeared in the open doorway. The mottled little terrier peered inside, then, tail wagging wildly, ran into the room and launched himself onto Bianca's bed, where he wriggled up to her and washed her face with his tongue.

"Enough," she cried, but the little scrap of a dog had managed to bring a smile to her lips.

"Geez, Cisco, give it a rest!" But she petted Cisco, not stopping as he nestled up against her.

Pescoli pushed herself to her feet. "Okay, gotta run. Please, don't discuss anything about this or post about it or tweet or whatever. Okay? Until we've sorted out what happened to Destiny."

"I think it's too late."

"Well, try." Bianca was right, of course. For all Pescoli knew, the story on Big Foot and the dead girl could already be trending. Closing the barn door now would do little good.

Another text came in.

Bianca was already on it.

"Who's texting you?"

"Lots of people."

In her mind's eye, Pescoli saw dozens of groups of kids, all with phones, all writing as rapidly as Bianca, misinformation and facts all twisted into multiple threads of conversation. That was how information was spread these days, instantaneously with the touch of a keypad, exponentially, with one phone linked to dozens and then again so that the conversations moved through the community like an insidious epidemic.

"Look, you can't text or talk about the case. It could be compromised."

Bianca looked up then, her eyes holding Pescoli's. She didn't say it, but the words *too late* silently passed between them. "Please, Bianca."

She dropped her phone onto the bed and stared

at it as another soft ding alerted her to a new text coming in.

Great.

"Look, I gotta go. There's stuff for breakfast or lunch in the fridge, yogurt and cheese, bread and I think some tuna. Eggs if you want to make them. And some cocoa mix if your brother didn't wipe me out."

Ignoring her cell, Bianca arched a brow and met her mother's gaze. "What're the chances of that?"

"Not good."

"Zero."

"Probably. Call me if you need anything, okay? And oh, someone from the department will be wanting to talk to you. You know, for your 'official' statement."

"I already talked to you," Bianca protested.

Pescoli nodded. "I don't really count this time."

"Because I'm your kid."

"You got it."

"Fine. Doesn't matter. I'll tell whoever the same thing."

"I know. But if you want me around . . . ?"

"I can handle it, Mom," Bianca said as Regan made her way to the door. Bianca had scooped up her phone again, her thumbs working fluidly over its surface, her head somewhere else.

Pescoli called over her shoulder. "I'll check in with you later," and picked her way down the steps, careful to avoid Bianca's pink Nikes and two dog toys. "Bye!" she yelled to utter silence.

Bianca hadn't heard or had decided not to reply.

No big surprise there.

CHAPTER 7

Pescoli's mood hadn't improved by the time she arrived at the station. She was hot and tired, and the cup of decaf coffee she'd bought at a drive-through kiosk wasn't doing the job. Today she needed high-octane rocket fuel, which this cup of Mellow Morning was not.

Carrying the paper cup, she walked into the office, where the air-conditioning unit was struggling to keep up with the stifling August heat. The department was teeming with officers, some in uniform, others in street clothes. Conversation buzzed, cell phones beeped, fax and copy machines chugged, and footsteps shuffled down the polished hallways.

As she passed Blackwater's office, she noted his door was ajar. His voice drifted through the crack as he assured someone "it would be taken care of." No one was in his office, but Blackwater was holding a cell phone to his ear as he stared out the window. "Yeah, I know. No worries. Everything's under control." A small laugh. "Yes, you can quote me on that."

Yeah, right. Everything was just peachy-keen, wasn't it? A dead girl found at an underage party with drugs and alcohol and some huge, hairy creature scaring the bejeezus out of kids on top of the usual cases of domestic violence, assault, robbery, and a handful of other miscellaneous crimes in the county. Sure. No worries.

As she continued to her office, hugging the wall as a detective with a suspect in chains clanked past in the opposite direction, Pescoli reminded herself not to be irritated that Blackwater was sitting at Dan Grayson's desk. It wasn't as if Grayson were ever coming back. Like it or not, she'd better get used to Cooper Blackwater because she figured he was here to stay.

If he was actually elected sheriff.

So far, no one was opposing him.

"Detective!" Joelle Fisher's high-pitched voice was punctuated by the click of her ever-present high heels. Hurrying in Pescoli's direction, Joelle waved a manicured hand. As the receptionist for the Pinewood County Police Department, Joelle always dressed as if she were attending a ladies' luncheon, circa 1955. Today she wore what Pescoli's mother would have classified as "an ensemble" in pale yellow. Knit suit, white blouse, yellow heels. The shoes actually had a bit of a platform, a surprising nod to the 2000s, or maybe the 1970s.

Joelle's hair was short and blond, a shade of

platinum closing in on silver, her lips glistening with freshly applied pink gloss.

"Do you have a minute?" Joelle asked as they met at the door of Pescoli's office. Then, quickly, as if anticipating Pescoli's negative response, she added, "Look, I know you're busy, but this will just take a sec." Without an invitation, she followed the detective inside.

There was just no fighting Joelle when she was on a mission, which, it seemed, she was today.

Pescoli placed her unfinished coffee onto a desk that needed some serious organizing. "What's up?" She tried and failed to keep the impatience out of her voice. It wasn't Joelle's fault Pescoli had been up all night, or that her daughter was embroiled in what in all probability was a homicide.

"It's about the baby shower."

Oh. Pescoli inwardly groaned. "I thought I already said I didn't want one."

"I know, but it's been years since you had a child." Joelle stood on the visitor's side of the desk, as if pleading her case before a judge. She loved anything to do with holidays, birthdays, or special occasions and intended to celebrate each and every one. From New Year's Day until the next New Year's Eve of the same year, there were multiple events that gave Joelle cause to bake, craft and decorate. A month didn't have a chance of slipping by without some celebration.

The walls of the lunchroom and hallways were usually covered in snowflakes, or sunflowers, or four-leaf clovers or reindeer, depending on the season. Small flags were strewn upon desks on the Fourth of July and Veterans Day, eggs and bunnies appeared at Easter, and even leaves decorated the lunchroom tables on Arbor Day. A birthday was never missed, so a new infant's imminent arrival was certainly reason enough to start knitting and baking and planning a baby shower.

Joelle's smile was almost as bright as the diamonds winking in her earlobes. "I thought that anything you did manage to hang on to from your earlier pregnancies is probably terribly out of date, or unsafe. I mean it's been *years*."

"Decades," Pescoli corrected. With more effort than usual, she slid into her chair and noticed that it wasn't as comfortable as it had been before she'd gained thirty-plus pounds.

"Yes, well. Exactly. I mean, do you even have a layette or a breast pump or a baby monitor that actually has a camera in it?"

"No . . ."

"The advances in technology these days makes things so much easier, and . . . and . . . well, there have been dozens of recalls on cribs and car seats and infant carriers, so you're best with something brand new."

"I think we've got everything covered," Pescoli lied. The thought of a roomful of women, or maybe men and women, all giggling over cute little onesies printed with sayings like LOOK OUT, LADIES, or DADDY'S LITTLE PRINCESS, or BORN TO BE ADORABLE was more than she could stand right now. To be feted by Joelle—Pescoli couldn't imagine.

"Now, Detective, let's be honest. Even if you did have any baby stuff, it's probably packed away where you can never find it." Joelle skated a quick look over the cluttered surface of Pescoli's work space.

Oh, come on. The mess wasn't *that* bad.

"You haven't even told us if you're having a boy or girl."

"We don't know."

A hand flew to Joelle's chest, her splayed fingers tipped in polish the exact match to her lipstick. "But everyone knows ahead of time these days!"

"Santana and I are a little old school."

Joelle sighed. "I don't get it. If you knew the child's sex, you could decorate the nursery appropriately and buy little outfits and be ahead of the game, you know?" Pescoli tossed her purse into a desk drawer as Joelle asked, "Why don't you want to know?"

"We want to be surprised." Why was she even having this conversation? "Look Joelle, I appreciate the offer, for the shower. Really. I think I told you that already?" She eyed the woman still standing resolutely on the far side of the desk. "But seriously, no thanks. I'm just not up for it."

The twinkle went out of the receptionist's eyes as she realized she wasn't going to talk Pescoli into changing her mind, and it was that moment Pescoli realized that Joelle had already made serious plans involving invitations, menu, party games, and gifts. Oh. Dear. God.

Before she could say anything else, quick footsteps in the hallway heralded her partner's arrival. "Hey!" Alvarez, looking fresh as a damned daisy, stuck her head through the open doorway. "How's Bianca?"

"She'll live. Out of the hospital, now at home, nursing a cut on her chin, sore shoulder, sprained ankle, and bruised ego."

"Your daughter?" Joelle said with a small gasp. "What happened?"

Just check Facebook for the latest, Pescoli thought, surprised that the receptionist, who was always first to know the local gossip, had missed any news. "An accident at a party. She's okay."

"What accident?" she asked. "Oh . . . did this happen at the party where they found the body of that poor girl?" From the outer reaches of the hallway, a phone started ringing insistently. Joelle caught the noise. "Damn." She hated to be left out of the gossip loop but duty was calling. "Please, Detective, just think about the shower."

Joelle maneuvered past Alvarez and started down the corridor. "When you change your mind, just let me know," she said with a smile as she bustled toward the reception area of the department.

"I will," Pescoli said, then, as the familiar clicks of Joelle's high heels faded, added, "Just after hell freezes over."

"I heard that!" Joelle's voice reached Pescoli.

Alvarez cast a final glance at the retreating receptionist. "What was that all about?"

Pescoli finally settled into her chair. "Long story." At the curiosity in Alvarez's expression, she rolled her eyes. "It's the same thing she's been bugging me with ever since my pregnancy seemed to go viral around this office." She scowled. "Joelle wants to throw me a baby shower. Invite everyone who works here. Can you imagine?"

"And that's a bad thing?"

"Yes, it's a bad thing. I told her I'm not up for it. Pink and blue streamers and balloons and a silly game or two? Come on."

"So Joelle gave up without a fight?" Her voice was full of disbelief.

"Probably not. As I said, we've been having this discussion for months." She stretched out her back and heard it pop.

"Maybe you should just give in."

Pescoli shot her a look. "I'll think about it. Maybe." She paused. "Then again, maybe not.

So, why don't you bring me up to speed on the Montclaire case?"

"It's the reason I'm here." While Alvarez explained about meeting the grieving parents as they'd ID'd their daughter's body, then compiling a list of possible suspects and evidence while waiting for the autopsy results, Pescoli listened and sipped the so-called coffee. With zero kick, the decaf blend didn't have the desired effect that caffeine would have supplied to her bloodstream. She really shouldn't have bothered except that the scone she'd devoured on the ten-minute drive had temporarily quieted the rumble in her belly.

Alvarez finished with, "Then the mayor called. Right after eight this morning."

"Did she?" Not much of a surprise. Pescoli was definitely not a fan, but, for once, she tried not to show her distaste of the new mayor of Grizzly Falls.

Carolina Justison had once been a stockbroker in New York. About fifteen years ago, after a scandal at the brokerage both she and her husband had worked for, she'd divorced the "lying bastard," packed up her son, who just happened to be her ex's namesake, and headed west. She'd landed in Grizzly Falls. Though she had insisted she was in search of a simpler life, she'd fallen back on her old ways and opened her own investment firm before eventually running for mayor. She'd squeaked by in an election that had been so close a recount had been initiated.

So much for her supposed dream of the simple life.

"She talked to Blackwater and he relayed her message." As a fax machine screeched and burped in a nearby office, Alvarez balanced on the arm of one of the visitor's chairs. It was damned amazing how irritatingly thin and agile the woman was. "Then, she called again. This time to speak directly with me."

"Fabulous."

"She wants to let us know that—"

Pescoli held up a hand. "Let me guess. This has something to do with her son being caught and cited up at Reservoir Point."

"Bingo."

"Another stab in the dark: she's not happy."

That scared up a smile on Alvarez's lips. Pescoli already knew her partner had been up all night, but looked fresh and ready to take on the world. How was that even possible? The room was hot and stuffy, the air conditioner rattling but unable to compete with the heat from a glaring Montana sun.

"She's not just unhappy, she's 'absolutely mortified' and I quote, that her son could be considered a part of this 'difficult situation.' And yeah, she called it that. The 'difficult situation up at Reservoir Point.' I guess she heard herself, though, because she did acknowledge that it was a tragedy, of course, but that her Donny had nothing, absolutely nothing, to do with what happened to the 'poor girl,' even though Donald Junior dated Destiny Rose for nearly a yea before he broke up with her. Destiny was a little broken-hearted, but 'you know how that is with teenagers.' "

"She wasn't exactly empathetic."

"No."

"Trying to cover her son's ass." Pescoli leaned back in her chair. "You think he's involved some way?"

"Too early to tell. But Glenn Montclaire, Destiny's father, mentioned Donny. And he said the break-up was the other way around, that Destiny cut Donny loose and he didn't much like it, even started stalking her."

"So Donny said he was the dumper, rather than the dumpee, but Glenn Montclaire says otherwise."

"And Helene Montclaire as well."

"The Montclaires actually pointed at Justison?"

Alvarez nodded. "Said if there was any evidence of foul play we should take a long, hard look at Donald Justison Junior."

"Then I guess we will."

"Already on the top of the list."

The case was morphing into a true mess. The mayor's son and a dead girl?

"And Carolina Justison was only the first parent to call."

"I'm not surprised."

"It started early." Alvarez had made notes and checked a memo-taking app on her cell phone. "Besides Mayor Justison, I had a pretty lengthy conversation with Billie O'Hara. She's actually a twofer."

"Twofer?"

"Two-for-one. Assured me that both her sons, Alex and TJ, are totally innocent." Alvarez glanced up from her cell. "Of what I'm not sure. She wasn't specific, so I'm going with innocent in general."

"Of all criminal activity or mischief or whatever," Pescoli thought aloud. "Sounds like her. Pretty high-maintenance and by the book. Rigid. Type-A through and through, and a fitness instructor to boot. Participates in triathlons, maybe even an Ironman or two, I don't really know, but I think she hauls her bike over to the West Coast every year and rides it all over the state in some organized race."

"Cycle Oregon?"

"You know it?"

"Heard of it."

Pescoli nodded, her damned stomach rumbling again despite the protein bar she'd devoured driving to work. "They ride over mountains and by the ocean and across the desert, all across the state. Hundreds of miles. Route changes each year. Takes like a week or something. I know because, when Joe was alive, he was always trying to talk me into it," she said, bringing up her first husband, Jeremy's father. "He took up bicycling for a while. That was twenty years ago or so, but I think it's basically the same," she said a little sadly. Theirs hadn't been an even-keeled marriage, not by a long shot. They'd both been young and bullheaded and, she had to admit, she'd been even more volatile then than she was now. But Officer Joe Strand had been a pretty good man, a great officer of the law, and a so-so husband. Both he and Regan had fought the bonds of marriage and parenthood. Then, suddenly, just when she'd hoped the marriage would straighten out, he'd been killed in the line of duty. Her heart still twisted a bit. Survivor's guilt never quite let go of you.

She took another sip of her now-tepid coffee and snapped herself out of her melancholy thoughts. "Anyway, Billie O'Hara is into fitness in a big way," she said.

"Isn't that a good thing?"

"The point is that whatever she does, whatever Billie focuses on, she has the intensity of an eagle diving for a fish in a lake. Whether it's an athletic event, or a position on the school board, or her job at the athletic club, she makes certain she wins. Always ends up on top."

"And expects the same of her boys?"

"Yep."

"Sounds like you know her. Personally."

"I did. A while back. Before she got into the fitness thing. She was just another mom at the preschool. A widow. Lost her husband to a logging accident when the boys were still in elementary school. She's always been fiercely protective of her kids. Never saw that they did any wrong and I think, for the most part, she's right." Pescoli shifted in the chair. "Is it just me or is it like the middle of the Mojave Desert in here?" To cool off, she lifted her hair off her neck.

"It's you."

Of course it was. She found the tiny fan situated on the far side of her computer and pressed the switch. Air started flowing, blowing across her face and ruffling some papers. She adjusted the direction and the pages settled back down. "So the deal is that I know most of the parents of the kids that were at the party last night, or at least I've been introduced to them over the years. I met some when our kids were in preschool, then saw them over the years as my kids went through elementary and junior high school. The O'Hara boys, both of 'em, attended Good Feelings."

"Good Feelings?"

"The preschool."

"Seriously?"

"I know, I know. Sounds a little granola."

"A little?"

"I think the owners were trying to do something with the letters in Grizzly Falls, and since the image of a grizzly bear doesn't quite fit with the warm and cuddly tone of preschool, they took the letters G and F and came up with Good Feelings." At Alvarez's smile, Pescoli added, "Yeah, it was a little 'Kumbaya' for me, but everything else was too strict or too religious or too expensive. Anyway, the O'Hara boys, Lara Haas, Bryant Tophman—for a while before his dad's church came up with their own—and Kywin Bell all went to Good Feelings at one point or another. Austin Reece and Simone Delaney, and oh, Maddie Averill, too, I think, but I'm not sure how long some of them were there. It was a long time ago. I guess all that 'peace be with you' didn't rub off on all of them."

"Teenagers are a whole different breed of cat from who they were as preschoolers."

"Can't argue there." Both Jeremy and Bianca had once been sweet and innocent as young children, only to turn into rebellious hellions in high school. She took a final sip of her decaf and drained the paper cup before crushing it and tossing it into the trash. "I'm thinking you might have a few more parents who phoned in. I'm willing to guess that Wilda Wyze called too."

"Kywin Bell's mother." Her gaze slid to her notes. "Yep. Bright and early."

"So her son is misunderstood as well?"

"She actually wasn't all defensive. Just wanted to know the score and seemed worried. Said she was afraid that he had some bad influences in his life."

Pescoli said, "She's talking about her ex?"

"Franklin Bell. Yeah. He's called about three times, but I've missed him. I have a list of parents to call back. But first things first."

"Destiny Rose Montclaire."

"Yeah."

"So, what's next?"

"A little bit of a waiting game." She explained about the parents ID-ing their daughter, that the autopsy hadn't been started despite the "rush" that both she and Blackwater had requested. "Later today, I'm told," she added, then shared a partial list of persons of interest, those who were closest to the victim, including the Justison kid, should it be proven that Destiny had been the victim of foul play.

"She was on the periphery of the crowd that gathered last night," Alvarez wound up. "Knew some of the kids, such as Justison and the O'Hara boys. But the others claimed they were basically only acquaintances. They knew of her, but had never hung out."

"Like Bianca. She had her in an English class."

"I'm going to have to speak to her," Alvarez reminded her.

"I know. I told her someone would call and set up an interview. You need her cell number?"

"Already got it."

"Okay, just let me know when you set it up."

"Probably this afternoon," Alvarez said as her phone buzzed. Answering, she held up a hand to end the conversation, then walked into the hallway, leaving Pescoli to really dig in to her work day a few minutes after noon.

CHAPTER 8

Bianca slept until nearly four in the afternoon, only waking when she tried to turn over and the pain in her ankle brought her to the surface. Or the nightmares of monsters and dead girls with flaxen hair and black empty eye sockets startled her awake. Each time, she would fall back to sleep. She finally roused and found Cisco curled up next to her. After her mother's pointed comments earlier, Bianca had turned off her phone and now clicked it on. It had blown up with messages while she'd been asleep, dozens of texts and four unanswered calls. Despite what she'd halfheartedly promised, she checked her texts and listened to her voice mail, but whoever had been calling hadn't left a message.

"Your loss," she said to the empty room.

For now, she ignored the texts. She wasn't in

the mood to rehash what had happened the night before.

And she was still mad at Maddie for ditching her.

She rolled over, and Cisco, who had snoozed the day away with her, gave out a startled yelp, then bounced to the floor.

"Sorry," Bianca said around a yawn.

She felt awful. Groggy and sore. In a bad mood.

Clumsily, because of the damned cast that couldn't get wet, Bianca wrapped her ankle in plastic, then forced herself through the shower. Afterward, she found a pair of shorts and a T-shirt, then managed to get dressed. Her hair was wet, curly, and currently a dark blond that she wasn't that crazy about, but she couldn't worry about that now. She pulled it away from her face into a wet, messy bun and didn't bother with makeup. She looked like a freak anyway with the scrapes and bruises visible on her face and bare arms. And where could she go with the stupid soft cast?

Nowhere.

Not that she had anywhere she needed to be.

She worked part-time as a waitress at a local diner, but had already left a message with the manager that she'd be out of commission for a few weeks, so she was stuck here, at home with the dogs and her cell phone.

"Lame," she said into her reflection, then grimaced at the sight of her messed-up face. She felt bad about Destiny. Dear God, no one should end up rotting in a creek. And though she hadn't admitted it to her nosy cop of a mother, the kids who'd been up at Reservoir Point were asking her a million questions about the girl. Somehow they'd all figured out the victim was Destiny, long before Mom had shown up in Bianca's room this morning.

She hobbled down the stairs, made her way into the kitchen, and then, hearing her phone ring again, cursed herself for leaving the damned thing on her bed. She muttered as she grabbed a container of mixed berry yogurt and a spoon, then headed up the stairs again. Of course she didn't reach her room by the time the phone had stopped ringing, and of course whoever it was who'd phoned—PRIVATE CALLER was listed on the small screen—didn't leave a message.

As she dug into the yogurt, she perused her texts, discovered nothing new, and switched on her television, a recent addition to her room, compliments of Dad and Michelle, a gift for her seventeenth birthday.

The phone rang again, and this time, she snagged it from the bed and answered with one hand while muting the TV with her other.

"Is this Bianca Pescoli?" a husky male voice asked when she answered.

"Yes."

"My name is Carlton Jeffe, and I live here in Grizzly Falls. You may have heard of me."

She hadn't but didn't say so and waited for him to go on.

"Well, see, I'm the president of our local club, the BFBs. Y'know, the Big Foot Believers."

Her stomach tightened. So that's what this was about. "Okay."

"And I heard that you had a close encounter with a Sasquatch last night, that one of them chased you up around Reservoir Point. Is that right?"

Again, she didn't answer.

Jeffe said, "You saw one."

"Where did you hear that?"

"Well, honey, it's all over town. Bryant Tophman is one of our members. He let me know. Me and some of the other guys, organizers, y'know."

Tophman? Crap. That jerk-wad!

"And he gave you my number?" She was pissed.

"Yes, he did."

"Why?" she asked, getting a bad feeling about all of this. "Why are you calling me?"

"Well, see, Bianca, I'd like to talk to you, in person. Hear your story and, y'know, I thought maybe you'd like to come speak at our next meeting."

"Speak? As in give a lecture?"

"Nothing that fancy." He gave a raspy cough. "Just come in and tell the group what you saw. Over at the Sons of Grizzly Falls Hall. Tuesday night. Seven sharp, but you should show up a few minutes earlier, y'know, to get set up."

Was he crazy? Probably. She was shaking her head.

As if he could see through the wireless connection, Jeffe upped the ante. "We serve coffee, soda, and cookies. And we've got some people who're interested in what you've got to say. Important people."

Oh. Like. Sure. "No."

"Now, darlin', come on, it would really help us. There's been a rogue Big Foot seen up around Cougar Pass, and this may be the same one. A rogue. Loner. Any information you might have would be a big help."

Darlin'? Seriously?

No way would she be a part of his carnival. She flashed on the massive smelly beast and his one glowing eye that had crashed through the underbrush while running after her. A shiver ran up her spine. "I don't know what I saw last night," she admitted.

"Maybe I can help you with that."

"No!" she said, then, "No," again and hung up. She dropped her phone as if it were radioactive. It was one thing for her to "think" she may have been accosted by a creature that was more myth than substance, another to have a complete stranger call her and invite her to speak at a meeting.

And the next time she ran across Bryant Tophman, she was going to ream him out but good for giving out her number. "Idiot," she muttered and glanced at the TV with its silent screen. A yearbook photo of Destiny Montclaire filled the screen. Bianca turned on the sound.

". . . discovered last night at Reservoir Point. Police are still searching the area where the body was found, trying to determine if the girl died from natural causes or if foul play was involved. If anyone has any information—"

Her phone rang and she saw her mother's number appear on the screen. "Hi," she answered, still watching the newscast.

"How're ya doing?"

"Okay."

"The ankle?"

"Still hurts. Bad."

"Probably will for a while."

"Great."

"How about the rest of you?"

"My lip hurts, too and my shoulder—" She glanced in the mirror, where she saw a bruise forming under the strap of her T-shirt. "It's turning black and blue. And *green.*"

"I was talking about your emotions. How're you feeling? Detective Alvarez needs to talk to you and so we'll be home in . . . probably about forty-five minutes. Maybe an hour."

"I know. She called." She glanced at the television again. A video of Reservoir Point rimmed in trees, the reporter walking up the path that bordered the creek where Destiny's body had been caught in the roots of a tree.

"I'll be here," she said and clicked off the television.

Pescoli hung up from Bianca and tried to tell herself that her daughter's conversation with Alvarez was no big deal, that it happened all of the time, but she couldn't convince herself. The fact that her daughter's name was in the slightest way linked to the homicide investigation was unsettling.

Bianca wasn't under suspicion of anything, of course, but still . . . it was hard being on the other side of the interrogation table.

Her stomach rumbled, reminding her that the scone on the way to work and a candy bar later in the day weren't enough to sustain her and the baby that was due to arrive in the next three weeks. Scrounging in her bag, she located a protein bar deep in the bottom of her purse, then made a trip to the lunchroom, where she found a jar of instant decaffeinated coffee crystals that made the low-octane cup she'd grabbed at The Buzz seem like rocket fuel.

Back at her desk, she'd no more than unwrapped the oat and peanut butter bar when her phone rang. She answered only to discover Manny Douglas on the other end of the connection.

Her already bad day took a decided turn for the worse.

The reporter was always looking for a big scoop, and she wasn't in the mood today. Nor was she any day for that matter. She didn't have a lot of use for the press and certainly not for Manny Douglas. He was a weasel of a man, a reporter who slanted everything he wrote while looking like a model for L.L. Bean or Orvis with his ever-present khakis, flannel shirts, and down vests.

After identifying himself, he got right down to brass tacks. "I'm working on a piece for the *Reporter* about the body found up near Reservoir Point this morning. A young girl, in her teens, who has been identified as Destiny Rose Montclaire. Can you confirm?"

"I'm sure the sheriff will hold a press conference about it."

"When?"

"I don't know."

"Cause of death?"

"Unknown."

"But there's going to be an autopsy, yes?" he asked.

"Yeah."

"And then you'll know cause of death and whether or not this is a homicide."

"You know how it works. Again, the sheriff, or maybe the PIO, will speak to the press." Currently there was no public information officer—the last one had quit earlier in the year—but Pescoli wasn't about to elaborate.

134

Ignoring her dodge, he plowed on, "There was a teen party up at the reservoir last night. Drinking, drugs."

"I can't confirm that."

"And your daughter, Bianca, she was up there?"

Pescoli's irritation catapulted to anger. "No comment," she said tightly. Bianca was a minor, and her name would be kept out of the papers. At least for now.

"Rumor has it she thinks she was chased by a Big Foot."

"Where did you hear that?"

"It's all over social media. Could go viral."

"Oh, come on."

"People all over the world are interested in the creature."

"The 'creature' doesn't exist."

"Is that what your daughter says?" he asked.

She wasn't going to be lured back into that conversation. "Look, Manny, I'm busy here with a homicide investigation. If you want more information, call the sheriff." She hung up, steamed, then forced herself to relax. There was a helluva lot of work yet to be done, and she didn't have time for Manny Douglas and the *Mountain Reporter*.

She was just closing her computer screen when Alvarez poked her head into the room and said, "Preliminary autopsy's in on the Montclaire girl."

"That was quick. Good."

"I guess when Sheriff Blackwater speaks . . ."

"Mountains are moved in the morgue."

"Seems so. As I said, just a preliminary, not complete. Toxicology won't be for a while. You've got a copy. Email." She pointed to Pescoli's computer. "Definitely homicide."

"I just turned it off," she said, switching on the monitor again. "Cause of death?"

"Asphyxiation." Alvarez's face was grim, her eyes dark as ebony. "She was strangled. Pressure so hard her neck snapped."

"Ugh."

"Takes a helluva lot of strength," Alvarez said. "Super-human."

"What about time of death?"

"With the water and decomposition, it was impossible to pin down, but she'd been in the creek a while. The coroner's saying a week, and I'm guessing she was killed the same night she went missing, or soon thereafter, so a week ago Friday, but who knows? Could have been Saturday or possibly even Sunday."

"We need alibis for the weekend."

"Uh-huh. Let's start with Friday night, work our way into Saturday. I've already asked Zoller to double-check all the people who knew the victim, those we won't get to today."

"Good."

"And there's something else that came up."

"Yeah?"

"She was pregnant. About two months along."

Pescoli let out a low whistle, unconsciously touching her abdomen and thinking of the baby soon to be born. "So that makes it a double homicide."

"Yes." Alvarez was grim.

"If Donny Justison's the father, the mayor's son just moved up on the suspect list."

She nodded slowly.

"He could have known about it; she could have told him." Pescoli didn't like the turn of her thoughts. "Could be our motive."

"Or, it could be the killer didn't know."

"This just keeps getting worse."

"That it does."

"Do the Montclaires know?"

She nodded. "I thought they should be the first to find out."

"You talked to them?"

"Mmm. Just a second ago, on the phone. Actually spoke with Glenn. At first he denied it could be possible, but then he turned right around and said that Donald Justison Junior was the . . . let's see, 'son of a damned bitch' who was responsible and that I should just go out and arrest him before something happened to him."

"Glenn threatened to do something to Justison?"

Alvarez tipped her hand back and forth in a "maybe, maybe not" gesture. "Worth watching."

"Crap."

Alvarez glanced at the clock. "You ready to go?"

"More than ready. God save me from more paperwork."

"I told the Montclaires we'd be over, to go through their daughter's room, double-check for the missing phone, and grab her laptop. Then, I want to talk to Bianca, but now, in light of this recent development, I want to check in with Donny Justison."

Pescoli slipped her cell phone into her bag. "I thought the mayor wanted us to stay away from her kid."

Alvarez's lips twisted into a cold smile. "All the more reason to talk to him ASAP, don't you think?"

"Didn't Carolina call Blackwater and tell him to back off or something?"

"She sure did."

"And what did he say?"

Alvarez's smile became icier. " 'Put him at the top of the list.' "

"Good." That was a surprise, she thought as she found her sidearm. Maybe Blackwater was more of a cop and less of an ass-kisser than she'd originally imagined.

"Justison may have been the last person to contact Destiny," Alvarez said. "I'm still waiting for her phone records. The cell carrier promised them today."

"We haven't located her cell phone?"

"Not yet. The parents had a GPS tracker installed, but somehow it was disabled."

Pescoli clicked off the desk fan. "Destiny was probably a hell of a lot more technologically savvy than her folks. She could have turned it off herself. There's an app for everything these days."

"Glenn Montclaire even went so far as to call the phone and walk around his house and property, hoping to hear it, but no answer. Our guys did the same thing in the area where the body was found. Nothing. Either it's turned off or lost or . . ."

"With the killer," Pescoli said before snagging her bag and following Alvarez out of the building to a blast of August heat. Though shadows were lengthening from the trees planted at the edges of the parking lot, the asphalt was sunbaked, the street shimmering with heat waves.

With a click of a remote, Alvarez unlocked her Subaru, an SUV she'd purchased recently. She'd parked the Outback nose-in, the front bumper nearly touching the brick wall of the backside of the station. Black and gleaming, the car soaked up the rays from the afternoon sun.

As they slipped into the sweltering interior, Alvarez said, "Did I forget to mention that Donny Justison was on the wrestling team in high school? He made all-state."

"So strong as an ox."

"Maybe superhuman," Alvarez agreed as she twisted her key into the ignition.

Was Alvarez buying into the whole "Big Foot in the woods" theory? No way. Not down-to-earth, stick-to-the-facts Selena Alvarez. "Don't even go there," Pescoli growled as she yanked her door shut.

"Don't go where?"

"To the far-fetched. Okay?" Sweat was beading on her brow and between her shoulder blades. "Bianca's already mentioning monsters chasing her, and Lex Farnsby is talking Sasquatch. You know, like there's a Big Foot running around the foothills. Holy crap, it's boiling in here. How about some air?"

"Just give it a sec." Alvarez fiddled with the temperature controls. "I'm not talking about Big Foot. What do you take me for? I'm thinking maybe our guy, a big, strong guy, is hyped up on drugs. I knew a guy in high school who snapped a guy's forearm during a wrestling match and he wasn't trying to do his opponent harm, not really, just wanted the pin." She adjusted her sunglasses before backing out. "And you always hear about in times of great stress like during an accident, with adrenaline pumping through his body, a guy's able to lift a car off a kid or rip a door from its hinges. Superhuman strength." She shot Pescoli a look. "So, let's just say, we've got a guy who's intent on murder, and he's already fired up anticipating the crime."

"Maybe someone who doesn't want a baby screwing up his plans?"

She twisted her neck to look out the rear of the vehicle, rammed the gearshift into reverse, and began backing out. "So, now he's pumped up, right, in a rage? Adrenaline flowing through his bloodstream, maybe steroids or whatever's amping him up adding to the mix, and good old testosterone driving the show. Just how tough would it be for a big guy, a trained fighter, to snap a small woman's neck?" She hit the brakes and put the Outback into drive. "Piece of cake."

A bad taste filled Pescoli's throat as she wrestled into her seat belt and flipped down her visor. At least a waft of cool air had begun to filter through the vents.

As Alvarez eased on the gas and pulled out of the lot, Pescoli's cell phone buzzed. Plucking it from her bag, she glanced at the screen and inwardly groaned. Her ex-husband.

Great. Just what she needed. A chat with Lucky.

Because of Bianca's recent trip to the hospital, she took the call. "This will just take a sec," she told Alvarez, then answered: "What's up?" No need for pleasantries.

"I was checking on Bianca."

"She's at home. You could call her."

"I did."

"And?" She slid on a pair of sunglasses and

stared out the window. Despite the heat, the sidewalks of the upper level of Grizzly Falls were crowded with pedestrians and skateboarders, women with strollers, joggers, and a few people walking dogs. Strip malls and restaurants lined the street, where traffic moved smoothly. This part of town, sprawling toward the foothills, was the newer area of Grizzly Falls. The older, original section of town lay upon the banks of the Grizzly River, just below the falls for which the town was named.

"I wanted your take on things," Lucky said.

That was a surprise. In their few years of a tumultuous marriage, he'd rarely wanted to hear what she had to say. A truck driver who was handsome, charming, and as slippery as an eel, he had been a big believer in asking forgiveness rather than permission. In Pescoli's opinion, it hadn't been a question of permission or forgiveness, but rather what should have been a discussion. Instead of a meeting of the minds, she and Luke had been forever butting heads. Still were. And she didn't trust him.

"She'll survive. Despite what she says, she won't be scarred for life."

"Physically, ya mean."

"Right. I think she'll put everything else in perspective, though. It'll take time."

"Pretty tough."

She thought about the first time she'd seen a

body. It had been her grandfather in a casket, and even that had been creepy for an eleven-year-old. "Real tough. And, she thinks she may have known the victim."

"The victim? Oh, the dead girl? Yeah . . . yeah, of course." He cleared his throat. "Real hard."

Something was off here. "What did you think I was talking about?"

"Come on, Regan. Bianca was chased through the woods with a Sasquatch bearing down on her. Has to be traumatic."

"Oh my God, you too?" She nearly clapped her hand to her forehead in exasperation.

"They've been spotted all around here," he said defensively.

"But no one has pictures or bones or even any spoor."

"Not yet."

"Please."

"They're real, Regan."

"Says who?" She caught herself being sucked into an argument. Again. "Never mind. Look, I'm working. I'll check on Bianca. Alvarez needs to talk to her."

"You mean like, interview her?"

"Yes." Was he being even more dense than ever?

"Because of the dead girl."

Two for two.

"Shouldn't I be there? She's underage. Needs a parent."

"I'm her parent," she reminded shortly.

"You're a cop."

She let that settle in for a few beats. Didn't immediately rise to the bait.

"I'm on my way," Lucky told her.

"Not necessary. Really." The last thing she needed was Lucky all of a sudden playing daddy.

"She needs an advocate. A real parent."

"One who believes in Big Foot?"

"Face it, Regan, you're a cop first and a parent second," he said tightly.

"What?" she nearly shouted. She thought of all the years that she'd raised the kids alone while holding down a full-time, more-than-demanding job as a homicide detective. The carpools, the shuttling kids, the school meetings, the sports or dance performances, the tears and laughter. How she'd dealt with Jeremy and his girlfriend and his once-upon-a-time affiliation with alcohol and marijuana. How she'd worried over Bianca's self-esteem and the boys who were forever sniffing around her.

And where had Lucky been?

Living his life. Free and easy. Married to a woman barely older than his stepson, a life-sized Barbie doll who spent hours getting "mani-pedis" and facials and spent her days tanning or reading online celebrity blogs.

"I am Bianca's advocate," she asserted, stressing every word. Out of the corner of her eye, Alvarez slid her a questioning look. "I'll handle this, Lucky." She didn't bother saying good-bye, just hung up. "All of a sudden, that deadbeat's worried about Bianca."

"She *is* hurt."

"I know, but she's been hurt before and he's always thought a quick phone call and an even quicker 'Love ya, princess' were the extent of his fatherly duties. And he acts like this Big Foot thing is real."

Pescoli shook her head in frustration. Damn Lucky. He always knew how to complicate everything. And if he played into Bianca's fears with this Sasquatch stuff . . . it would make her want to rip her hair out.

But Bianca saw something . . . something large and frightening. . . .

Whatever it was, it sure as hell wasn't good.

CHAPTER 9

The Montclaires were devastated and numb at the murder of their child. They wanted their daughter's remains released so that they could plan a service, but could barely talk about Destiny without breaking down. Helene had a washed-out look. In jeans and a blouse, she hadn't bothered with makeup, her thinning blond hair lank, her eyes red-rimmed. Glenn was a big man with the beginnings of a belly hanging over his belt, his hair thin though he appeared to be in his early forties.

He talked to Alvarez and Pescoli while his wife worked hard to stem the tears. Twisting a nearly shredded Kleenex, she remained on a worn leather couch as Glenn led the detectives down a short hallway to Destiny's room.

Pescoli's heart was heavy as she eyed the room, neat and tidy, probably straightened up, with a twin bed with a thick black and white striped quilt and tall posts that had once, it seemed, held a canopy. A dresser and night table were the only other furniture atop a vinyl floor softened by a white shag rug that was starting to gray. A poster from *Frozen* seemed at odds with the head shots of teen heartthrobs that decorated the walls. A corkboard held ticket stubs and photos, a report card and a wrist corsage that had long wilted and dried—memories of a life cut short. But not one picture of Donald Justison. There were a few shots of friends tacked to the corkboard. Donny wasn't in them.

Odd, Pescoli thought as she searched a pillow-case and the pillow inside.

Glenn Montclaire stared into the room where his daughter had grown up and Pescoli guessed he was seeing his child in his mind. "Have at it," he said, as if suddenly snapping to. "Just please respect our daughter, okay? Her mother . . .

Helene would be very upset if things were disturbed too much."

"We'll be careful," Alvarez said.

"Fine." He blinked, fighting tears. "Then get on with it."

"Did she have a laptop or tablet?" Alvarez asked.

He nodded, walking to the nightstand and opening the top drawer. A small, silver laptop was tucked next to a box of tissues, some open packs of gum, and change.

Pescoli asked, "What about credit cards?"

"She would borrow ours if she was going shopping, but no, she didn't have her own. I told this all to the officer when I gave the missing persons report."

Alvarez nodded. "Thanks."

"I just want you to know she was a good girl. Good. Despite all this talk about her being pregnant." His voice cracked.

Pescoli had thought he might stick around, but he held on to the doorframe for a second, then, with a sad shake of his head, said, "You get the guy who did this. You get Donny Justison."

"We're not sure who did this," Pescoli said.

"Justison," he repeated, then left them alone. They looked through her closet and bureau, the nightstand and the bed, underneath the mattress and box springs, even searching for hidey-holes in the walls or floor.

Other than the laptop, they found nothing that

would help. They took the computer with them, leaving the Montclaires to their grief.

"It never gets any easier," Alvarez said as she climbed behind the steering wheel and started the engine.

"Never." Pescoli slid into the passenger seat, buckled in, and stared out the window. "Justison place?"

"Let's see what Donny has to say." She threw a look toward the house, where, through the picture window, she could see Destiny's folks seated on the couch, close together. "The Montclaires, or at least Glenn, think he's the doer."

"Early days yet."

"I want to know what his alibi is. Wish we had a time of death."

"Yeah, stop by Midway okay? I'm starving." And that was the truth. At least it felt that way. Ever since she'd learned she was pregnant, she couldn't inhale enough food and it was a problem. But not one she could solve today.

Alvarez made the stop, and inside the small burger joint with its 1950s motif, they found a table near a bank of windows. A long L-shaped counter guarded the area leading to the kitchen, and a handful of patrons were sitting on stools, while other diners filled the tables scattered between the counter and windows.

A tall redheaded waitress with a bad attitude and a name tag that read MISTY took their orders.

Pescoli asked for a cheeseburger and a sparkling water while Alvarez settled on a chicken Caesar salad, dressing on the side, and an iced tea with lemon.

While waiting to be served, Alvarez and Pescoli talked over the case and the suspects, and then Alvarez went over the autopsy. "No water found in her lungs, so she probably wasn't killed in the creek. Her hyoid bone was crushed, consistent with strangulation, and the only thing of any significance was a tiny bit of what looks like latex found under two of her fingernails."

"Latex?" Pescoli repeated, then thought about it, how Destiny had probably been trying to pry the killer's hands from her neck. "As in gloves?"

"Maybe. The lab is looking into it. The pieces are tiny. But definitely latex as opposed to nitrile or vinyl."

"Or cloth or leather."

"Uh-huh," she said as a sizzling noise emanated from the kitchen, as if a fresh batch of sliced potatoes or frozen shrimp or the like had been lowered into the deep fat fryer.

"Could be a break?" Pescoli asked.

"All of the hospitals, clinics, dental offices, you name it, use latex gloves. You can pick up a pack at your local supermarket, or drug store, or online, so they're easily attainable."

"Still . . . it's something."

"Yeah." Alvarez nodded. "Something. I hope."

Misty returned with their orders. "Can I get you anything else?" she asked without a lot of enthusiasm.

Pescoli eyed the pieces of her put-it-together-yourself burger. "Just ketchup."

"I'm good," Alvarez said, and Misty, slanting a look at Pescoli's belly, turned to a table tucked near the swinging doors to the kitchen, where rows of condiments were lined like tiny plastic soldiers getting ready for a twenty-mile march. She retrieved a squirt bottle of ketchup and dropped it onto the table as Pescoli began placing the sliced onion, lettuce, and tomato on the open face of her cheeseburger.

Pescoli asked, "No DNA?"

"No. And due to decomp, not much we could find on the body, like blood from the assailant if there was some. The only reason we got the bits of latex is that it doesn't decompose quickly, even though it's biodegradable."

"Long shelf life."

"Yeah." Alvarez drizzled a little dressing onto her salad and dug in.

Once her sandwich was stacked and the French fries covered with ketchup, Pescoli took a bite and nearly sighed in relief. The burger tasted like heaven. As for the fries, she might taste them all afternoon, but she didn't care. For now, she could quiet the rumbling in her belly, satisfy her hunger, and regroup before the next interview.

· · ·

The Justison residence was one of a dozen or so imposing houses that had been built along the ridge overlooking the river, all with views of the falls for which the town was named. Most of the homes had been built before the turn of the last century, and from the street they stood, constructed of brick and stone, their mullioned windows sparkling in the afternoon sunlight.

"What do we know about this kid, other than that he dated the victim, graduated from the local high school, and was a wrestler?" Pescoli asked.

"Is. He still wrestles for the University of Montana."

"So not that far away," Pescoli said. "A road trip to Missoula, weather permitting, takes less than an hour."

"Uh-huh. He lives near campus during the year, but, as I understand it, he's home for the summer. He's had a few minor brushes with the law, but Mom and Dad have worked hard to make sure all charges have been dropped."

"What's he doing this summer?"

"That's what we're about to find out." She pulled into the drive.

The Justison home was a boxy Georgian building constructed of red brick, paned windows, and a wide front porch flanked by gas-lit conces. Black shutters framed floor-to-ceiling windows, a wrought-iron balcony rail stretched overhead and matched the fence surrounding the yard. A huge chandelier was poised to illuminate the porch, and a fountain splashed and bubbled in the center of the lawn. All in all, the home was imposing, a mansion by Grizzly Falls's standards.

Alvarez parked in front of a building that appeared to be a carriage house that had been converted into a garage. Out with the horses, in with a Ford Minivan or Ferrari or Prius, depending on one's taste. The mayor, who had once proclaimed to want a simpler life, had apparently done very well for herself since her move to western Montana.

A dusty four-by-four was parked in front of the garage. A Jeep Wrangler. The same rig had been parked at Reservoir Point the night before and, as they'd already discovered, was registered to Donald Justison Junior.

So, unless Donny had gone off with a friend or his mother, he was home.

Good.

Alvarez and Pescoli headed to the grand porch with its front door—actually, two huge doors— flanked by narrow beveled windows and guarded by flowerpots overflowing with blooms of red, white, and blue. The sidelights offered a glimpse into a marble-floored foyer with a sweeping stair-case. Alvarez poked the doorbell and heard the peal of chimes from within. Then silence. No footsteps. They waited on the brick stoop, Alvarez noting a few honey-bees buzzing through the hedge of lavender that grew beneath the windows of the first story, Pescoli tapping the toe of one boot impatiently.

Still no sign of life from inside the house.

Selena exchanged a look with Pescoli, who, swearing under her breath, hit the bell and held it down for a full five seconds. She was sweating, now shifting from one foot to the other, as the chimes rang. "He's here," she said. "The little coward. Probably saw us pull up."

Selena wasn't so sure.

Pescoli shook her head in frustration. She was due to have the baby within the month, her leave of absence slated to begin next week, all things being equal. Which they weren't. But now, despite the impending birth, she knew she wouldn't want to leave the department until the case was solved.

"Screw this," Pescoli muttered and took a swipe at the perspiration beading her brow. "He's not home or not answering . . . or—wait a sec." Holding up a finger, she cocked her head, and that's when they both heard the familiar slap of a basketball hitting concrete, then the accompanying *thwang* of a hoop as a ball bounded against it. With a hitch of her head toward the corner of the house near the garage, Pescoli said, "Let's go."

They skirted the house, followed the driveway to the backyard, then stepped through an open wrought-iron gate, which had been cut into a ten-foot-high hedge of arborvitae. Inside, they saw Donald Justison Junior, shirtless, in basketball shorts, shooting hoops at a private sport court that, Alvarez noted, appeared to be multipurpose, if someone preferred tennis over basketball.

Only nineteen, he was definitely a man, and a big one at that, several inches over six feet. With a mop of brown hair, now covered in sweat, and sculpted muscles that gleamed beneath hair that grew not only on his legs but on his arms and the backs of his hands, he moved quickly around the court. His chest was shaved, but growing back to shadow his pecs and arrow down into his shiny silver shorts, which hung low on his waist.

He must've caught sight of them from the corner of his eye as he launched an arcing shot that hit the rim, robbing him of his expected three points. He swore under his breath, then jogged after the ball, which was bouncing toward a corner of the court. He grabbed it, spun, tried for a short jumper; missed. Another quiet oath under his breath. No wonder he was a wrestler rather than on the basketball team.

"Donald Justison Junior?" Pescoli asked.

"Yeah?" He snatched the retreating ball and tucked it under his arm before turning to face her and the badge she was holding up. He actually rolled his eyes. "I know who you are, Mrs. Pescoli. Bianca's mom."

"Today I'm Detective Pescoli," she said without the hint of a smile. "Just so we understand each other. This is my partner, Detective Alvarez."

He nodded. "We met."

"Last night at Reservoir Point," Alvarez clarified.

Pescoli said, "Good. We just need to ask you a few questions."

"My mom said I wasn't to talk to anyone without a lawyer present." He headed for the shade cast by the overhang of another huge porch. Its ceiling was extended to cover part of a patio where lounge chairs were arranged near side tables. Holding the ball between his knees, he snagged a T-shirt that had seen better days and yanked the worn cotton over his head.

"Do you need a lawyer?" Pescoli asked.

" 'Course not." He jabbed first one arm, then the other, through holes where once there had been sleeves.

Alvarez said, "We just need to clarify things."

"I said, I need—I mean—I should have a lawyer here, okay? I heard that the girl you found is Destiny. And yeah, we were a couple. But we broke up weeks ago. I can't help it if she was still hung up on me. Still hanging around." He swiped his sweaty face with the hem of his shirt. "She thought we were gonna get married or some such shit. Couldn't take no for an answer." He stopped himself and smiled humorlessly. "Didn't I just say I can't talk to you?"

"We can wait," Alvarez said.

"Wait?"

"For the attorney you don't need," Pescoli helped out.

"Shit, no . . . I mean . . . oh, hell." He flopped into a lounge chair positioned near a glass-topped table, where a water bottle was perched by a cell phone, a pack of cigarettes, and a lighter. With a hungry glance at the Winstons, he uncapped the bottle and took a big gulp. "What do you want to know?" he asked, checking his phone just as it beeped, indicating a text had come in.

Alvarez was taking notes and didn't bother hiding the recorder.

"You're taping this?" he asked.

"Unless your attorney won't allow it."

"I don't give a . . . I've got nothing to hide. So, go right ahead," he added expansively.

"When was the last time you saw Destiny?"

"Uh, God, when? I don't know. Sometime last week. No . . . Friday. A week ago Friday." He squinted into the sun, sweat rolling into his eyes. "I remember because it was the weekend, y'know, the start of it. She called and came by here."

"You remember the time?" Alvarez asked.

A lift of a massive shoulder. "Maybe four . . . or no, had to be after five, cuz she was off work." His gaze slid away from hers and Pescoli guessed he was lying or working on one, testing it in his mind to see if it would hold water. "Oh, no, wait," he said, holding up a finger. "It was later than that. More like eight. After dinner." He nodded, satisfied. "Yeah, that's right. Getting dark." A bounce of the basketball. "She worked that day—she did volunteer stuff at the hospital, in the kids' ward, I think—and she went home and had dinner with her family and then she came over."

"So she works at the hospital," Pescoli interjected. "What about you?"

"What do I do?" Then, at the slight tilt of Pescoli's face, he answered his own question. "I work construction. Well, in the summer, when I'm not in school. Mostly cleanup around the sites, y'know, but I'm learnin' to frame. So I get off earlier than Des does—uh, than she did, I mean. At my job, we start early, real early, like sometimes before seven, y'know, if my boss can get away with it, like there are no noise restrictions or whatever. It's a killer getting up that early, but then we knock off around four, sometimes four-thirty."

"What did you do after work that Friday?" Pescoli figured this was where the real lying would start.

"Came home," Donny said. He was frowning, as if trying to remember. "I, um, showered, then got pizza at Dino's with a couple of friends."

"Who?" Pescoli asked.

"Uh, there were four of us. Alex and Teej and Tophman. And me."

"The O'Hara brothers and Bryant Tophman were with you?" Pescoli knew them all.

Donny was nodding, warming to his story. "That's right."

Alvarez asked, "How long did you hang out?"

"Until . . . I dunno, we played video games for a while. Here, and then . . . then they all left and Des called. Then she texted, I think, wanted to come over. So she did."

"How long did Destiny stay?" Alvarez asked.

"Maybe half an hour? Forty-five minutes?" Again, he bounced the basketball. "Not long."

"What did the two of you do?" Pescoli asked.

"We hung out." He grew a little belligerent, his dark eyebrows pulling together as if by purse strings.

Pescoli believed he was still trying to work things out in his mind, figure out how much they, the cops, knew, how to make his story believable. "Did you talk?"

He shot her a cold look. " 'Course." Another swallow from his bottle.

"What about?" she pressed.

"Nothin'. Just that she wanted to get back with me." He shrugged. "She kinda cried because I told her it was over. I was interested in someone else."

"Who?" Alvarez asked.

"Does it matter?"

"Maybe," Pescoli said.

"It's personal," he said. "And complicated."

"Okay," Pescoli agreed.

"It doesn't matter because this girl, she doesn't even know. I said it mainly to prove to Des that I was serious about the break-up. Geez." He took another swig from his bottle. Appeared nervous.

Alvarez asked, "Did Destiny drive over here?"

He hesitated, then shook his head. "I think she walked."

"And when she left?" Alvarez again.

"She just left. Yeah, on foot. I don't know where she went."

"Did you offer to give her a ride?" Pescoli asked. "By the time she left, it would've been dark."

"No. Sorry. I didn't," he snapped. "We'd broken up. She didn't want it, and neither did I."

"Her folks said she took off across the field, as if she were going to go walking in the woods, up by Reservoir Point, where she was found, where you all partied the other night," Pescoli said. "If she was coming to visit you, here"—she pointed at the baking concrete at her feet—"it seems odd that she wouldn't take the road, save herself the hill to climb, cut off what? Half an hour or so."

"She did what she did," he said, but his jaw worked and he looked away, rotated the ball in his hands, then grabbed his water bottle and lifted it to his lips.

Alvarez asked, "Did she tell you she was pregnant?"

He choked on the water. "Wh–what? Pregnant? No. What? No! You're lying!"

"So you didn't know?" Pescoli asked, pushing.

"I don't believe it." His face had turned to chalk.

"Could the baby be yours?" Alvarez asked.

"Baby? Jesus. No . . . I mean, we were careful. She told me she was on the pill, for Christ's sake." Panic rose in his eyes and his knee was jumping frantically. "You mean she lied to me?"

Pescoli said, "I mean we'll need to take a swab of your mouth for a DNA sample."

"Oh, God. No." He was wagging his head. "My mom can't find out about this. She would kill me. I mean it."

"Come in to the station," Alvarez suggested. "Or we can send a tech out here."

"No! Don't! *Shit!* Can't you just do it right now?"

"We prefer for it to happen in the lab." Alvarez didn't want any chance for some lawyer to scream about lack of control or any question of the chain of evidence. "By a tech."

"Oh . . . okay."

"Today." Alvarez met his eyes.

"Yeah . . ." He licked his lips as if they were suddenly dry, and his eyes rounded. If he'd known about the pregnancy, he was certainly putting up a pretty good act. "I just can't believe it," he said, hanging his head and shaking it slowly, as if he were trying to put things right in his mind and kept failing. "Knocked up? Des?" He clasped his hands over his eyes. "How the hell—?"

Alvarez heard the sound of a motorcycle, engine racing loudly on the street in front of the house.

Donny's head snapped up. "Look, this"—he moved his hands back and forth to include both of the police officers—"is over. I gotta go."

Pescoli didn't budge. "You'd better not be lying to us, Donny, because we will find out and then, if you haven't been truthful with us, we'll wonder why and we'll be back."

"Come into the station for that swab," Alvarez reminded.

He nodded and his Adam's apple bobbed.

The roar got closer, coming from the driveway on the other side of the hedge, only to stop suddenly as the engine was cut.

"Can you just leave now?" Donny pleaded, climbing to his feet.

Footsteps approached, and a second later Alex O'Hara stepped through the open gate to the back-yard. In faded jeans and a black T-shirt printed with an image of a Harley-Davidson, Alex was a little leaner than Donny and two or three inches shorter. His dark hair was clipped tightly to his head and he definitely resembled his brother, TJ, but Alex seemed older and, if not wiser, then cagier. At least in Alvarez's opinion. It was the way he carried himself with a bit of bravado, and the too-quick grin, eyes hidden by reflective shades. But he was here and that was good luck.

CHAPTER 10

Alex O'Hara almost stumbled when he caught sight of the cops. "Whoa," he said and sent a quick look to Donny, who gave an almost imperceptible shake of the head.

A warning.

These two, and God only knew how many others, knew more than they were saying.

"Alex O'Hara," Alvarez said as the kids started to back up. "Stick around."

"Didn't mean to interrupt." He was still back-pedaling.

"You're not interrupting at all. In fact, you saved us a trip, as we were going to talk to you next." She was stretching the truth a bit, but he didn't know that. "We met last night," she reminded him, though she doubted he'd forgotten. "I'm Detective Alvarez and this is Detective Pescoli." She motioned to Pescoli, who was studying the newcomer.

"Yeah. I know." He nodded. He stopped heading for the gate, folded his arms over his chest, and waited.

She said, "Since you're here, we'd like to ask you a few questions."

"About Destiny Rose Montclaire," Pescoli added. Even in the shade of the porch, she felt like she was melting, the edges of her hair around her scalp moist.

"I barely knew her," Alex said, then glanced at Donny, as if to confirm, but this time his friend just stared at his clasped hands, which were now hanging at his knees.

Alvarez said, "But you'd met."

"Yeah." One more look at his friend. He got no response. Donny, it seemed, was lost in his own world. "Look, I only met her a couple of times, I think." His gaze swept from one cop to the other. "Wait a minute. Don't I need a lawyer or something to talk to you?"

"That's your choice, if you think you need one." Alvarez didn't intend to back down.

"You mean like if I'm guilty?" His eyebrows shot up over his glasses to make furrows across his forehead. "Well, I'm not. No way." He turned to Donny. "You know that, man. I mean, Destiny, she was cool and all . . . but . . ." His lower lip protruded a bit and he lifted his shoulders up to his ears. "I just didn't know much about her."

"You didn't know that she was pregnant?" she asked.

He visibly started. "Like as in knocked up?" The skin on his face tightened. Either he hadn't known or he hadn't thought anyone would find out. He turned his head, and this time the look that passed between the two friends was unreadable. "How would I know that?"

"When was the last time you saw her?" Pescoli asked.

"I dunno . . . maybe two weeks ago . . . maybe longer. I can't remember. She was always hanging around."

"But you'd only met her twice?" Pescoli pressed. "That's what you said."

"I meant, I really didn't know her. Sure, I saw her. With Donny or . . . or whoever, but I never spoke to her but a few times. But, yeah, she was around a lot."

"So you weren't with Donny, here, when he met up with her, a week ago last Friday?"

Alex wagged his head. "Uh-uh."

"Were you over here playing video games that evening?"

He flicked his gaze at Donny, eyes locking. "Yeah?" It was more of a question than a statement.

Donny said, "After Teej, Alex, Tophman, and I grabbed some pizza, we played games, then they all took off. After that, that's when Destiny called me and came over here." It sounded like he was giving Alex the story, so that he could back Donny up. The kid was just digging himself a deeper grave.

"So you were never at Reservoir Point?" Pescoli pressed. "You and Destiny didn't go up there?"

Donny's jaw worked and he thought about lying again; Pescoli could see it in the way his eyes shied away from hers. But he said, "Nope. Her folks don't like me much so we met here." He looked pathetically miserable.

"Anyone else here?" Pescoli asked.

"No," he shot back. "Like I said, we wanted to be alone."

"What did you talk about?" Alvarez asked, her voice calm.

"Nothing."

"The baby?" Alvarez prodded.

"No! Jesus. I didn't . . . I didn't know about that." He rubbed his chin. "She wanted to get back with me. I said no. We argued."

Pescoli asked, "Did it get physical?"

"No! Fuck. I told you. I didn't hurt her. Never laid a hand on her!"

"So you talked and fought," Alvarez said, sending her partner a silent warning glare to be cool. "What then?"

"She left. Mad."

"How long was she here?" Alvarez clarified.

"About an hour, I guess, maybe a little longer. I dunno."

"So now it was dark," Pescoli said. "And you just let her go. By herself."

"Yes!" Donny was getting angry, color tinging his cheeks and the back of his neck. "That was the whole point. She wanted to talk to me alone, to, you know, work things out, but it didn't happen. That's it. She was there, we talked, fought—just words—and then she stormed off. She always did that, just left, sometimes maybe slammed a door. That's all I know. What she did afterward, I don't know. I never heard from her again."

"She didn't call or text?" Alvarez said as she heard the smooth purr of another engine coming close.

"What part of no don't you understand?" Donny demanded. "That's all there is."

"Would you mind showing me your cell phone, so I can confirm?" Pescoli asked.

"What? No." Panic in his gaze. "I erase everything."

Another lie. Pescoli said, "We can get them from your cell phone carrier."

"Is that even legal?" he asked. "Don't you need like a warrant or something?"

Pescoli said, "We haven't found Destiny's phone yet, but when we do, we'll be double-checking her records, calls, texts, searches on the Internet."

He blanched.

"And even if we don't find it right away, we'll be checking with her carrier and getting the records from them."

He opened his mouth, was about to say something, probably change his story, when the idling engine stopped. A car door opened and slammed shut.

"Oh, shit," Donny said just as Mayor Carolina Justison stormed through the open gate.

"Whose car is blocking the—?" She let the sentence die when she recognized the two detectives. "Oh."

Wearing a slim navy skirt and white knit top, a computer bag slung over her shoulder, she advanced on the group gathered in the shade of the back porch. Her lips were compressed. Her eyes, behind rimless glasses, snapped angrily. Her blond hair, cut at an angle to her chin, whipped away from her face as her red pumps pounded along the cement path past the basketball court.

"I thought I told the sheriff that my son was off limits," she barked at Pescoli. "I made it very clear that Donald wasn't going to talk to the police without an attorney present!"

"I didn't say nothin'," Donny protested as Alex edged away from the group and toward the gate.

"Anything!" she corrected automatically, swinging around to glare at her son. "You didn't say 'anything' and that's good. But it's not the point. We all know you have nothing to hide. But there is a protocol to follow." Her gaze sharpened on Alvarez. "I talked to the sheriff directly, and I spoke to you. I thought we were all on the same page about this."

"New information came to light," Alvarez said, not backing down an inch. "We just wanted to clarify a few things. Donny and Alex both knew the victim."

"Donny will speak with you, but only with an attorney present. Is that clear?" She turned her attention to her son. "I think you should go in, take a shower, get cleaned up. We're going out for dinner. With Bernard."

As in Bernard Reece? Senior partner of a local law firm? Father of Austin Reece who seemed to be the ringleader of the group? Alvarez made a note.

Donny's expression turned put-upon, as if his mother were really stepping into his private space and time. "I can talk to them. I've got nothing to hide . . ." At his mother's sharp glare, he clammed up and scooped his things from the table, but not before Carolina's sharp eyes noticed the pack of Winstons.

"Donald," she said tightly. "Really?" She plucked the pack from his big paw. "We talked about this."

"You smoke!"

Her cheeks tinged pink. "It's not a habit." She slid her eyes toward Alvarez to see if she noticed. "And it's different. You're an athlete."

Donny, red-faced, didn't argue and hurried off, making his way toward a large sliding door flanked by a wall of windows. As he yanked it open, Alvarez caught a glimpse of a large kitchen that appeared to be recently remodeled, and opened to an adjacent family room where leather furniture was clustered around a fireplace, an oversized flat-screen mounted over the mantel.

From the corner of her eye, Alvarez saw Alex O'Hara easing toward the hedge.

Mayor Justison noticed also. "Good-bye, Alex," she said in a singsong voice. As he disappeared through the hedge, she tucked the pack of cigarettes into the side pocket of her computer case, then made sure that Donny had shut the family room door. "Kids," she whispered, as if the three women remaining were in a tight-knit little coffee klatch that understood the foibles of teenagers. She seemed less tense and, with another glance at the family room, Carolina scrounged in her bag and withdrew a cigarette and Donny's lighter. With her back to the house, she lit up. "Since my little secret's out, right?" Exhaling a lungful of smoke, she flashed a smile as a motorcycle's engine came to life, wheels chirping. Presumably, Alex O'Hara had made good his escape.

Carolina said, "I rarely buy a pack, but today, I think I owe myself a wee little shot of nicotine."

The motorcycle was now racing away, engine whining to a higher pitch as Alex O'Hara put the bike through its paces.

"Did you know that the victim was pregnant?" Pescoli asked.

Carolina was about to take another drag but stopped, the cigarette halfway to her lips.

"Two months along," Pescoli added.

"Oh, dear God. Oh, no." She was visibly shocked.

Alvarez said, "Preliminary autopsy's in. Looks like her neck was snapped. She actually died of asphyxiation. She was strangled. But whoever choked her was strong enough to break her neck."

"I thought she drowned."

"No water in her lungs," Alvarez said. "Someone killed her and tossed her into the creek."

Carolina's knees looked about to give way and she placed a hand on the top of a table to steady herself. "Oh Lord." She took a seat as well as another hit from her cigarette. "Oh, dear Lord." Then it hit her. "But you don't think . . . that Donald Junior . . . that he was involved?"

Alvarez said, "He admitted to meeting her that night, here. Claims they talked things out. No one else was here. They fought. She stormed out, that was the last he saw of her. He never went to Reservoir Point that night, or so he says, but it seems he may well be the last person to have seen her alive."

"Aside from the killer," she said weakly.

Pescoli said, without inflection, "We're asking for a DNA sample. And need to see his cell phone records."

"Now, wait a minute. You can't possibly think that Donald Junior had anything to do with what happened to that poor girl."

Pescoli said, "He agreed to come to the station and give a DNA sample."

"No," she stated firmly.

"We're just trying to get to the truth," Alvarez assured her. "Eliminate suspects."

"Oh, for the love of . . ." Carolina rubbed her forehead with the fingers of her free hand, then steadily climbed to her feet. "My son is innocent of any wrongdoing. I can't speak about paternity of the baby. That I don't know, but I assure you Donald Junior would have stood by his child, if—and it's a big if—he was the father. From what I understand Destiny was . . . loose with her favors."

"Her 'favors'?" Alvarez repeated.

"As in *sexual* favors. You know what I mean. The way I understand it, she kind of got around. I think it was one of the reasons Donny broke up with her."

"Then a DNA test will straighten all that out," Pescoli pointed out. "And the text and phone information on his cell will help clear him as well."

For a second, Carolina studied the lit end of her filter tip, then took another long drag and, in the stream of smoke that ensued, said, "I think we're done here, detectives." Though she'd calmed considerably, there was still an edge to her voice. "We all know that Donny is innocent except for being a slave to his raging teenage hormones, as we all once were. That girl Destiny, poor thing, just wouldn't leave him alone. She was obsessed. Donny tried to let her down easy, but, of course, that just didn't work." She sighed heavily, took a final pull on the Winston, then let it drop to the concrete, where she crushed out the burning butt with the toe of one pump. "Now, if you'll excuse me, I'm sure you can find your way out."

With that, she plucked the remains of her cigarette from the patio and dropped it into a trash can tucked behind a fence near the hedge, then, back ramrod straight, clipped her way into the house.

Pescoli said, with no inflection, "Bitch."

Alvarez smiled faintly. "All right. Let's go." They would learn nothing more. Alvarez suspected Carolina had put a gag order on her son, and even now, she was probably on her phone, trying to connect to the sheriff to ream him out but good.

Fair enough.

That was all part of Blackwater's job.

Still ruminating about Carolina Justison's mention of "Bernard" in the same breath as "dinner," Alvarez followed Pescoli back to the Outback and slid behind the wheel. The interior was oven-hot, but before her partner could complain, she started the engine and hit the fan to full speed.

"What do you think?" she asked, backing around a newer white Mercedes, the mayor's sporty two-door, which she had been unable to slide into the garage. "About the kids?"

"Donny's lying through his orthodontist-straightened teeth. Alex O'Hara, too." Pescoli rolled down her window. "I just haven't figured out what it is they're hiding."

"Everything." She checked the street and wheeled out, then put the Subaru in drive and caught a glimpse of the curtains moving in the big window not far from the front door. Carolina Justison, cell phone pressed to her ear, was standing on the other side of the glass and peeking through the drapes to make sure the cops were leaving. "What about the mayor?"

"Piece of work." Pescoli wasn't one to hold back. "Thinks her kid is innocent."

"Or knows he isn't."

"A mama bear."

"Hmmm." Alvarez thought of the other calls she'd received earlier in the day. "Lotta them around."

Pescoli brooded. Held her hair off her neck to try to cool down. Glared out the window but didn't see any of the buildings as they passed. "Bianca was up there at Reservoir Point with the rest of them."

"Teenagers aren't known for using the brains God gave them. I'm not worried about Bianca. We'll get this over ASAP."

Pescoli gazed through the bug-streaked windshield and let her wild mass of curls fall back around her face.

CHAPTER 11

This was dangerous.

Marjory Tufts peered through the blinds of the French doors. She checked the long drive, but the asphalt cutting along the side of the manicured lawn was empty and, aside from some humming-birds flitting around the shrubbery and the neighbor's black cat stalking birds splashing in the fountain, there were no signs of life.

The motor home was parked in its slot, the end of the boat trailer visible in the extra garage, and everything else was buttoned up tight.

They were alone.

She smiled. Felt naughty, even a little dirty.

Someone could come by, of course, but the gardener had been here early, fixing the sprinkler system and mowing the grass. No one else was scheduled to come by, but . . . one never knew.

"Come here," he called from the bed, and she turned to spy him on the mussed covers, the smell of sex still lingering, his tall body naked and tanned, legs wound between the sheets, his eyes following her every move. He was handsome, she thought, and muscular, the veins beneath his skin bulging a little when he flexed, the outline of his muscles visible. She loved running the tips of her fingers over the washboard of his abdomen or the sinewy strength of his back and shoulders.

She, too, was wearing nothing, and at the abject lust in his eyes, she felt her nipples tighten and a warmth invade her most private of parts.

While she still felt a little bruised from his more than enthusiastic penetration, she felt a thrill go through her. Yes, she could be ready again, and to show him just how interested she was, she arched an eyebrow, took her thumb and stuck it in her mouth, then slowly trailed it down to her breasts.

She caught her reflection in the mirror over the bureau, saw that the tip of her tongue was visible between her teeth, and felt sexier than she ever had in her life.

"We don't have much time," she said, still planted by the shaded doors.

"I'm quick." A cocky smile, a quick flash of white against his tanned skin. "When I want to be."

"And do you . . . want to be?"

"Slow would be better, but . . ." His voice was low and sexy, and she still felt the rash of whisker burns all over her body from where he'd run his face against her abdomen, breasts, and the inside of her thighs.

At that thought, she began to pulse inside.

"It's dangerous."

His gaze wandered hungrily up her body. "Just the way *you* like it."

She started for the bed. "You think you know

me," she whispered as he grabbed her hand and she tumbled onto the length of him. But he was right, and maybe the risk of getting caught, the knowledge that they were breaking so many vows, the pure indecency of having sex with another man in her marriage bed, maybe that's what made it so delightful, so damned hot.

Because she was on fire again. As his hands and tongue poked and prodded, licked and caressed, and his teeth nibbled at her nipples, causing just the tiniest bit of pain, she wanted him. Again and again and again. Wanted to feel him on top of her, mounting her, taking her, making her feel as if she were the most primal and sexy woman in the world.

And he did. Over and over again.

Until she heard the sound of the garage door lifting on the floor below and they both froze.

"Get out of here," she whispered, suddenly panicked.

"Is it—?"

"Yes!" she hissed. "Now, leave!"

He flew off the bed, his eyes wide as they both heard the kitchen door open from the garage.

She placed a finger to her lips as he gathered his jeans and T-shirt. She was already straightening the covers, and sliding open a window. "Go into the next bedroom. Hurry! Hide there. I'll . . . I'll think of something. I'll distract him and you can leave. Wait until you hear him up here. With me."

He slipped through the doorway and tiptoed down the hallway as her husband's tread echoed in the mudroom downstairs. Frantically she found her perfume atomizer and gave the room a spray, then flew into the bathroom, sprayed again, twisted on the shower, and stepped inside. The water was cold, and she gasped as the needle-sharp spray slashed against her skin and into her eyes.

Oh, God, she hoped Richtor didn't see him on the landing, didn't guess.

She thought of the lovemaking and bit her lip. Why had they been so reckless? They both knew the consequences. Richtor Tufts had a mercurial temper. Oh God, she could never let him find out.

And, this, the cheating, could never happen again, even if her lover did have a way of turning her inside out.

She grabbed for a bar of soap, but her hands were shaking so badly, the bar toppled from her fingers and hit the tiles of the floor. "Damn it." She was losing it. Scared. All those happy little feelings of being "bad" disappeared at the thought of her husband's reaction if he knew she'd been sleeping with . . .

She took in a deep breath and, as the spray started to warm, snatched up the slippery little bar and began lathering her body. The spray and lather would hide the marks on her skin, the smell of the soap and perfume hiding the scent of sex, and she could say she'd taken a nap while reading a book. That's why the bed wasn't perfect.

Forcing herself, she began to hum as steam roiled over the glass door of the shower.

"Marjory?" she heard her husband call from the bedroom. Her insides twisted. "Marj?"

And then he was poking his head into the bathroom.

"Hey. What's going on?"

"What's it look like?" She smiled through the foggy glass.

"It's the middle of the afternoon."

"I know. Didn't feel well today." She sent him a look. "You know."

"Are you okay?" He was looking at her body, the shower door not quite opaque, and she felt a little jab of guilt. It wasn't that she didn't love Richtor. She did. In a way. Just not all that passionately. He was a big man, tall and good looking, though of course he was graying, his goatee almost silver. But he'd kept himself in shape. Sort of. And he owned the Ford dealership in town, so he could afford this house and the motor home and the boat and fabulous vacations and . . .

"I'm fine."

"Good. Good. Sooo . . . maybe I should join you," he said through the glass. He was already toeing off one loafer with the other, then pulling his blue polo shirt with its TUFTS FORD logo over his head. Well, why not? Didn't she need to find a distraction? He would never guess that she'd just been made love to three times already this afternoon. What would a fourth hurt? And he'd be less inclined to be suspicious.

"Maybe you should," she agreed as he tossed the shirt across the room and began working on his pants. In a second, he was in the shower and standing under the spray.

"I think you should do me first . . . with your mouth," he said. "You know, to get me going."

He was having a bit of a problem in that department lately. She didn't really want to give him a blow job in the shower, but it was something she'd done before they were married, in this very shower, in the middle of the afternoon when his first wife, Terri, had been out of town for a couple of days and Richtor had never forgotten, never let her forget it.

At every opportunity, he thought she should nearly drown while going down on him just so he could get it up enough to penetrate her.

She wanted to refuse, but thought about her lover's need to escape.

"Sure," she said, lowering herself to her knees, clinging onto his thick thighs, and feeling his strong fingers curl in the wet strands of her hair.

For the rest of the afternoon, Pescoli managed to avoid Joelle, who was being ever persistent about the damned baby shower. She conducted a few phone interviews, studied the autopsy herself, double-checked some alibis, then checked in with Sage Zoller, who was running through all of the statements of the kids who had been at the party Saturday night. After spending fifteen minutes being "briefed" by the sheriff, who thankfully didn't bring up the Justison interview, she was on the road again, this time in her own Jeep. Alone. Heading for home. Alvarez was following in her Subaru.

She'd been right. The taste of greasy French fries kept coming back on her, and she was beginning to regret that particular choice for lunch. Or maybe it was because she was nervous about Bianca being interviewed. Or maybe just the fact that she was so bloody pregnant. Whatever the reason, she decided French fries were going the way of cigarettes, alcohol, and caffeine. At least for a while.

She turned off the main road and onto the long lane leading to her house. The sun was lazying down around the mountain tops, and as she rounded a final bend she spied her house and the lake nearby. Ducks were skimming across the water, and the house, really a large cabin they'd recently built, was a sanctuary for her, a place she could relax with Santana and the kids and dogs while leaving the stress of her job at the office.

Well, usually.

But not today.

Not when she recognized Lucky's yellow Corvette squatted in the space usually reserved for Jeremy's battered old pickup. The low-slung sports car was parked as if it had every right to take up space at her house and probably anywhere else on the entire planet for that matter.

"Awesome," she said, and hit the remote clipped onto her visor. The perfect ending for a perfectly miserable day. The last person she wanted to deal with today was her ex. She was tired, starting to get hungry again, and worried about her daughter. So, no, she really didn't need to see Luke Pescoli.

But it looked like she'd have to.

The garage door rolled open and she drove into the yawning interior. The area reserved for Santana's pickup, an older Dodge Ram, was empty. She didn't know if that was a good thing or bad. Probably bad. Though there was no love lost between the two men, she always felt a little stronger with Santana by her side, though, of course, she was loath to admit it, prided herself for being a strong, independent, free-thinking woman, and she was.

But dealing with Luke was always a challenge, and though Santana never got into their heated discussions, his presence seemed to keep Luke a little more in line.

Cutting the engine, she checked her rearview

and spied the nose of Alvarez's Subaru, head-lights burning though it was still daylight, making the final turn through the trees.

She walked outside and waited for Alvarez to pull into a vacant spot near Lucky's dream car.

"Luke?" Alvarez slid her sunglasses onto the top of her head.

"Yeah," she said with a scowl. "Just what we need."

"Maybe it won't be so bad."

"And maybe I'm not pregnant. Let's go. Get this over with."

They headed inside through the garage.

Stepping into the mudroom, Pescoli was assaulted by three dogs. Cisco spun in tight little circles, all the while yipping frantically. Sturgis wagged his tail back and forth in an arc that could have swept a coffee table clean, and Nikita, Santana's large husky, nuzzled at Pescoli's thigh and whined a little. "Hi, hi, hi," she said, bending over as best she could, scratching each pup behind his ears, then reaching for a box of dog biscuits she kept in a cupboard. Still barking, Cisco went out of his little mind, toenails clicking madly on the hardwood as Pescoli dug out three various-sized treats. Biscuit clamped between his teeth, Cisco took off to hide under the kitchen table, the lab swallowed his cookie whole, and Nikita carried his to a dog bed positioned near the fireplace in the family room.

At Alvarez's amused expression, Pescoli straightened with difficulty and explained, "Priorities."

"I get it."

They stepped into the kitchen.

As expected, Pescoli found Lucky and Bianca seated on the sectional in the adjacent family room. Her ex leaned back with his legs stretched onto the ottoman, a beer can resting on the side table next to him. She was curled up in an opposite corner of the couch, her booted ankle elevated on a fat throw pillow.

Bianca was pale and tired-looking while Lucky appeared right at home, his eyes straying to the muted television, where some baseball game was playing out. His left hand found the can of Coors, no doubt one he'd scrounged for and found in her refrigerator, his favorite MO. With a glance at her, he took a long swallow.

The only good news was that Michelle didn't appear to have come with him. Pescoli didn't think she could handle bubbly, all-smiles wifey right now. Sometimes the woman's bright smile, dancing eyes, and ever-present effervescence were damned irritating. Well, most of the time. No, make that *all* of the time. Michelle bugged the crap out of Regan, and she didn't hide the fact well.

But Luke's current wife wasn't in evidence, so Pescoli pushed the woman out of her mind and concentrated on her daughter.

"How're ya doing?" Pescoli asked, rounding the extension of the couch where Bianca's foot was elevated.

"She's doing okay," Lucky answered for Bianca. "She's a trooper. A real Pescoli."

Regan had to bite her tongue as he took a long pull from his beer can and lounged with that easy-going Lucky manner, his near-blond hair a little too long, the tiniest of crow's feet cut into the skin at the corners of his hazel eyes. "Bedroom eyes," she'd once heard a friend comment, only to learn later that the friend who'd made the remark had been sleeping with him during his marriage to Regan.

Lucky hadn't thought his affair was that big of a deal, certainly not grounds for divorce, but then, she'd learned later, he, a long-haul truck driver, had kept girlfriends tucked away in various towns and cities along his route for years.

Yeah, she thought now, he was a real charmer.

Pescoli raised an eyebrow at her daughter.

"I'm fine. Bored mainly." To prove her point, Bianca let out a long-suffering sigh, and Pescoli was struck, not for the first time, by how much Bianca took after her father, at least in the looks department. Her hair was curlier and tinged with red, like her mother's, but otherwise, Bianca was a petite, feminine Lucky with smooth skin and a smile that wouldn't quit. That was, when she deigned to offer it up, which wasn't often. All in all, Bianca looking like her father wasn't so bad, really. Luke Pescoli was certainly handsome enough, but that narcissistic attitude . . .

"Detective Alvarez is here," Pescoli said as Alvarez came in behind her. "She's going to ask you some questions about last night."

Bianca sighed again. "I know."

Alvarez said, "It won't take long."

"That's why I came over." Luke swung his feet to the floor. "To be here for her."

That irked Pescoli anew. "She's not a suspect. She's just making a statement, for God's sake. You've been watching too much *Law and Order*, or *NCIS* or whatever." She thought about pointing out that he'd been an absentee parent for much of Bianca's life, but reading her expression, Luke got the message and rather than argue, took another swallow from his beer. "Just lookin' out for my kid's interests."

Sure.

Alvarez intervened before the discussion turned into a full-scale argument. "We can talk over here," she suggested, already setting up on the kitchen table.

"Fine." Regan nodded and Bianca, grumbling a little, hobbled to the scratched table that had been in the family for decades. She sat with her back to the bay window, her injured foot resting on the seat of another chair, and Pescoli stood behind her, stretching the kinks from her back and feeling the baby move. The pending interview made her nervous; she was used to doing the asking, and not worrying about the answers. But this was her daughter.

"Let's get started," Alvarez said, scraping back a chair and sitting down across the table from Bianca.

CHAPTER 12

As Alvarez set a small recorder and her phone on the table, then pulled a notepad and a pen from her bag, Pescoli crossed her arms over her chest, making her blouse bunch, and her belly seemed to protrude even farther. She dropped her arms to her sides and smoothed her maternity shirt.

This wasn't her first time defending her children or watching them be grilled by another detective. In high school, Jeremy had walked a thin line with the law, which made his current interest in law enforcement as a career all the more ironic. Pescoli had tried to talk him out of it to no avail. Even when she brought up his father, her first husband, Joe Strand, who had been killed in the line of duty. The thought that Jeremy, who looked so much like Joe, was following in his father's footsteps chilled her to the bone. She was a cop herself, knew the pitfalls and the dangers. Currently Jeremy was enrolled at the local community college while volunteering at the sheriff's department. If he didn't change his mind in the next couple of years, he'd become an officer of the law, like both his father and mother.

What goes around, comes around.

"I know you've been through all of this before," Alvarez was saying to Bianca, "but let's go over it again. Start with how you ended up at Reservoir Point and how you found the body."

Bianca took a deep breath, then launched once more into the tale: how she'd made plans with Maddie, been ditched in the guys' game of hide-and-seek, been chased by an incredibly huge beast from the top of the ridge down to the creek, where she'd literally stumbled on the dead body of Destiny Rose Montclaire. She wrapped up with, "Of course I didn't know who she was then, just that she was dead and rotting. . . ." Her voice lowered. "It was awful," she admitted on a shudder, then told Alvarez about running into Rod Devlin, their argument, how she'd snatched the phone from him to call 911 and then had run back to the main area, where kids had been madly scrambling around, trying to take off as the cops arrived. "You know the rest," she said, rubbing her arms as if suddenly cold when the temperature in the house was over seventy-five degrees and Pescoli was still sweating. But then maybe the perspiration was, at least in part, due to her case of nerves. She listened as Alvarez asked her daughter the same questions she had earlier: How do you know Destiny Montclaire? Who were the kids at the party? Who was connected to Destiny? Did she have any enemies?

Finally, Alvarez asked, "Did you know that Destiny was pregnant?"

Bianca's jaw dropped. "Pregnant?" she repeated. "No. I mean, I hadn't heard that." She glanced up at her mother. "Really?"

Pescoli nodded.

"So there was no talk about it?"

"None!" Bianca said. "Well, at least I hadn't heard anything. I wasn't friends with Destiny, but she dated Donny Justison and even though he's a year older, he runs around with my crowd, so . . . I think I would have heard something."

"Did she date anyone else?"

"I don't know," Bianca said, shocked. "That's kinda sad."

"All of it is," her mother agreed.

"So you didn't hear any rumors from any of your friends, or from people who knew her?" Alvarez asked.

"No." She shook her head, and after a few more questions about Destiny, Pescoli's partner seemed satisfied. Only then did she ask about Bianca's reference to being chased down the mountainside by a hairy monster.

"You don't know who was behind you?" she asked.

"No. It . . . didn't seem human."

"Not one of the other kids?"

"I don't think so. I don't know. It was huge and hairy, and I know it sounds crazy, but I didn't think it was a person."

"An animal?"

"Or . . . maybe a Big Foot?" she said tentatively.

Pescoli forced herself not to make a disbelieving snort.

Alvarez didn't so much as react, but Luke did. He crushed his beer can and was on his feet, heading to the table. "That's one of the reasons I'm here," he announced.

Perfect.

"Carlton Jeffe, you know him," he said to Regan animatedly. She reluctantly nodded. Jeffe had worked at a sporting goods store in town for the last decade or so. A Montana mountain man, his family had farmed outside of Grizzly Falls for over a century. While his brothers ran the wheat farm, Carlton had worked his way up to become manager of the hunting and fishing area of the store and was an expert on firearms, ammo, bows, and any other kind of weaponry a hunter would want. He was also in charge of the Big Foot Believers, a local group here in town that met once a week to play poker, discuss Sasquatch sightings, and shoot the bull. "The BFBs put together a group every year to go hunting for one, y' know—"

"And every year have returned empty-handed," Pescoli cut in.

"Well, maybe that'll change now. Because of Bianca."

Pescoli didn't like the sound of this.

Lucky went on, "Carlton called me. The BFBs want Bianca to come to the next meeting and tell her story, what happened to her."

"You have to be kidding," Pescoli said.

"He called me, too," Bianca said.

"Oh, for the love of—no way. No effin' way." She looked from father to daughter and back again. "This is where I put my big parental foot down. Bianca is not talking to those nut jobs."

"They're not all crazies," Luke said. "I know there are some like Ivor Hicks and Frank Nesmith who have a few screws loose, but most of the members are okay."

"They are *not* okay if they believe in Big Foot and want Bianca to come and, what? Talk to them about being chased and terrorized by a mythical creature that anyone with a brain knows doesn't exist?"

Luke bristled. "I think that's for Bianca to decide."

"I wasn't going to but . . ." Bianca lifted a shoulder. "Maybe it wouldn't be such a bad idea."

"No. Forget it. You're laid up." To Luke: "She's a minor. Remember? Isn't that why you said you were here in the first place?"

"She can speak for herself," he said, then regarded his daughter with a coaxing smile. "Bianca, what do you say? You know that Sphinx is going to be there, right?"

"Sphinx?" Regan repeated.

"As in Barclay Sphinx, the TV producer." Lucky gave her a pitying look, as if he could not believe how out of it she was. "Tell me you've heard of him."

In her peripheral vision, she saw Alvarez give a barely perceptible shake of her head. But Bianca was listening raptly, and Pescoli finally understood her daughter's reasons for entertaining the idea of speaking to the group. Bianca had always had an interest in acting.

"Sorry," Pescoli said tightly. "What has he done?"

"Most recently, reality shows. His most popular one is *Big Foot Territory: Oregon!*, filmed in the Cascade Mountains. He's from Seattle, I think, but he's got ties to Hollywood." Luke was earnest. "Michelle is all over this—she's a major fan."

"Of the Big Foot series? Seriously? Doesn't sound like her kind of thing."

Luke ignored that. "Sphinx has done other things as well. Auction stuff, I think, and a reality show looking into the daily lives of celebrities once they lose some of their star-power, how they try to reinvent themselves. *Tarnished Stars: Where Are They Now?* She loves that one."

Bianca visibly brightened. "I do, too!"

"Still not ringing any bells." Pescoli shook her head.

"Doesn't matter. He's coming to Grizzly Falls. This week. Or that's what Carlton implied." Lucky was on a roll now, more excited than she'd seen him since he'd hit a thousand-dollar jackpot in a casino when Bianca was a baby.

"Implied?"

"It's not a 'for sure' thing, but if Bianca comes to the meeting, Sphinx told Carlton he'd try to make it."

"Really?" Bianca whispered.

How had this become a thing? Alvarez thanked Bianca and made her escape, shooting Pescoli a look of commiseration on her way out. As soon as she was gone, Pescoli rounded on Luke. "And you think . . . what? That because some Hollywood type blows into town that it means . . . money? Fame?"

He lifted his chin like a stubborn little boy. "Maybe."

So there it was; the real reason Lucky was in her house, swilling her beer and being the attentive parent.

"I'm afraid everyone, including Sphinx, is going to be disappointed. Bianca's not going."

"You can't just say that. Bianca can make up her own mind," Luke shot back.

Again, he gave his daughter an encouraging do-it-for-Daddy smile.

Pescoli growled, "Stop it, Luke. We're done here. Bianca's recovering. It's been a long day and—"

"What would it hurt?" he demanded.

"—we've got a murder investigation, so the answer is no," she barreled on. Enough of this nonsense!

Lucky was eye-to-eye with Bianca. "Carlton says you don't have to get up and give a formal talk. Just go to the meeting, talk to some of the people, meet Mr. Sphinx. It could be fun and you know . . ." He winked at her. "You'll be a celebrity. Think on it."

It broke Pescoli's heart to see the light in her daughter's eyes at her father's show of tenderness. "I want to go, Daddy."

"Bianca," Pescoli began.

"Mom," she angrily shot right back.

Pescoli clamped her teeth together. She knew better than to get between father and daughter, but it was nearly impossible to hold her tongue.

Luke bent down and placed a kiss on Bianca's head, then started for the door.

"Jer's here," Bianca said at the sound of an engine fast approaching. Pescoli glanced out the window to catch a flash of metal, followed by dust kicking up from behind the tires of Jeremy's truck. He parked next to the Corvette, threw himself out of the cab, and was up the path to the house as the truck's door slammed behind him.

Inside, he nearly ran into Luke, who was on his way out. At six foot two, he had a couple of inches on his once-upon-a-time stepfather.

"Hey!" Jeremy said and gave Luke a high five as the dogs, barking and wagging their back ends, greeted him enthusiastically. Cisco acted as if he hadn't seen Jeremy in years rather than hours.

"Back atcha," Luke said after the slap. "So, your mom's got you working for the sheriff's department now?"

"Nope. All my idea." Jeremy shot Regan a quick smile, took time to pat each dog on the head, and then beelined for the refrigerator. "Hey, Mom," he said as a greeting, then to his sister, "How ya doing, brat?"

"Not great," Bianca muttered with a glare at her mother.

"When are you ever?" He opened the refrigerator door and hung between the door and the body of the appliance as he studied the shelves.

Bianca threw him a look. "Very funny."

He wasn't cowed in the least. "So, you can't walk or drive for the next six months?" He grabbed a pizza box, pulled it out, and examined the contents.

"You're such a douche," she muttered. "I can drive. The splint is just kind of a reminder to take it easy or something. I'm fine."

Grabbing three slices of the cold pie, he took the time to dump two into the microwave, hit the button, and while the slices warmed, ate the third in two bites. Then, without missing a beat, he opened the pantry door and retrieved a full pack of Oreos.

"Those are poison, you know," Bianca warned. Her healthy diet was on-again, off-again, but currently, it seemed, back on.

"Really?" he mumbled around the sausage and pepperoni pizza while ripping the bag open. "Somebody should let the FDA know because there's no warning on the package."

"Read the damned contents."

He ignored her suggestion as the microwave dinged, and he retrieved the rest of his snack, placing the cheesy slices on a napkin. "What's going on?" he asked, holding a pizza slice and two cookies in his hands.

"I just had to talk to Mom's partner about Big Foot."

"She's speaking to the BFBs this week." Luke rushed in, bringing Jeremy up to date and couldn't help but mention the possibility of a reality show and dropping Barclay Sphinx's name.

Jeremy gaped. "Are you kidding me?" he said, awe in his voice. "Barclay Sphinx is a genius."

"The reality show producer?" Regan asked in disbelief.

"Oh, he's a lot more than that, Mom. He worked on some other TV stuff. *Zombies Among Us* and *Ghosts of the West.* Docu-drama/reality or non-reality shows, whatever you want to call them, but they're all high intensity." He was impressed. "You have to meet him," he told his sister, and he was so intent he momentarily forgot about the pizza and Oreos. "I mean, the man's a genius," he said again. "I can't believe he's here."

"Oh, he's apparently here," Regan said.

"I'm gonna go to the meeting," Bianca declared. "Mom can't stop me!"

Jeremy looked at Regan. "You're trying to stop her?"

Luke put in smoothly, "Your mom's got a lot of things to think about, and I remember what she was like at this stage when she was pregnant with Bianca. It wasn't pretty."

"Thanks for that, Lucky," she said through her teeth.

But there was no fighting all of them. Jeremy and Bianca were starstruck and Luke, well, she'd known him long enough to see that he was smelling easy money. There was no talking to him when he caught that scent. "Fine," she said, and then walked out of the room.

CHAPTER 13

Hurry, hurry, hurry!

Bianca was running, faster and faster, though her legs felt like lead. Her heart was racing, fear driving her forward, the feeling of impending doom surrounding her. The forest was dark. She couldn't see where she was going, but she kept running, slogging through thickets and weeds, brushing the spider webs from her face, knowing she was about to die.

She felt the breath of the beast upon her. It snarled and snapped, growling and thundering through the woods. Was it a bear? A cougar? A massive wolf, or a rabid Sasquatch?

Or a monster? The stuff of horror movies.

She didn't wait to find out, just kept racing through the night-shrouded timberland, over rocks and stumps, avoiding the edge of the cliff that fell sharply to the creek below.

Run! Don't stop!

Heart in her throat, she tried to make her legs respond.

The thing behind her was getting closer, its giant strides sweeping over the rough terrain, its booming voice echoing through the canyon.

Where were the others?

Where was Mom?

She felt a huge claw brush her shoulder and she screamed, but no sound came out of her mouth.

Again, the thing took a swipe at her and she shied away, her ankle twisting painfully, her arms flailing wildly as she pitched headfirst over the lip of the ridge and fell into the yawning dark abyss.

Help! she tried to scream. *Please, someone help me . . .*

She landed. Not on the hard pan of the canyon floor, but in a lake, the water breaking her fall as she slipped beneath the surface, where a light glowed brightly. For the briefest of seconds, she thought she would be safe, until she saw it: the grotesquely distorted and rotting body of a girl that twirled in the current, her dress and hair swirling around the moldering flesh.

Destiny Rose Montclaire, the pretty little mouse who had been in her class at school.

Bianca screamed, air bubbles rising as the light dimmed, the water darkening, her voice gurgling, her words indistinct. *Help me, please! Help!* Struggling for air, she kicked upward, toward the surface, trying to get away, desperate to escape, but her legs again were useless. As she gave a final kick, she felt a hand on her ankle, bony fingers clenching hard, dragging her down.

No, no, oh, God, noooo!

Another hand grabbed her thigh, and the thing that had captured her climbed up her body, rising with her toward the far distant surface. Another hand on her arm. Another on her shoulder, pulling her downward, scaling her torso.

Let go of me, she tried to scream, attempting to kick the thing off of her.

Destiny stared at her through the black pits in her skull where her eyes had been.

"Help me," she cried, echoing Bianca's own desperate pleas. "Help me, Bianca."

No. Oh, God, no. This can't be happening. It can't.

Bianca pushed and pushed, desperate to get the girl's remains off her. The bones fell apart, floating downward, being carried by the current, the ghastly skull following after but staring ever upward directly at Bianca and whispering, "Please, please . . . help me . . ."

Bianca woke with a start.

Her heart hammering, her breath coming in short, sharp gasps, she clutched the covers. Oh, God, she was safe. At home. In her bed. She let out a relieved sigh and saw that her bedsheet was twisted around her legs, the coverlet having slid off. Her ankle ached, and if she let herself, she could still feel the steely grip of the bony fingers encircling the spot where her foot joined her calf.

She shoved her hair from her face with fingers that still shook. She glanced at the clock. The digital readout told her it was one-seventeen in the morning. Not exactly the witching hour, but close enough.

Forcing herself to a sitting position, she tried to shake off the dream, but it clung to her, embedded in her mind. She knew she was safe here. Her mother, a cop, and Santana, as tough a cowboy as you'd ever want to meet, were both in the room down the hall. Jeremy, probably, was in his own room over the garage, and three dogs would sound an alarm if anyone or anything they didn't recognize should wander too close to the house. So, okay, Cisco was pretty much useless as a guard dog, but he could sure make a racket if he wanted to.

So she and the rest of her family were secure.

Still . . . she looked around her darkened room, zeroing in on spots where any kind of monster could lurk.

All in your head, Bianca. You're just letting your subconscious take over.

"Not on purpose," she said, as if the voice in her head could hear her. Geez, what was wrong with her?

Nothing. You're fine. You just had a horrifying experience. That's all. You used to think there were monsters under the bed or in your closet. This is no different.

But the horrifying images of the nightmare persisted, and as she reached to the floor for the comforter, she couldn't convince herself that this

200

house, her home, was as safe as she'd always thought. Wrapping the coverlet around her, she walked to the window and peered into the night, black as pitch, only a few stars winking between the film of clouds.

She didn't turn on a light, didn't want anything outside to see her silhouette, because deep in her heart, she knew that something or someone was watching. Why, she didn't understand, but intuitively she knew that whatever was skulking in the darkness was, without a doubt, the embodiment of evil.

For Pescoli, the next few days flew by. Most of the kids from the party were questioned again, but offered up nothing new. All that came of it was that Pescoli decided she didn't much like Madison Averill, who, at seventeen, seemed already able to use all her feminine charms to her advantage and did it willingly, even eagerly. A pretty girl who was smart enough, she wasn't looking beyond trying to gain TJ O'Hara's interest, which, as Bianca had told her, seemed to be zeroed in on Lara Haas. As popular as TJ apparently was, he might find himself having to stand in line, as a number of college boys had returned this summer to sniff around her.

Lara radiated innocence, but it was an act, Pescoli thought, after interviewing her—something she purposely played up. However, she had admitted to knowing Destiny a little, more than the rest of the kids had allowed. She'd sworn she couldn't shed further light on what had happened to her though.

"I hadn't talked to her for a few days. It's summer and so, with everyone's jobs and vacations, we don't see each other like when we're in school." Chewing gum, she had been seated in Pescoli's office, having opted to give her statement at the department rather than at home. Her sun-streaked hair had been pulled into a messy bun, big hoop earrings swung from her lobes, and though she'd been wearing makeup, it wasn't overdone. Didn't have to be. She'd been blessed with thick, sooty lashes, high cheek-bones, and pouty rosebud lips to go along with a killer figure. In skinny, holey jeans and a cropped tee, Lara elicited more than her share of sidelong glances from the male deputies and clerks who happened by. If she noticed, she didn't react, just held Pescoli's gaze and snapped a wad of green gum she was working on.

Pescoli had brought up the pregnancy.

Lara pulled a face as she chewed. "I wondered."

"You did?"

"Well, no. Not if she was knocked up. Not like that. I just sensed something was wrong. She was off, y'know. I thought it was because she broke up with Donny, but maybe . . ." Lara gave an exaggerated shrug. "Maybe it was the baby. Geez . . ." She'd bit her lip then, forgetting about the gum for a second.

"Do you have any idea who the father could be, who she was seeing?"

"After Donny?"

"Or . . . during?"

"Oh. I don't know." She shook her head, wispy tendrils of pale hair shaking about her face, earrings flashing under the fluorescent lights strung high overhead. "All of the guys thought she was okay, but if she was hooking up with someone, I didn't know about it."

She began chewing again. Thoughtfully.

Pescoli guessed that she was lying, that Lara had a few ideas. She pushed, but got nowhere.

"I suppose it could have been anyone," Lara finally admitted when Pescoli pressed her on Destiny's possible sexual partners. "Maybe one of the guys—they're always interested—or maybe someone else."

Pescoli had thought about that, but her social circle seemed to radiate from the same group of kids that Bianca knew, that Lara was a part of. She tried another tack, for now. "You said she broke up with Donny. Thought it was the other way around."

"Oh, no. She kicked him to the curb. And I don't blame her. He was screwin' around with some girl from college and she found out. Really pissed her off that he thought he could be with that girl in Missoula, then come back here and expect Destiny to . . ."

"Have sex with him?"

"Uh-huh. It just doesn't work out that way, y'know?"

"What about her seeing someone else? How would Donny feel about that?"

"Bad. Really bad. He freaked out when she talked to any guy, if he wasn't around. Real controlling, y'know. We were at a party once, and she was in a different part of the house from where the keg was, where Donny was hanging out, and she was just like talking to this guy, and Donny went crazy, started swearing at the guy, then punched him in the face."

"Who was the guy?"

"Bryant Tophman, I think. He was at the party with Austin, but for some reason he was alone with Destiny and Donny saw them and went off, mad as hell. He punched Bryant in the nose then tackled him, had to be pulled off him. There was blood everywhere. Bryant's nose gushed and gushed. Anyway, I think Kywin Bell actually broke up the fight—he was always kind of Destiny's protector because Donny has a temper. Especially when he drinks. A sweet guy who gets kind of mean when he's had too much."

It was on the tip of Pescoli's tongue to remind her that the whole group had acted as if they barely knew Destiny, when they'd been asked.

She decided bringing it up would be counter-productive, and said instead, "So Donny was drinking that night."

"We all were. Everyone was pretty wasted, y'know."

"Where did this happen? And when?"

"I dunno . . . oh, wait. Spring break, cuz Donny was back from college. So the end of March. We were all at Reece's cabin, but after the fight, Austin made everyone leave. He was really pissed, I mean like *really* pissed. He kept screaming about the blood and beer all over his parents' carpet. One of the guys actually had peed in the corner of the room, then the fight and Austin went ballistic, said he was going to sue everyone who was there, but he couldn't, could he? Without getting into major trouble."

"And Bryant didn't press charges?"

She was shaking her head. "It wasn't all that big of a deal."

Maybe. Maybe not.

"I think he was hoping his dad wouldn't find out. Reverend Tophman doesn't like it when Bryant gets into trouble. Bryant wanted to keep it all quiet. And he and Donny helped pay to clean up the mess. If Austin's parents ever found out, I never heard about it."

"So who did Destiny leave with?"

"That night?" She thought. Worked the gum. "I dunno . . . oh, wait. I think she got a ride with Alex and Teej. They said they'd drop her off."

"And did they?"

She paused. Thinking. No longer chewing. "I . . . I guess." She lifted her shoulders.

"Wouldn't Donny have been upset about her leaving with some other guys?"

"Yeah, but it was just Alex and Teej, y'know. Buddies of his." She chewed again. "I, you know . . . I don't know . . . I was a little wasted myself," she said with a sheepish smile.

Pescoli changed the course of the conversation. "Donny claims he was the one who broke up with Destiny."

She rolled her eyes, then looked more thoughtful. "Okay, I wasn't there, but I don't think so. She was the one who started it."

"What do you mean?"

She worked the gum to one side of her mouth. "I heard that she texted him first, to tell him it was over. Then they met up later in the day. She coulda texted him to break up, but then they maybe hooked up later to talk. Not a hook-up, hook-up. Just talk."

"No sex."

"Yeah." She chewed harder. "Maybe when they got together, they got in a big fight or something, and then he tells her *he's* breaking up with her. A pride thing, y'know." She blinked. "Does it matter?"

Maybe . . . if it went to motive.

Pescoli asked her a few more questions but got nowhere. When she said, "I think that's it," Lara straightened from her chair. But then she lingered a moment, one pink-tipped finger resting on the corner of Pescoli's desk.

"So is Bianca going to that meeting? The Big Foot thing?"

"I don't know." That was an out-and-out lie. Bianca had made it very clear that she was meeting with the Big Foot Believers tonight. Pescoli had argued against it; Santana had backed her up. But as of eight o'clock this morning, Bianca had claimed she was attending.

"I heard that Barclay Sphinx was going to be there."

"That's the rumor."

"That's so awesome." Lara actually beamed.

"Yeah?"

"Yeah. He's like a big deal in TV. Reality TV. Does all these celebrity things. And he makes celebrities, too. Y'know, people get famous on his reality shows and then they do more and are on cable TV and suddenly you see them everywhere."

"Wow." Pescoli stood, indicating the interview was over, and Lara skated a glance down Pescoli's body.

"Are you like due right away?" she asked, eyeing Pescoli's baby bump.

"Pretty soon."

"Wow. A lot of people pregnant, huh?" Lara said. "Destiny, I guess, and you, and Emmett's stepmom."

"Marjory Tufts?" Pescoli clarified, surprised. Marjory was about Jeremy's age. They'd gone to school together, but the name Marjory sounded wrong. Ah. Marjory had gone by Madge as a kid. Madge Vadala. She'd changed her name some-where along the line, but Pescoli didn't know when or why. Not that it mattered. What was odd was the fact that Marjory/Madge was only a few years older than her stepsons, Emmett and Preston Tufts. If Pescoli remembered correctly, Marjory had married their father, Richtor, shortly after he'd divorced their mother, Terri. Richtor owned the Ford dealership in town and after over twenty years of marriage, he'd dumped Terri unceremoni-ously, then married Marjory, a woman half his age, in a huge wedding not two months after his divorce was final.

Lara said, "It's kinda weirded Emmett out, to think he's gonna have a little brother or sister like seventeen or eighteen years younger than him."

"Hmmm." Pescoli knew the feeling. Bianca and Jeremy, when first told that they were going to have a new half-sibling, had been mortified. It had been bad enough to think their mother was sexually active, but to get pregnant . . .

Lara was still staring at Pescoli's belly as she

slid her phone into the back pocket of her pants and picked up her keys. "You can still work? They let you?"

"Yep, they still let me," she said dryly. Of course, there were some people in the department who thought she should already be on maternity leave. "Last I heard, pregnancy wasn't classified as a disability."

"Maybe it should be," Lara remarked before gathering her iPhone and keys and leaving Pescoli's office.

Pescoli shifted uncomfortably in her desk chair and had to admit, the sooner she birthed this baby, the better. The trouble was, she just had too much to do before a new little life took over hers.

"I'm scared," Lindsay whispered into her smartphone. She'd heard that the police were still conducting interviews, even going so far as to talk to some of her friends more than once. It had been almost a week since Destiny's body had been found, and in that time Lindsay thought she'd go crazy with worry.

Now, she was outside, near the old garage that had been converted into her father's "man cave." Inside, Roy Cronin was no doubt seated on one end of the couch that was really a series of recliners with a built-in table, cup holders, and even a mini-fridge. From there, he could smoke, drink beer, and have the volume on the fifty-odd-inch flat screen cranked as high as he wanted and didn't have to hear his wife's nagging.

So he wouldn't hear his daughter's conversation as she huddled in the bushes near the back of the building, the night closing in around her.

"Hey. Don't be scared. Just . . . hang tough. And don't say anything."

"But the cops are going to find out," she whined, nearly breaking down.

"They don't know anything."

"Yet, but they will. You know Bianca's mom, right? Or know about her? How she's like a great detective and has solved all of these murder cases, her and her partner, that Hispanic chick. They've been in the papers and in the news."

"She's just a cop. How smart do you really think she is? If she was all that great, she'd be working for the FBI or CIA or some big-ass police department. Don't worry."

"How can you say that? When they find out that we knew about Destiny, that—"

"Shhh!"

"But what if they find out?"

"They won't. Just be cool."

"I can't!"

A beat. "Fine." Another beat, and then he said, as if he'd just made up his mind, "Let's meet. I'll talk you off the ledge."

She bit her lip, glanced out across the backyard to the hedgerow of arborvitae, saw something—a rat? Squirrel? Small cat? She couldn't tell in the darkness. The shadowy creature skittered away, sliding deep into the undergrowth.

Goose pimples marched up the back of her arms and she shivered.

"Linds? You still there?"

"Yeah."

"Don't lose it. I'll meet you. Later. Midnight. You know where."

"Not at the Reservoir—"

"Of course not. The other place!"

And then he was gone and she was left with the muted sounds of a crowd roaring its approval from her dad's TV, and the smell of cigarette smoke curling through the cracked caulking surrounding the old garage's only window.

For the first time in her life, she envied her parents with their drab, boring lives. He worked for the railroad, had for as long as she could remember. His thrills were double cheeseburgers at Shorty's, the all-night diner, playing pool with his buddies, or just hanging out in his man cave.

Lindsay's mother still worked part-time at that preschool Lindsay had attended years ago, volunteered at the local animal shelter, played Bunco with a group of friends one Monday night a month, and sang in the church choir. Their lives were planned out, no worries, no damned drama.

She felt a tear start to well in the corner of her eye, but she willed it backward. No time for that. She had to meet him in a little while.

Hopefully he had a plan.

CHAPTER 14

Since Pescoli couldn't beat 'em, she decided to join 'em and attend the meeting of the Big Foot Believers with her daughter. They parked in the courthouse lot as it was after hours, then hiked the two blocks to the building that had originally been built by the Sons of Grizzly Falls, a fraternal organization with secret meetings where, it had been rumored, men had met, drank, played cards, and brought in prostitutes all under the guise of working for the betterment of the community. The organization slowly dissolved and the building had been sold to the city. Since World War II, the Sons Building, as it was called, had been city hall, the police department, and the town library, but over the years each of those entities had moved on, and now the building was used to house meetings, art festivals, adult education classes, and the like. The latest rumor was the city was ready to sell the building to a developer who wanted to turn it into a mall of some sort. As far as Pescoli knew, negotiations on the sale were stalled and specific groups such as the Big Foot Believers were still able to rent out space.

Bianca tried not to limp on her way into the building, but she winced a little as she headed though the massive double doors and into a wide hallway with soaring ceilings, complete with stained-glass skylights. The architect who had designed the edifice had spent three years in Europe and had been greatly influenced by medieval architecture. While most of the buildings in Grizzly Falls were constructed with wooden western facades, even, in some cases, adorned by hitching posts, or were long and low, built in the style of mid-century strip malls, not so this enormous structure. The Sons of Grizzly Falls building was thick and square, like a fortress. Built of concrete and stone with huge, exposed cross timbers and high ceilings reminiscent of a cathedral, it had withstood two fires and over a hundred and fifty Montana winters.

Wide stone steps led to huge doors, through which they entered into a grand hall with thick columns and a marble floor inlaid with tile. People were milling around the center area, some climbing the steps, voices muted but echoing slightly.

Smaller rooms branched off the cavernous hallway. One door was shut firmly, a handwritten sign posted over the carved panels:

BIG FOOT BELIEVERS MEETING
MOVED TO ROOM 211
Come and meet
Hollywood Producer Barclay Sphinx
Visitors Welcome!
Please: No cell phones
No firearms

Up the stairs they trudged and followed the signs to room 211, where a door stood open. Just as they walked inside, they were met with an obstacle, a long folding table manned by a heavyset woman in jeans, a T-shirt, and a vest. Her face was square and tanned, blue eyes a shade bordering on green and covered by cat's-eye glasses. Over one ample breast was a button that read I BELIEVE in red letters over the silhouette of a black Sasquatch. Upon the table was a stack of brochures about Big Foot, a cash drawer flipped open, and a stamp resting on a pad oozing green ink. "Are you two together?" she asked, peering upward through her glasses while motioning in an arc between Pescoli and her daughter Bianca.

"Yes," Pescoli said.

"That'll be fifty dollars. No student discounts tonight."

"Fifty bucks?" Pescoli was outraged. "We were invited by Carlton Jeffe."

The woman squinting behind her glasses said, "And I was told to charge for everyone who wants in. We've got serious entertainment tonight and," she said, on eye level with Pescoli's belly, "you're lucky I'm not charging you for a third. You look like you could pop and have that baby any minute."

Pescoli was getting real tired of being reminded of her condition.

"So that'll be fifty. Cash only."

"Wait a second." Pescoli was seriously thinking about reaching for her badge while Bianca died a thousand teenage deaths of embarrassment beside her. "I didn't want my daughter to come down here in the first place but—"

"I'm Bianca Pescoli," Bianca cut in. "I was asked to speak by Mr. Jeffe."

The woman's mouth rounded into a silent O just as Carlton himself squeezed through some men who had gathered around the other side of the table. The noise from within was a cacophony of serious voices punctuated by occasional bursts of sharp, short laughter.

"Is there a problem, Edie?" Carlton asked. He was medium height, maybe a couple of inches under six foot, wiry, with near-black hair that matched his eyes. In his early forties, he was a man who looked like he took himself seriously. His nose was hawkish, his skin stretched tight over his sharp features, and when he smiled, it seemed forced, a hasty stretching of the lips to show peg-like teeth.

"This woman doesn't want to pay. Says she was 'invited,' whatever the hell that means." Her voice dripped skepticism.

But Jeffe recognized Bianca. "She's right." His gaze moved from her daughter to Pescoli. "They are special guests."

Behind the slanted glasses, Edie's eyes were flint. "Well, someone shoulda told me, don't ya think?"

Carlton reached across the table, grabbed the stamp, and pressed it onto first Pescoli's, then Bianca's wrist. "Okay, you're in. Sorry, Edie, it's been crazy, you know. What with Barclay coming."

Wending through a couple of guys who looked like members of ZZ Top, Carlton rounded the table. "Bianca's our guest, and she's here with her mother."

"Fred told me to charge *every*one, and that's what I was trying to do," Edie muttered, irked that her authority had been usurped. "That's the problem, Carlton. I hear one thing from Fred and Ivor and those guys with their rifles and scopes out to hunt down and kill a Sasquatch"—she flipped her hand to a group of a dozen or so bearded men in trucker's caps, jeans, and T-shirts who were huddled into a group—"and then I hear something else from you tree huggers who just want to capture one on film." She twisted the same hand toward the other side of the room, where there was a smaller contingency. Groups

A and B didn't look much different aside from the fact that there were more women in the cluster identified as tree huggers. "So, you tell me, Carlton," Edie went on. "You tell me, who am I supposed to listen to?"

"Well, I am the president of the club, elected, mind you, this past January, and I did set up this meeting with Mr. Sphinx, so you tell me."

Red color climbed up her neck and suffused her face, and she turned aside. Jeffe either ignored her or didn't notice as he ushered Bianca and Pescoli inside. "I'm sorry," he said. "Everyone's on edge. Not only is Barclay arriving, but when we moved the meeting to this room, we discovered some of our decorations, the things we usually have at meetings, were missing." He was obviously disturbed. "It's irritating as hell to spend hours looking for a folding table we need and can't find it and, God, the costume. Where the hell is it?"

"What costume?" Pescoli asked.

"We have a Big Foot costume, you know. For plays and reenactments. Parties. Whatever. Very expensive. Very lifelike. Supposed to be locked up, but it's missing. What're ya gonna do?"

"You're missing a costume and there have been Big Foot sightings? Don't you think someone took it and used it? That it's what someone was wearing when they chased Bianca?"

"Why would they do that?"

"Maybe a prank." Or, worse, she thought. "Which of the members have access to that closet?"

"Anyone who's a member, I guess."

"You said it was locked. Where are the keys?"

"Well . . . they're in a box in the regular meeting room, and before you ask, the key wasn't missing. I used it earlier when we were setting up."

"I need you to get me a list of members and note on it anyone who was in the closet recently, or since you last saw or used the costume."

"Oh, come on." She stared at him and Jeffe shrugged. "I'll *try*," he said, then led her through the crowd that was, for the most part, about seventy percent male. There were women, of course, but most of them seemed attached to one of the men.

Pescoli had expected all the members to be mountain men, and there were definitely those who looked like they could be a part of the cast of *Duck Dynasty* or *Swamp People*. With long, unkempt hair, bushy beards, trucker's caps, old T-shirts, and faded jeans, they seemed intense and what she would consider part of the outdoorsman landscape. But the rest of the crowd could have been found in any town in America. Men in khakis and work shirts, some wearing glasses, others in slacks, with wives, some even looking as if they were heading to church or, alternatively, a rock concert.

There were those who had tattoos visible, metal studs in their faces, and those clean shaven with trimmed hair, checking their smartphones. The ages ranged from preteen to an old guy in a wheelchair hauling an oxygen tank who didn't look to be long for this world. But he was here, at the meeting that seemed, to Pescoli, more like some kind of rally.

Despite the vastness of the room, it felt stuffy and close, almost claustrophobic, and there was a definite buzz to the conversation. She heard Sphinx's name said with what was almost reverence, and she recognized more than a few familiar faces. Lex Farnsby, the crime scene tech, was chatting up Jenner Stevenson, an accountant of about fifty who was standing next to his wife, Barbara, a schoolteacher. Along with the Stevensons was Ivor Hicks, who now sported a short white beard and yellow-tinted shades. Ivor was one of the local nuts and had suffered his own set of tragedies. Pescoli made a note to avoid him, along with the others gathered nearby. She also spied Sage Zoller, a junior detective with whom she worked at the sheriff's department. She'd known Zoller was a bit of a conspiracy theorist but hadn't realized she, too, was a Big Foot Believer.

Fred Nesmith was in a heated conversation with Otis Kruger. Nesmith lived off the grid, was an anti-government type who'd fathered six kids and probably would have had a dozen more if his wife hadn't died in labor with the sixth. He hunted for meat and pelts and didn't give a damn about the local laws. Like Nesmith, Kruger was also a known poacher and proud of it, another guy who considered the wilderness his own personal realm. Once again, no laws mattered to Kruger, a bean-pole of a man whose face was weathered, his hair long enough to show where it had started to turn from brown to gray, his temper mean.

She recognized some of the kids, too, those she'd recently interviewed. Kywin Bell, a big, blocky guy stood out. He and Donny Justison were hanging out with the O'Hara brothers. Not far away, Maddie Averill sipped from a water bottle, her gaze drifting to TJ. Lindsay Cronin and Seneca Martinez were in attendance as well, huddled together and talking with Bryant Tophman and Rod Devlin near a table where T-shirts and Big Foot paraphernalia were for sale. Lindsay kept looking around, as if nervous, or more likely searching for someone she deemed more popular than Seneca. Tophman was a football player and looked the part. In the past year or so, he'd bulked up, developed a lot of muscle. Devlin, in contrast, was a little taller, but whip-thin, his skin acne-prone.

Pescoli caught glimpses of the others, as well, and decided that nearly everyone from the party at Reservoir Point had suddenly taken an interest in the Big Foot Believers, or, more likely, the rumors of a television show being filmed in the town and the fact that Barclay Sphinx was here.

Shifting from one foot to the other, she glanced back at the group of boys. Austin Reece, all smug smiles and obvious sense of privilege, had joined his friends and wasn't far away from TJ and Alex O'Hara, the ubiquitous Madison standing by.

Rod Devlin and Austin Reece stood near the table with Simone Delaney, who caught Pescoli's eye and quickly looked away. A second later, she disappeared into the crowd, and Pescoli wondered if her mother, perfect Mary-Beth, knew her daughter was attending the event.

Probably not.

"I'd like to talk to you before we get started," Carlton said to Bianca just as Regan spied Luke moving toward them. In one hand, her ex held a water bottle, his other fingers laced with those of his wife, Michelle, who, in five-inch-heeled boots, was having some trouble keeping up with him.

Bianca nodded. "Okay."

"There's a connecting room behind the stage." He offered a smile. "It's kind of like our green room. Barclay's already there."

"What?" Luke asked, joining the group. Then, "Hi, Carlton. You've met Michelle."

Carlton brightened. "Several times. I was just telling Bianca that we should go meet Barclay before the meeting gets going."

"I'm in!" Luke was grinning from ear to ear and Michelle was nodding. Aside from the high heels, she hadn't over-glammed herself and was wearing a yellow shell and tight white jeans that funneled into her short, suede boots.

Pescoli just wanted her ex to butt out, but decided not to make a scene. Santana and Jeremy, who had both insisted upon joining, were meeting her here. Santana had to finish overseeing a project at the Long ranch and Jeremy had a class that wouldn't be over until 8 p.m.

So, she'd have to go it alone.

Single-parent it one more time.

Well, fine.

CHAPTER 15

Bianca and Regan followed Carlton Jeffe toward the stage at the far end of the room, where the crowd was mostly gathered. The room they walked through was cavernous, with high ceilings and velvet curtains that appeared as old as the building itself. Those curtains were currently drawn, and the room was dark aside from the illumination cast by hanging chandeliers that looked as if they belonged in a ballroom rather than over a meeting of the Big Foot Believers.

They passed a refreshment table pushed against a side wall with a coffee urn, bottles of water, and an array of cookies. A second table held CDs and T-shirts from some of Barclay Sphinx's reality shows. Throughout the seating area, where the crowd was still milling, life-sized photographs of Big Foot had been placed, as if the tall mythical creature were actually attending the event.

The stage was elevated only about a foot off the main floor. It was set up with several chairs facing the audience, a podium with a microphone, and a few posters from Barclay Sphinx's television shows. The podium itself was decorated with a large head shot of the guest of honor.

Despite the ceiling-mounted fans slowly whirling above, the room was hot, and Pescoli was glad when Jeffe said, "This way," and led Bianca and her away from the crowds, circumventing dozens of folding chairs that had been set in a semicircle around a small stage with a microphone and an amp, circa 1970. A projector on one side of the stage was showing films of Big Foot on a drop-down screen. The images were grainy and unclear, pictures of the beast from a far distance, forever looking over its shoulder and always alone in the woods, footage even Pescoli had seen a number of times.

The "green room" was simple and small. Empty except for a few folding chairs and a low table where more refreshments had been placed— cookies fanned upon a plastic tray, two carafes of coffee marked decaf and regular, and about twenty water bottles that were chilling in a large tub of crushed ice.

Barclay, a tall, thin man in his mid-thirties, was standing, and despite the heat he wore a gray jacket over a black T-shirt, jeans, and leather flip-flops. His head was shaved and gleamed under the lights overhead, almost as if it had been polished. Clean-shaven except for a reddish soul patch, he wore John Lennon glasses.

"You must be Bianca!" he said as they approached. "I heard about the accident." One long finger motioned to her booted foot. "You all right?"

"Yeah." Bianca nodded. "Will be."

"Barclay Sphinx." He shook Bianca's hand and then snapped his head up to survey the room. "Maybe you should sit down. Hey," he said sharply to Luke, as if he were a gopher on a movie set. "Can we get a chair here?"

"Sure, sure." Juggling his water bottle in one hand, Luke snagged one of the folding chairs and placed it near Bianca.

"Let me help," Michelle said and adjusted the chair.

"And you are—?" Sphinx glanced at her, then grinned. "The sister?"

"Stepmom," Michelle simpered, extending her hand. She couldn't help but gush, "I can't tell you what a pleasure this is, Mr. Sphinx, I am *such* a fan!"

"Thanks." They exchanged glances.

"I *adore Tarnished Stars*. It's brilliant!" Michelle breathed, and Lucky actually shot her a slightly irritated glance.

Sphinx's lips twitched, bemused, and Pescoli fought the urge to roll her eyes.

"Oh, let me introduce you all!" Carlton, ever energetic, stepped between Michelle and Barclay as Luke's wife reluctantly, it seemed, let go of the tall man's fingers. He made hasty introductions among the producer, Bianca, and what must have appeared to be her entourage, adding at the end, "And this is Fiona Carpenter, Mr. Sphinx's assistant."

"Executive assistant," she corrected. Fiona was compact and petite and radiated competence. Her brown hair was cut short and highlighted with thin streaks of red, and her outfit was composed of a gray long-sleeved T-shirt, tunic length, and black leggings that tucked into her boots. She didn't smile, wore no visible lipstick, just a sheer gloss, and appeared to be all business.

Sphinx was sharp, remembered everyone's name and said to Pescoli, "You're the cop, right? A homicide detective?"

"Yes. With the Pinewood County Sheriff's Department."

"Perfect," he said, nodding to himself.

She didn't really see how her career path could be considered "perfect" by anyone's standards, much less a Hollywood or Seattle producer of different reality shows for cable TV, but what the hell.

Carlton interjected, "As I said before, Bianca's . . . uncomfortable telling her story to the group, a little shy, so I thought you could speak, Barclay, and then later people could ask Bianca some questions."

"How about this?" Sphinx asked, as if the idea just occurred to him. "What about if I ask Bianca questions on stage, kind of a personal interview in front of the group, and then I could say a little bit about her responses." His eyes, behind the round glasses, found Bianca's. "You would only have to answer with a word or two. I read your story in the papers and online from all of the posts from your friends, so I have a pretty good idea what happened. That way it's a little more intimate, not so nerve-wracking."

Bianca's eyebrows drew together. "I'm not shy."

"All the better," Sphinx said. "We'll set up as an interview and you can expound to your heart's content." Then he looked directly at Carlton. "Set it up on the stage. Just that way. Now." He didn't smile, didn't frown, just gave the order, as if he was used to barking out a command and expecting people to scramble to do his bidding.

"Good. Sure. Sounds great." Carlton was starting toward the stage in the other room.

"Oh, and Jaffe—?"

"Jeffe," Carlton corrected quickly.

"Yeah, maybe another chair. I'd like Mom to join us." He swung his gaze to Pescoli, flashing his most sincere grin. "I understand you're involved in a murder case as well. That your daughter found the body of a classmate while running from Sasquatch."

"I am investigating a murder and yes, Bianca did find the victim, but there was no Big Foot, and I'm not getting on the stage to discuss an ongoing investigation." To Carlton Jeffe, she called, "You won't be needing that extra chair."

"Oh—okay. I'll set up now. We'll be on in five." With that, he bounded out of the room.

Sphinx pulled a face. "You sure you don't want to be a part of this? Someone in the crowd might know something that could help you solve this murder. I heard that you're kind of a rogue cop, that you don't always play by the rules, that you'd bend them to close a case and bring a killer to justice."

"I think I'll just hang with the crowd, stand in the back and watch."

"Not a believer then?"

"Of Big Foot? No. Definitely not." From the corner of her eye, she spied Lucky, his face a mask of horror that she was actually standing up to the producer, and Michelle, too, looked appalled.

Sphinx was unfazed. "You probably know I'm

considering a second series, *Big Foot Territory: Montana!* I think your daughter's story would be a great pilot. It has all the dramatic elements the audience loves. A pretty girl at a party in the mountains, chased down a mountain by a monster to end up finding a corpse in a stream, a dead girl, a classmate. Her mother is a cop, doesn't believe her, but together they search for a killer and a rogue Sasquatch who just may or may not be the killer." He was actually caught up in his own story, talking faster, as if convincing himself as he spoke. "We'd do a reenactment with Bianca. Up at the site where the Big Foot was seen, I think it's called Reservoir Point? The pilot would start out with a Handycam, shaky, raw, a little like *The Blair Witch Project* maybe. Because of the murder, it would be two programs, one that ends with the discovery of the body and the next with the aftermath, Big Foot in the shadows."

Michelle actually clapped and bounced on her heels, like a twelve-year-old spying a teen idol. "I'd watch that! In a heartbeat."

One of Sphinx's eyebrows raised over the tops of his glasses. "There you go. The fans, at least one, have spoken."

"You want me in the TV show?" Bianca asked a little breathlessly, and she, like Michelle, had stars in her eyes.

"No." Pescoli had to stop the madness. "Bianca's still in school and . . . no. Just no."

"Mom!" Bianca protested.

Sphinx offered Pescoli a conspiratorial smile. "Look, Detective, this could help your investigation. If the homicide isn't solved by the time of the airing, I'd be willing to put a tag at the end of the second episode, explaining the circumstances about the murder and, should anyone know anything, a number they could call along with a website dedicated to solving the case."

Michelle actually gasped. "Oh! Perfect."

No way. They weren't going to sensationalize a fresh case with grieving parents. "Thanks, but I think the department can handle it," Pescoli said dryly.

From the main room, after a screech of feedback, Carlton's voice rang over the speakers. "Can I have your attention? Hey! Could everyone take a seat now? We're ready to start with the program. Mr. Carlton Sphinx will talk with us, and he's going to ask Bianca Pescoli about her close encounter. She's agreed to let him ask her questions, so if you could all just take your seats. I know it's standing room only, so those of you on your feet, please take a spot near the walls and please don't block anyone's view. Okay? . . . yes? Okay, we're ready. So, without further ado, Big Foot Believers, let me introduce you to Bianca Pescoli and Barclay Sphinx!"

Amid a roar of clapping, Sphinx led Bianca to the stage, and as she sat in one of the chairs, he replaced Carlton Jeffe center stage, standing at the podium.

Michelle and Luke moved into the main area, the larger room filled with cheering, standing fans, but Pescoli grabbed a couple of cookies and hung back, grateful to stand behind the stage in the doorway and observe the performance while being able to watch everyone who was in attendance. The audience, after the heartfelt welcome, took their seats.

Carlton Jeffe hadn't been kidding. The place was packed, standing room only. Three, or maybe closer to four hundred people filling the space. She picked out many faces she recognized, including Santana as he walked inside and, a few minutes later, Jeremy. Closer to the stage, Manny Douglas was chatting up a woman reporter for a television station based in Missoula, a reporter who'd interviewed Pescoli on more than one occasion.

As Pescoli munched on a dry store-bought gingersnap, she saw that Alvarez, standing next to Dylan O'Keefe, was already in the crowd, keeping back, but viewing the event as it unfolded. Even Blackwater had shown up, taking a position in one of the dark corners, for once, it seemed, content to blend into the surroundings and not try to be center court or in the limelight.

Shifting from one foot to the other, trying to stand beneath a cooling AC duct, Pescoli finished the first cookie and started on the second, all the while observing the proceedings. For the first forty-five minutes, Barclay Sphinx talked about his career, the shows he was working on and specifically the success of *Big Foot Territory: Oregon!* The crowd was quiet, aside from a few whispers and, despite the warning, a couple of cell phones that jangled and were quickly quieted. Sphinx was an accomplished speaker, gave anecdotes and examples and proved to be able to laugh at himself. He drew everyone in. All in all, the spectators were rapt, hanging on his every word.

". . . so it only seemed natural," he said, "that we do a spin-off. The network is pushing for it, and we've got a production crew ready to go. I mean they are already teed up. The only question was . . . where? We discussed Alaska and Northern California, but there was talk of Montana and when we heard, just recently, about several sightings in the area, capped by Bianca Pescoli's encounter, we thought, well, *I* thought Grizzly Falls would be a perfect location for *Big Foot Territory: Montana!*"

The crowd went wild.

They hooted and hollered, and someone actually started a chant: "Big Foot! Big Foot! Big Foot!"

"And I'm thinking this group, the Big Foot Believers, could be a big help. With your knowledge of the area and history of sightings, your intense interest in Big Foot, I think we could find one and catch it on film!"

More shouting and yelling and clapping and whistling. Like a damned revival meeting.

Pescoli half expected to hear, "Amen, brother!"

Instead she saw Fred Nesmith approach the stage. "I need to ask you a question," he said to Sphinx.

"Shoot."

"That's exactly what I hoped you'd say!" Nesmith was a tall man, and thin, with a long face, an Abe Lincoln beard, and deep-set eyes. Pescoli looked past him but didn't see Otis Kruger, who'd been with him earlier. "Cuz this is a real reality show, yeah?" Nesmith questioned.

Ivor Hicks had joined Fred. He said, "Not scripted or nothin', so we can really hunt the sumbitches. Like they do on that gator show."

"Excuse me?" Sphinx said. "You want to kill a Big Foot?"

"Absolutely!" Nesmith said, and a handful of men nodded their agreement. Nesmith went on, "How else ya gonna prove that they exist? What we need is the real thing. A carcass."

Carlton Jeffe stepped in. "Fred, let's not start all that killin' talk up again."

"I'm tellin' ya, we need proof. This here's our chance to finally get it." To Sphinx, Nesmith said, "You all got a chopper, right? For the production. And tents and SUVs—the country around here is pretty damned rough."

"Whoa, there." Jeffe's jaw was tight. "Not now, Fred. Let's hear what Mr. Sphinx has to say. You and Ivor, take your seats."

"We're just sick of sittin' around and havin' damned meetin's," Hicks grumbled. "We need some action!"

"You tell 'em, old man!" a voice yelled out from the teenage boys who'd been at the party over the weekend. Pescoli zeroed in on Bryant Tophman. "That's right!" Bryant averred.

His friends were agreeing as well, nodding and holding their fists in the air. "Let's get 'em!" Austin Reece said, inciting the others, who reacted by shouting:

"Yeah!"

"Let's kill 'em!"

"Find those bastards!"

Jeffe was shaking his head, and some of the others were doing the same. "Let Mr. Sphinx explain what he wants to do," he nearly shouted.

"Goddammed sissies!" Ivor cried.

Fred joined in, "Yer all a bunch of blowhard pussies."

"Hey! Watch your language!" Rod Larimer reprimanded. Owner of the Bull and Bear Inn, he was in khakis and a dress shirt, his sleeves rolled to his elbows. "We've got women here. Let's keep this civil."

"Civil, my ass!" another guy yelled. He was hidden by the others, but when Ivor moved, Pescoli caught sight of Otis Kruger's red face. Ah, there he was. An instigator if there ever was one. He looked ready to charge out, guns blazing.

But Sphinx was cool, lifting his hands, then patting them downward, indicating that everyone should quiet, which they did, some grumbling, a few chanting a few final "Big Foots!" before trailing away as he spoke again.

"By now you've all heard about this most recent sighting that I mentioned," he said to a murmur of agreement. "Bianca Pescoli, a local teenager, was chased by what she thinks was a Sasquatch, late Saturday night. The beast charged at her and forced her to run down a steep hillside, where she was injured and, believe it or not, nearly stumbled over the body of another girl, a classmate."

Sphinx was solemn now. Sober as a judge. And appeared troubled.

"The girl, Destiny Rose Montclaire, was mercilessly killed, the victim of homicide. An innocent young life cut short. Someone or some*thing* strangled her and was strong enough to break her neck."

Pescoli thought she should stop this and took a step forward, but she caught Alvarez's eye and the quick little shake of her head. The meeting-goers were quiet, listening, all eyes on the speaker. It was so quiet that Pescoli heard her own breathing above the humming AC.

"Was her murderer a rogue Big Foot?" he threw out to the group.

More whispering and one loud, "Hell, yeah!"

Sphinx shook his head. "We can't go there . . . at least not yet. And I'm not so certain. There's a chance Big Foot just might be a gentle creature." He paused for effect, then said, "But who knows? Maybe we can find out. And yes, we'll use the most sophisticated technology: tracking systems, night vision, drones, whatever it takes. We'll find 'em."

More murmurs of agreement. He had them. Everyone in the room was rapt, and Barclay Sphinx knew it.

Gripping the sides of the podium, he swept his gaze over the crowd. "But we owe it to Destiny to help the police catch her killer."

Whispered agreement swept through the audience.

"Along with the new series *Big Foot Territory: Montana!* I'm putting up a website connected to the show, but also to the Pinewood County Sheriff's Department, for people to access easily and offer up anything they might know about the tragedy. I've already talked to Detective Regan Pescoli, lead investigator on the case, and I'll work with her to make sure the website is up to date, the best technology available."

"Wait a second," Pescoli said, but her voice was drowned by the roar of approval from the crowd. She hadn't agreed to any of this.

Sphinx bent into the microphone. "It just so happens that Detective Pescoli is Bianca's mother, so it's one tight little family. Let's get started, shall we?"

And he did, sitting in a chair and facing Bianca as if they were alone, as if there weren't three hundred people plus hanging on their every word. He began by asking Bianca question after question, leading her through her story so that she told exactly what she saw and experienced. He was good, Pescoli gave him that, even though her stomach was in knots as Bianca described the "monster with an eye that seemed to glow," its incredible height, and how it smelled. With soft-spoken questions, he asked how she'd found the dead girl, and Bianca, white-faced, her splint visible, relived her terror and the sheer horror of finding the dead body, a classmate, as it turned out, in the water.

At that point, Sphinx turned to the crowd and said, "We're not going to go into this any further. There's an ongoing homicide investigation and a family that is devastated and grief-stricken, so we'll confine the rest of this meeting to Big Foot." To Bianca, he said, "I believe that's what you saw up on the mountain, at Reservoir Point, a

Sasquatch. A very close encounter. Thank you."

His statement caused a fresh murmur to race through the crowd, a new jolt of electricity. "Don't you?" he said to the group as he stood at the podium again. "Don't you think Bianca, here, came across Big Foot?"

Whistling and clapping and hollering were the enthusiastic response.

Some of Bianca's friends sidled closer to the stage. Pescoli made eye contact with Austin Reece and TJ O'Hara, but the others, including Lara Haas, Lindsay Cronin, and Maddie Averill, didn't notice her and inched ever closer to the podium.

"I think setting *Big Foot Territory: Montana!* right here in Grizzly Falls is a great idea, and I think that Bianca Pescoli should relive her adventure, her encounter, on screen. Don't you?"

More wild applauding. Even Bianca's friends, the kids who'd been busted up at Reservoir Point, were clapping. Lara Haas and Maddie Averill were nodding enthusiastically, TJ sending Bianca a thumbs-up signal.

Pescoli realized then that her daughter was a hometown celebrity. Her stomach clenched. This was not good.

Sphinx stood and then, as Carlton Jeffe took command of the event again, the audience was allowed to ask questions. They fired them mainly at Sphinx, thank goodness, though Lucky had made his way onto the stage to sit next to his daughter and hold her hand in between his—ever the doting father.

At his side was Michelle.

When Sphinx asked Bianca if she'd like to star in the first episode of *Big Foot Territory: Montana!* she seemed to hesitate a minute. Did Luke actually squeeze Bianca's hand? Oh, for the love of God! And then Bianca, staring straight at Sphinx, started nodding. "Yes," she said. "Yes. I—I'd love to."

Luke nodded and grinned.

Michelle was absolutely radiant.

Sphinx seemed pleased with himself.

The crowd let up a cheer of approval.

And Pescoli thought she might be sick.

CHAPTER 16

Alvarez didn't like the feel of the meeting. Aside from the airlessness of the room, there were too many people packed into too tight a space, all of them riled up, some of them agitated. She felt the tension sizzling through the crowd, and it was more than just the excitement of something new happening in town. This new, electrified buzz wasn't just because Grizzly Falls might become the center of a "reality" television show. No, there was something else, an uglier current rippling through the crowd that was contentious, almost antagonistic. The people packed into the hall tonight weren't part of a congenial gathering, not a crowd of like minds.

O'Keefe felt it, too. "Not exactly a unified group," he observed, leaning close so that he could be heard.

"Nope."

"Militants and pacifists, all loving up Big Foot."

"The militants are definitely hating on Big Foot."

"Held together by belief, but at each other's throats," he said dryly.

"Like all of life." Her gaze traveled over the gathering. Some of the more vociferous members had the mentality of a lynch mob, like the townspeople carrying torches and spears in old monster movies to "take the sumbitch down." The other faction appeared only interested in proving the myth reality, and that Sasquatch was a shy, almost intellectual beast, smart enough to hide any trace of its existence. But all of the members of the group believed that Sasquatch lived and breathed —that was the uniting factor.

"I have to run. See you this weekend?" he said.

"Okay." She was a little disappointed. She loved being with him, but he still resided in Helena, where he was a private investigator, and though he talked often of moving to Grizzly Falls, of setting up shop here and living with Alvarez full time, so far it hadn't happened.

She worried a little about that. If they truly wanted to be together, to take the relationship to another level, then they should try harder to make it happen. Right? There shouldn't be the convenient excuses of conflicting jobs and career paths. They should want to be together all the time. Wasn't that the way it was supposed to be?

He planted a kiss on her cheek and said, "I'll call."

She wanted to say, "Stay," or "Let's make this coming weekend special," or "I hate it when you leave," or even, "I love you," but she didn't, not here in this crowded, loud room overflowing with people rabidly intent on proving Big Foot existed. Or was that an excuse? It didn't matter. He was already moving away from her, through the crowd, and she watched him disappear past the cashier table and through the main door.

Her heart twisted a bit.

She'd known him for a long while. They'd been partners in the San Bernardino Police Department years before. He'd saved her life. Nearly lost his own. She swallowed hard, told herself not to be maudlin and to concentrate. She had a homicide to solve.

So what was she doing at a damned Big Foot Believers' meeting, where it was so hot and stuffy she was actually fanning herself with a brochure she'd picked up on the main table?

The answer was simple: Almost everyone who

was associated with Destiny Rose Montclaire, aside from her parents, was in attendance.

Maybe it was just a coincidence.

Maybe not.

As the meeting broke up, some of the attendees swarmed the stage, hoping to get closer to Sphinx, a man who could bring fame to Grizzly Falls and validate the members' beliefs. Others stopped by the table to buy Big Foot mugs and T-shirts. Another group grabbed refreshments and chatted, while the people she was interested in, the swarm of teens or post-teens who'd been at the party on Saturday night, milled within their own private circles.

She'd interviewed all of them, studied their statements, felt she knew some of them inside out and was surprised that after being busted the past weekend and being involved, at least peripherally, in the discovery of a body of one of their own, they would be here in what seemed an almost celebratory mood.

They're kids, one side of her mind reminded her.

The other said: *Yeah, but nearly adults.*

"You think Destiny Montclaire's killer is here?" a male voice asked, and she turned to find that the sheriff was standing next to her. His gaze was fixed on Kywin Bell and Donny Justison, who were standing next to each other, two big men. Friends? Or rivals?

"I don't know. Maybe," she said, watching as they were joined by Austin Reece and Alex O'Hara.

"No one looks like they're in mourning."

She'd been thinking the same thing. As scared as the kids had been on Saturday, as somber as they'd appeared while being interviewed, the boys now were all laughing and joking, male bravado, camaraderie and animosity, hitting each other, giving fist bumps, glancing over at a group of girls, the center of which was Lara Haas. But the females, tonight, weren't showing any interest in the boys' antics. To a one, their attention was focused on Barclay Sphinx, who held an edge over the locals, an air of mystique, a bit of sophistication, an association with the glitter of Hollywood. He was the peacock tonight, and he knew it.

"This is such bullshit!" a voice nearby yelled, and she caught sight of Kruger again, standing with Nesmith and Hicks near the back of the crowd. "I'm sick of meetings and talk, talk, talk. We need action, that's what we need. We should be out huntin' Big Foot right now instead of sitting around like a bunch of women talkin' about it." He snorted loudly. "And talk of a fuckin' TV show? What will that do? Only bring more outta towners in."

"And that would be a bad thing?" Sandy Aldridge, the owner of Wild Wills, a local restaurant, asked. She was tall and thin, and wore heavy makeup and a tough-as-nails attitude.

" 'Course it would. We don't need no more people up here, and no goddamned TV cameras and crew scarin' off the Big Foot! This"—he made a wide arc with his arm to indicate the interior of the meeting hall—"this is nothin' more than a publicity stunt, a goddamned fiasco, that's what it is!" Kruger was practically roaring now, and Alvarez was standing close enough to smell the alcohol. His face was red, his eyes bloodshot. "It's about money, people, not about Big Foot!"

"Oh, stuff it, Otis." Sandy was having none of it. She was used to dealing with disgruntled loud-mouths at the bar in her establishment. "Just shut up and listen to what the man has to say."

"I did and he's done! Paid my goddamned twenty-five bucks just to hear him peddle the same old shit I've heard a million times."

"If you don't like it, just leave," Sandy snapped as a few others turned their heads. "You're making a scene."

"I said I paid my money!"

"You need to show some respect."

He spat out a stream of tobacco juice, which arched upward before hitting the floor with a splat.

"That's it, Otis!" Alvarez stepped in. "Time to leave."

"Who the hell are you?" He whirled and she

saw the outline of a pistol in the pocket of his baggy jeans.

"The woman who's going to escort you out of here quietly," she said, and he snorted derisively.

"Sheeiiit."

Ivor warned, "Jesus, Otis, watch out. She's a goddamned cop!"

"You got that right. Detective Selena Alvarez, Pinewood County." She showed him her badge, and Otis stared at it long and hard.

"Fuck me," he said, tottering a bit, and she pulled his gun, a small pistol, from his pocket.

"Hey, wait!"

"You got a permit to carry?" she demanded.

"Damned straight. Give that back to me."

"Tomorrow, you can pick it up at that station."

"You can't take my gun! It's legal! I told you, I *have* a damned permit to carry a concealed weapon."

She made sure the safety was on and slipped it into her bag. To Otis's stunned friends, she said, "Anyone sober enough to give him a ride home?"

Ivor Hicks only blinked at her through the yellowish lenses of his glasses. No help there.

"Yeah, I can get him home," Nesmith said reluctantly. "But I really wanted to talk to Sphinx." He gave a nod to the stage, where people were still swarming. "Find out if he's the real deal."

"He's not!" Otis spat. "Goddamned panty-waist. Gonna just poke around the woods, have the actors hear somethin' or spy a shadow flittin' by. Maybe a bear messes with the camp or somethin'. Make a big deal of it on the show when it's probly jest the stage crew. That's all that'll come of it. Trust me, he ain't gonna find no Big Foot. Not with his cameras an' lights an' microphones, all that crap production gear." He glared at Nesmith. "Has he found one in that Oregon show? Huh? No. Just a damned footprint or two, right? He finds an actual Big Foot and his show is over. Kaput! Mystery solved. Ratings gone. End of the fuckin' story."

"Come on, Otis," she said, nudging him firmly.

"I'm not goin' anywhere," Otis protested and tried to wriggle away, the reek of alcohol mixed with the pungent smell of his body odor. She rewarded him by twisting his arm behind his back. "Shit! Goddamn it!" he squealed.

"This way, Otis." She was pushing him toward the main entrance. Nesmith, muttering under his breath, followed behind.

"I don't need a ride! I just want my damned gun!" Kruger was angry enough, she thought, to maybe take a swing at her with his free arm.

Just try it, she thought, aware several people had turned to stare at them. "Go home, Otis."

And then he rounded on her, twisted faster than she expected, his fist coiled. He swung. "No way, you bitch, I want to—"

She feinted and he stumbled, dropping to a knee.

"To what?" Blackwater demanded, his black eyes flashing. He grabbed Kruger by his free arm and hauled him to his feet. "To talk to her superior? Well, you got him. Now, let's go. Move it!" To Alvarez, he said, "I've got him," and she gave up her grip on the drunk. People nearby who had witnessed the scuffle stepped back, the crowd parting as the sheriff marched Otis out of the room and down the stairs. Alvarez, Hicks, and Nesmith followed after.

"This is police brutality!" Otis screamed as they reached street level and he was forced toward the exterior doors. "I'll sue. Swear to God I'll sue you and the whole damned sheriff's department. Don't think I won't!" He was blisteringly angry now, spitting nails.

"You can have the papers drawn up from the drunk tank." Blackwater, jaw tight, gave the older man a little tweak to his arm, and Otis grimaced but quit resisting.

"Okay, okay!" he said, "I'm goin'. Home. But I want my damned gun."

"Tomorrow. At the station. Talk to Detective Alvarez. She'll deal with you."

"You can't keep my weapon! Son of a bitch! Son of a fuckin' bitch!" Kruger spat out as Alvarez followed them through the front doors, Nesmith and Hicks in tow.

Outside, the evening was still warm, but far cooler than the stuffy interior of the meeting room, and Alvarez felt as if she could finally breathe again. Streetlights began to glow as dusk settled, and a few cars and trucks rumbled slowly by.

"Go home," the sheriff told Kruger. "Sleep it off. Come to the office in the morning."

To the others, Blackwater asked, "Who's driving him?"

Nesmith said, "Rode with me. We heard there might be a parking problem. All came together. I'm stone-cold sober."

"Good. Take him home and then take his keys. We don't want him to get any ideas about driving back."

"You can't do that!" Kruger was outraged.

"Sure I can. And you can get them back tomorrow."

"I can't drop 'em by," Nesmith protested. "I got work!"

"Then have Ivor do it. I don't care. Figure it out," the sheriff said as he released Kruger. "I don't want to hear about any trouble, or some-body gets arrested." He swept his gaze over the three men.

Ivor was shaking his head, then, as if realizing his response was negative, quickly started nod-ding while some of the combative fire disappeared from Nesmith's eyes.

Alvarez did notice that the corners of Nesmith's lips were still tight, but he didn't argue as he herded Otis down the block toward the king cab of a huge black pickup. Once Kruger was in the back seat, Nesmith climbed behind the wheel and Ivor Hicks took his place riding shotgun.

"Troublemakers," Blackwater muttered to Alvarez as he watched the pickup pull away from the curb, and drive down a nearly empty street.

"I could have handled them. You didn't need to step in and take over."

"I noticed he had a gun. Saw you take it from him, but thought a little assistance wouldn't hurt. The place was crowded, and I was afraid someone else might think it was a good idea to get involved. Start something. The smell of a fight was in the air. You could feel it."

"Yeah." He was right. Tensions had been running hot. Another punch could have been thrown, this one landing, and all hell may have broken out as others joined in the fight.

"Didn't want to have a riot on our hands." They walked toward the building together. She noticed some people had followed the altercation outside, including a couple of kids who'd been at Reservoir Point. Preston Tufts and Donny Justison stood on the steps, smoking cigarettes and blatantly watching her. She sensed they had been hoping for more of a fight. As they eyed her, she saw the bloodlust in their eyes, the desire for more action and violence.

"Besides," Blackwater continued as the boys each took a final drag, then tossed their cigarettes onto the steps and ground them out, the smell of smoke still lingering as they disappeared inside, "we're not out of the woods."

"What do you mean?"

"I came here from the office," he said quietly. "Wanted to tell you, the paternity test came in on Donny Justison. The lab compared his DNA sample with that of the fetus."

She waited, feeling a cool breath of a breeze roll off the river two blocks north, but she knew from his expression what he was going to say and he confirmed it a second later:

"Donald Justison Junior is not the father of Destiny Rose Montclaire's unborn child."

Lindsay Cronin left the Big Foot meeting more worried than ever.

She'd seen the cops looking over at her, all of them. No matter what *he* said, they were all suspects, every last person who knew Destiny, and sooner or later, the truth would come out. It always did.

The cops wouldn't let it go.

The Montclaire family wouldn't let it go.

She drove home, parked her Ford Focus on the street and, with the excuse that she was tired, went directly to her room.

Her mom checked on her, of course. Darlie Cronin was nothing if not a perfect, doting mother, and she expected great things from Lindsay.

"You'll be the first woman in the family to graduate from college," she'd said often enough. Her eyes had always shined at the thought, and though she didn't think her father really gave a crap if she went off to Montana State, or Oregon or even UCLA, he always went along. Lindsay knew he was worried about money; he always was. He was pushing for a junior college and Lindsay living at home, but she really didn't think she could stand another year or two in Grizzly Falls.

But that all seemed so far away now. Her life was a cluster-fuck. Make that a *major* cluster-fuck.

She waited until she heard her mother go into her bedroom, where she'd probably read for an hour. A while later, she caught the sound of her father coming in the back door, his footsteps pausing in the kitchen, then trailing past her room to theirs.

She gave them another half an hour to settle in, until she could hear the rumble of her father's snoring. She couldn't imagine how her mother could stand it, sleeping in a queen-sized bed, right next to the old buzz saw, but at least Roy's snores made it easy for Lindsay to leave without detection.

She created some bumps in her bed with some pillows to make it look like someone was actually sleeping in the bed. It kinda looked like a person. Then she made certain the window was unlatched and raised a little, in case, on her return, she didn't want to risk using the door, like if one of her parents couldn't sleep and went into the living room to watch TV or whatever.

Gathering her courage, her nerves stretched thin, she sneaked out of her room, tiptoeing down the hallway, through the living room and small entry hall, then outside and into the night. She closed the door softly behind her and dashed to her car, letting out a pent-up breath she hadn't even known she'd been holding.

She drove down her street and the next without her lights. Once she was out of the neighborhood, she flipped on the beams and headed out of town to Horsebrier Ridge, where they'd met before. Already, she was feeling a little better. He would take care of everything; he always did.

She was still panicked, of course, but less so as she drove out of town, then sped up the long road to the ridge. On this side of the hills, the road was straight, like an arrow, the climb slow and easy, but once she reached the ridge and started down the steep side, the narrow lanes twisted and looped, like a sidewinder. No one was following her on the straightaway. In fact, it was eerily lonely.

"That's good," she told herself and yet was spooked, her fingers circling the wheel in a death grip.

Something jumped out of the shadows and

she hit the brakes, skidding a little as a coyote darted across the road. Her heart slammed into her throat. And she swore as she saw the shaggy beast stop and watch her from the ditch on the far side of the road.

"It's nothing," she told herself, but her pulse had skyrocketed, her case of nerves taking her anxiety to the stratosphere.

Calm down. Just take a deep breath. You'll meet with him and he'll make things better.

She crested the top of the craggy ridge, then started downward into the canyon. Rolling down the window, she smelled the dry forest and felt the night air seep into the car, the wind snatching at her hair. That was more like it. Cool. Calm. Rational.

She hit the brakes repeatedly, keeping her little Ford on the road, hugging the center line. Still, she met no other cars, but as she rounded the tight curves she thought she caught the flash of headlights in her rearview. Odd. The car hadn't been behind her on the straightaway. Had it pulled behind her here in the mountains, or had she slowed so much that someone she hadn't seen before, a speeder, had caught up to her?

She kept driving, but her concentration was distracted, caught between the empty, winding road ahead, and the quicksilver hints of head-lights behind. She'd thought the beams weren't steady because of the trees and hills and curves in the road, but maybe it was because the driver was turning his headlights on and off, trying to chase her down.

No way.

No one knew she was on the road.

Except him.

And he was her ally.

Could her parents have found her out? Gone into her room and discovered that she'd sneaked out? Even if they had, how would they know that she was on this road? No, that wasn't feasible. But if they called the cops . . . ?

Wouldn't a cop use his lights? Maybe a siren?

So what then?

She kept driving, the lights behind her flickering on and off, distracting her.

Putting her more on edge.

She should never have agreed to meet out here in the middle of no-damned-where. Why hadn't she had him swing by and talk in the damned "man cave"? Her parents wouldn't have heard her. But, of course, it would have been dangerous.

Nervously chewing on the inside of her mouth, Lindsay squinted into the darkness. Her thoughts were a jumble, and she wondered if she should have just called the cops. Told them what she knew. With difficulty, she focused on the road ahead, where her headlights cut through the darkness and the double yellow line was nearly mesmerizing in its snake-like path.

Again, she saw lights in the reflection of the mirror.

Distracted, she cut a corner a little tight, then swung wide and saw the S-curve ahead. She braked, attempting the first sharp turn, pulling hard on the wheel, seeing a glint of light behind her again, cutting the corner too close as the vehicle behind her appeared.

Big.

Lights on bright.

Accelerating on this twisting snake of road.

"What the hell?" she whispered. "Back off jerk-wad!" As if the driver could hear her.

She glanced through the windshield again and screamed.

In the wash of her headlights, she saw a body. Stretched out across the center line, a human form lay, unmoving. Dead? Alive? She didn't know.

Oh, God. *Oh, dear God!*

Lindsay stood on the brakes.

Nooo!

Jerking the wheel, she tried to avoid hitting flesh and bone, all the while seeing the girl's face turned toward her, her eyes rounded and staring blankly.

"God, no!"

Her car fishtailed.

She couldn't slow down fast enough!

Thump!!!

She hit the body.

Thunk!

Oh, Jesus! Her tires squished the girl, rolled over her, pushing the body as the brakes seized.

Screaming, disbelief and terror scraping through her brain, Lindsay twisted on the steering wheel and the back tires came free, bounced over the body.

Oh. Dear. God. No. No, no! Oh . . .

Headlights appeared behind her. Bright. Glaring.

Shaking, crying, and shrieking, she saw the side of the cliff rushing at her. She cranked the wheel. The Focus hit gravel and began spinning. The beams of her headlights splashed over the cliff face, then the road, then the guardrail as the car spun around, swerving wildly. She saw the truck that had been following her stopped on the road, its headlights glaring at her, its driver watching.

Her fender caught on metal.

Scraaaape! The Ford slid along the guardrail, metal screeching and groaning, sparks flying until the old rail and pilings suddenly gave way and her little car sped over the rim of the ledge.

Lindsay screamed as she plunged down, down, down into the great, black, yawning abyss, while the driver of the pickup did nothing to help.

CHAPTER 17

The morning after the meeting with Sphinx, Pescoli made a stop at a coffee shop, where she picked up a breakfast sandwich, decaf coffee, and hash browns and devoured every last bite before she drove to the office. "This has got to stop," she said, aiming the conversation at her belly as she parked. She felt a gentle kick deep within her abdomen, as if her baby understood. "Yeah, I know. We were *both* hungry."

And so it begins with private conversations with an unborn child, all the hopes and dreams of the future wrapped into the baby growing within you. Then, in a blink, it seems you wake up one morning and your kid has discovered a dead body and is furious with you for standing in the way of her chance at reality TV stardom.

She made her way into the station and noticed the air-conditioner unit was acting up again, her office feeling like a sauna. She flipped on the desk fan and had just settled into her desk chair when Alvarez, looking trim in skinny jeans and a T-shirt and open jacket, popped her head into the office. "Seen your email yet?"

"Just got here. Something up?"

"Donny's not the baby daddy."

"Hmmm."

"The lab results came in late yesterday, Blackwater gave me the word last night and I double-checked."

Pescoli had hoped that the paternity test would confirm what she'd thought was obvious, one little mystery solved. "Doesn't mean he's off the hook for the homicide. He could have found out and killed her in a fit of jealousy."

"Possibly. Or . . ."

"Whoever the father is might have gone off when she told him. Killed her accidentally or intentionally. So who's next up?"

"The Montclaires have no idea," Alvarez said.

"You already talked to them?"

"I didn't want it to come from some other source, and I thought they might have some idea who she might have been seeing." Alvarez leaned a shoulder on the door frame. "When I gave them the news, they were on their home phone, a landline with an extension. Glenn was icy, acted as if I were accusing his dead daughter of being . . . promiscuous. As if I were making some judgment call. And Helene, on the extension, started crying about her 'baby' and 'grandbaby.' "

It all hit home with Pescoli, pregnant as she was, about not only losing the life of the nearly grown child, but the little unborn life as well. "Not pleasant."

"No. I tried to talk to them about other guys she might have been seeing, but all I got was that she had a lot of 'friends,' and the only names that he actually gave me were Kip and Kywin Bell and Bryant Tophman. When I mentioned some of the others who were at the party, he'd heard of them, but didn't think they were involved with Destiny. He reminded me that his daughter was a good girl and that Donny Justison was the reason she was dead. In Glenn Montclaire's opinion, the mayor's son is the embodiment of pure evil."

"But not the father of Destiny's infant."

"Glenn's not ready to acknowledge that."

"Even though you can't argue with science."

"Tell that to the creationists."

Snorting her agreement, Pescoli snagged her keys again. "Let's go have a chat with Kywin Bell. Lara Haas claimed he was protective of Destiny Montclaire, so I'd like to hear what he has to say."

"You think he might have been involved with her?"

"Or know who was." She was on her feet again and stopped dead in her tracks as a cramp rolled through her abdomen. As it passed, she leaned against the desk. "Whoa."

"You okay?" Alvarez asked, her eyes dark with instant concern.

"Yeah, yeah." Letting out a long breath, she said, "Braxton Hicks. I had 'em with both the other kids."

"A long time ago."

"Which everyone keeps reminding me." The contraction eased, and she straightened. Without missing a beat, she grabbed her sidearm, and together they walked outside.

"I'll drive," Alvarez said and for once Pescoli didn't argue. She'd had enough arguing last night when the discussion with Luke, Michelle, and Bianca had gotten hot and escalated in the parking lot of the Sons of Grizzly Falls building. Luke seemed to think Bianca's opportunity to be a part of the reality show was akin to finding a pot of gold at the end of the rainbow.

"Think of the money she could make. God, Regan, it might pay for her college. Maybe that's not a big deal for you, but I'm not a rich man and any little bit helps."

As if he'd paid for any damned thing since their divorce. They shared custody, and that appeared to mean that Regan shouldered all of the bills. But Luke was on the hook for college—that had been written in the divorce decree—and so, of course, he was squirming, trying to get out of it.

"Or starring in this reality show could be the start of something, maybe launch an acting career," Michelle had piped up, a bit of envy in her words.

"Why wouldn't you want her to do it?" Jeremy had asked. He'd shown up late for the meeting, but had added his two cents.

Only Santana hadn't argued with her, just kept

his silence as Bianca wheedled, "Mom, I want to do it. Come on. What would it hurt?"

That was it. She didn't know, but it had just felt wrong to her. Still did, she thought, as she stared through the Subaru's bug-splattered window at a line of clouds, thick and white, slowly inching across the blue Montana sky.

She and Alvarez continued to discuss the case on the way to the feed store, tossing out names of suspects and coming back to the big question mark that had eluded them: Who had Destiny Rose gone to meet, if anyone, on the evening of her disappearance? As far as they knew, Donny Justison was the last person to have seen her alive and therefore was still at the top of the suspect list.

They discussed potential motives for Destiny's murder. If the girl hadn't been killed by a random nutcase in a situation where she'd been at the wrong place at the wrong time, which seemed remote, then it was someone who knew her. The obvious motive was that she was pregnant. If the pregnancy wasn't the reason she was killed, then why?

Destiny didn't have any money, no trust fund. She had no known enemies, at least none that had surfaced yet, so that brought them back to the fact that she was with child.

"Maybe her cell phone records will give us a clue," Alvarez said. "There was some kind of hiccup with getting them to us, but they're supposed to be in today."

"What about her laptop?"

"Zoller's going through it as we speak."

"Good. I gave her another assignment. Because she's a card-carrying member of the Big Foot Believers, I asked her to check out who could have made off with the missing Sasquatch costume."

"Let's hope we catch a break."

The drive only took about fifteen minutes, as the feed store where Kywin Bell worked was only a few miles from the station, past the sprawl of strip malls and fast-food restaurants in the newer section of town.

Alvarez pulled into a two-tiered asphalt parking lot. The commercial part of the store was located on the upper level and faced the pockmarked asphalt lot. The lower level serviced farmers who came for truckloads of feed and heavier equipment.

Pickups, flatbeds, vans, and a couple of sedans were parked haphazardly in the upper lot. If there had been any lines delineating parking spaces, they had long since faded.

The building itself was built of concrete blocks and had obviously been constructed for function rather than form. While the Sons of Grizzly Falls building was ornate, this one was stark. A metal awning ran across the front of the structure, shading the large windows and glass doors guarded by pallets of bark dust, peat moss, and sand.

Pescoli and Alvarez made their way inside, where the air seemed dusty despite the efforts of fans mounted high overhead. The only cashier at the front register was a man of twenty or so, whose dark hair was clipped so short his scalp showed through, and whose thick beard was long enough to boast two little rat tails that had been braided beneath his chin. He offered them a smile as they approached and asked if he could help.

The smile faded as they identified themselves, showed their badges, and asked about Kywin Bell.

"He's in back. Loading," the cashier, whose name tag read BRYCE, said. His Adam's apple bobbed nervously and Pescoli wondered if he had something to hide, or if police officers in general sent him into overdrive. "I'll show you the way."

Quickly, head down, he ushered them along a wide center aisle that passed through sections dedicated to a variety of pets. They walked past stacks of bags of dry dog and cat food and shelves where dog toys, leashes, and collars had been suspended.

Through the pet area, they headed into another section dedicated to farm animals. Pescoli saw salt licks and saddles, veterinary and grooming supplies, pails and feedbags before Bryce showed them a staircase that looked to be a hundred years old. "Kywin's down there," he said. "In the grain depot." He looked over his shoulder to the front of the store. "I got to get back to the register."

"We can handle it from here," Alvarez assured him as they started down the steps.

"Okay." He hurried off.

"You know this kid, right?" Alvarez said. She paused on the bottom step to glance back at Pescoli, who was easing her way down the final stairs.

"Yeah, since preschool."

"And?"

"He was always a bully. One of two of Frank Bell's sons. Bell has been in and out of jail himself. Domestic violence. Of the two boys, Kywin, the younger, is probably more law abiding, but that isn't setting the bar all that high."

The stairwell opened to an expansive area that was complete with loading dock. All of the barn doors had been thrown wide, and a forklift was parked in one corner. Pallet after pallet of grain was stacked against each other: wheat, oats, barley, and corn. Inside an adjacent area, bales of straw, hay, and alfalfa were kept dry.

A small forklift carrying a single pallet piled with bags of some kind of grain slowly rounded the corner. Kywin Bell, wearing a hard hat, was at the controls and concentrating as he pulled into the covered area and carefully lowered the pallet into place, then backed up.

Alvarez flagged him down and he stopped, leaving the forklift to idle. Alvarez had to shout over the rumble of the engine, and Kywin, appearing to want to flee, glared at her. She identified herself, as did Pescoli. "We need to talk to you."

"I'm working," he called loudly.

"Only take a few minutes," Alvarez yelled back.

He scowled. "Give me a sec." He backed the forklift to a spot near the larger one, cut the engine, and hopped onto the dusty concrete. "This has to do with Destiny." It was a statement rather than a question, but Alvarez answered anyway. "Yes."

He tossed his hard hat onto the seat of the forklift and glanced around. Spying a string bean of a man sweeping near an open bin of corn, he yelled, "Hey, Zach. I'm taking five."

"Already?" The tall guy stopped pushing his broom and squinted.

"Won't be long." Bell glanced at Alvarez and said more softly, "Right?"

"Shouldn't," she agreed.

"Good. This way."

Pescoli had expected him to lead them inside, into some kind of break room. Instead, he strode outside, where the sun was already climbing high, beating down through the scanty clouds. He rounded a corner of the building, to the side road that connected this lower part of the business to the parking lot above. The road was chewed-up asphalt, cracked and dusty. A retaining wall ran along its length, up the steep slope. Here, at the bottom, Kywin hoisted himself easily onto a half wall and reached into his T-shirt pocket, withdrawing a pack of Camel cigarettes and a lighter. He lit up and blew smoke toward the sky. "What do you want to know?"

"How involved were you with Destiny Rose Montclaire?"

"Shit." Another drag, then he turned his hands, palms up, the tip of his cigarette clenched between two fingers as it smoldered upside down. "We were friends, okay?"

"Good friends?"

"I already told this to some cop that night. Last Saturday. At Reservoir Point."

"Detective Zoller."

"That's the one. Little. Like Destiny." He studied the smoke trailing from his Camel.

Alvarez nodded, her black hair glistening in the morning light. "I've seen Detective Zoller's notes."

"Then you know I had nothing to do with what happened to Destiny." He was sweating, hat ring visible in his short-cropped hair. "I liked her. I wouldn't hurt her." He paused thoughtfully. "Never."

Was he lying? Pescoli couldn't tell. She stepped closer, noticed that he was swinging his legs, his heavy work boots as dusty as everything else. And huge. "Some people claim you were her protector, that you stepped in when she and Donald Justison got into it."

"I didn't like him knocking her around. Donny's a mean drunk and she is . . . she was just a bit of a thing. Didn't seem right. Even though she never seemed afraid of him, didn't mind going at him, y'know? Setting him off." He squinted in the harshness of the morning light, took a final pull on his Camel, and tossed it into the dirt.

"When was the last time you saw her?"

"I *told* you all. I can't really remember. A day or two before she went missing, I guess. A bunch of us were at the diner and she came in."

"What diner?" Alvarez asked.

"Midway Diner."

"You and who else?" Alvarez pressed.

"Donny. TJ and Alex O'Hara and Kip, I think. Oh, and Tophman. Bryant Tophman. He was there, too, a little later. Came with Reece and Devlin."

"Austin Reece and Rod Devlin?" Pescoli clarified.

"Yeah."

Alvarez gave a quick nod. "The whole gang."

"Most of us," he agreed as a crow lit in a scrag of tree nearby and cawed loudly. "Is there anything else? I've really got to get back to work. I need this job."

"Just another couple of quick questions. Is there any chance you're the father of Destiny's baby?" Alvarez asked.

Kywin's lips tightened. "I said we were friends. I didn't say we were friends with benefits." When neither cop responded, he added, "We didn't get it on, okay? Maybe made out a couple of times, but no. Definitely not the father. I thought Donny took a DNA test."

Alvarez ducked that with, "We're just ruling out everyone. So, you wouldn't mind giving a sample?"

"A *sample?*" He shook his head vehemently.

"Saliva," Pescoli assured him.

"Oh." He let out a breath and fished in his pocket for another cigarette. "I thought you meant . . ."

"Yeah, I know what you thought," she said and smiled inwardly that Kywin had freaked a little at the thought of having to give a sperm sample. Pescoli didn't like him. Never had. Too cocky.

"No way that kid is mine."

"Easy to prove." Pescoli was tired and hot, the back of her blouse starting to stick to her. "Come to the station, give a sample. Do it today."

"I work," he complained. As if the rest of the citizens of the world didn't hold down jobs. The crow, still giving out raw cries, flew off.

"That's the beauty of the sheriff's department," Pescoli said. "We're open twenty-four-seven."

She eyed him through her shades. "Who do you think could be the father?"

"Donny."

"Anyone else?"

He screwed up his face. "Destiny . . . got around."

Pescoli pushed. "So give me another name."

Anger flashed in his eyes. "How the hell would I know?"

"Gee, I don't know. Maybe because you're her friend. Her 'protector.' "

"I wasn't her protector. I never called myself anything like that, okay? If I was her damned protector, I did a pretty lousy job of it, didn't I? She's dead." An emotion Pescoli couldn't name passed behind his eyes. He ran a hand over his head and swiped the beading sweat from his forehead. "Destiny could have hooked up with anybody. She was . . . kinda desperate, put up with Donny's shit and didn't like it when he started dating some chick in college, but hell, she wasn't exactly true-blue, if ya know what I mean." He jabbed the second cigarette into his mouth and flicked his lighter to the tip, drawing deeply.

Pescoli asked, "So where were you a week ago Friday night?"

"I don't know. Probably just hangin' out." He stared at them through the rising smoke. "Is that when . . . when she died?"

"Was killed," Pescoli reminded him. "Give us a recap of your weekend."

"I didn't kill her!"

"Well, come up with someone else besides Donny."

"When are you gonna get Donny's results back?"

Pescoli just shrugged, waiting.

"Well . . . a week ago Friday, I don't know. Uh . . . oh yeah, I was with Kip, for a while, Friday night, then later I went over to Reece's. It was Triple Pool Night, that's what we call it. We do a little betting, pool our money for lottery tickets, then play pool. We go there a lot of Friday nights. Reece's dad has a bitchin' rec room."

"With a bar?" Pescoli asked.

"Well, yeah, I guess, but they also have a swimming pool with a hot tub and waterfall. It's cool. We were there all night. Crashed and got up around eleven, I think."

"Everyone was there all night?" Pescoli asked.

"I think so. Like I said, I crashed."

"But when you woke up, the same people were there."

He shook his head. "Nah. Just Reece, of course, in his room and, uh, Tophman, I think—no wait, he had to get back. His dad's a prick."

"The minister?" Pescoli had met Reverend Raymond Tophman at various community events, starting with the Good Feelings Preschool years before.

He snorted. "Some minister."

"What's wrong with Reverend Tophman?" Pescoli asked. She had her own feelings about the severely strict man, but wanted to hear Kywin's.

"Doesn't it say somewhere in the Bible that it's okay to hit a kid or whale on him or something?"

Before Pescoli could respond, Alvarez said, "There's an old proverb, 'Spare the rod, spoil the child,' but I think the actual translation from the Bible, book of Proverbs, is a little more precise. It suggests that you need to discipline your children."

"Well, whatever. The preacher is all in his kid's business. If I were Tophman, I'd move out."

"What about the rest of the weekend?"

"I had chores. I always have chores. My old man doesn't care that I work my ass off all week, so I mowed the lawn, cut brush. A lot of fun stuff like that." When she didn't say anything, he said, "You can check with him."

"You live with your father?"

He squinted against the cigarette smoke. "Things didn't work out with Mom. She's got younger kids and thinks Kip and I, we should be on our own." He scowled slightly, and it was obvious to Pescoli that Kywin thought he'd been given a raw deal in life. Maybe he had.

Alvarez asked, "Did Destiny have any known enemies?"

His big shoulders lifted into a shrug. His neck

was thick, his entire body fit and packed with sinewy muscle, not the long muscles of a basketball player, but the shorter, denser muscles of a running back in football or a wrestler. "The girls were always fighting. Besties with this one for a week, then hatin' on her the next. Weird as shit, if ya ask me."

"Anyone in particular who didn't like her?"

"Nah . . . well, I did hear that Simone and she didn't get along all the time."

"Simone Delaney," Alvarez clarified.

"But Simone's a bitch." He took a deep drag and threw a glance over his shoulder to look at the loading area, where String Bean and another guy, older and with a big gut, were in discussion. "They fought a lot. At school and, I guess, at work."

"They worked together?"

"Volunteered at the same hospital, or somethin'. Oh, shit. Look, I *gotta* go." With that, he hopped off the wall and dropped his second cigarette, crushing it with the toe of one huge boot.

"What size shoes do you wear?" Pescoli asked as a flatbed truck turned from the upper parking lot and rumbled down the steep road, kicking up dust, the driver giving them a quick once-over from inside the cab.

"Fuck! That's my boss."

"About your shoe size?"

"I don't know. Thirteen. Sometimes a fourteen.

271

A real bitch to find some that fit." With that, he was off, jogging back to the overhang of the building where the truck was parking. The driver climbed out and stood with his hands on his hips, his face turned toward Alvarez and Pescoli. From his expression, Pescoli guessed he was none too happy. He turned to watch Kywin jog back to the shed.

Let Kywin explain to his boss why the police were talking to him, she thought, as she and Alvarez walked up the sharply inclined road to the main parking lot, where Alvarez's Subaru sat baking in the intense sunlight.

As they slid into the interior, Alvarez asked, "Next stop? A&B Painting?"

Pescoli nodded. A&B Painting was the establishment where Kywin's brother, Kip, worked.

CHAPTER 18

Bianca hunched down in the passenger seat of her dad's vintage Corvette. She was usually confident, but today, after last night's meeting of the Big Foot Believers, when she'd felt as if she were on display in front of what seemed to be the whole damned town, she felt unsure. She'd always thought she would love fame and the spotlight, but not like last night. It had been cool in a way, yes, to be the center of attention. Well, almost. Actually Barclay Sphinx had been the star of the night, but she still felt a little weird about it.

Which made this trip with Lucky all the more awkward, so she'd put on dark glasses and avoided eye contact with anyone else who happened to be driving around. Lucky was behind the wheel, taking her to meet with Barclay Sphinx. His side window was down, and he rested a tanned arm on the ledge and drove with one hand on the wheel. As much as she wanted to hide, her father was on display, grinning, joking, on top of the world.

But, of course, he wasn't nursing a sprained ankle, a split chin, and a few other bruises. Nor had he been chased by a monster and found a dead body floating in the creek.

Through the dark lenses, she hazarded a sideways glance at him. He was so pleased with himself, his hair blowing around in the breeze, his head moving faintly to the beat of a song from the eighties or nineties that was blasting from the speakers, some old Bon Jovi song. He sang along. ". . . had a job on the docks . . . down on his luck . . . someday . . ."

Bianca wasn't so pleased with herself. In fact, she felt kind of rotten because it seemed like she was sneaking around. Okay, sure. She did a lot of things behind her mother's back. It wasn't that big of a deal as a rule. Usually she felt that the less Mom knew about her life, the better. It just made things easier, but then she wasn't usually in collusion with her dad, keeping secrets from Mom. Even though Lucky denied that there was anything underhanded going on, she knew otherwise.

"Don't be so suspicious," he'd said when he called and told her to get ready, that they were going to meet with the producer. "This is a good thing."

"Mom won't like it. You heard her."

"Oh, she'll come around. It's just her nature, what with her being a cop and all, to be over-protective. And come on, her hormones are *all* out of whack with this pregnancy. I'm surprised they still let her work. She's big as a barn. Just get ready and I'll swing by and pick you up. I'll be there in half an hour. Let me handle Mom."

So here she was, driving with her father to a meeting with Barclay Sphinx at the Wilderness Motel. "It just feels like I'm lying to Mom," she said, reaching down to scratch her calf where the damned ankle brace rubbed. "You know, sneaking around behind her back."

"When has that ever stopped you?"

"Very funny," she said.

"We're not sneaking around, okay? You're with me. I said I'll handle your mother, and I will. But I can't bother her with this. She's in the middle of that homicide investigation, and she's pregnant, and you all just moved into that new house. She has a lot on her plate right now."

He was equivocating, making excuses, dancing around the truth, and they both knew it.

Nonetheless, Lucky wheeled into town, switched lanes, and stopped for a red light, his car idling loudly. On the other side of the highway, Bianca saw another car at the light and wouldn't you know, Emmett Tufts was driving with Rod Devlin riding shotgun. Lara and Maddie were in the back seat. She slid lower in the seat, didn't want them to see her and didn't understand why.

Lucky turned down the radio. "Now's the time. The opportunity. We—you might not get another one. Barclay called me this morning. He's had a change of plans and has to drive to Oregon for something, he didn't say what, but he's leaving town today, and he needs to nail down a few details, the biggest one being if you're going to be in his show. It's a 'go,' that's what he said, his exact words, 'a go,' but he has to figure out the first few episodes, what the story line is. He's already got a team on the way."

"A team?"

"I think a production crew. He's got the basic story in his head, but they have to completely work it out. He outlined it the other night, didn't he?"

"So it's a script."

He lifted his right hand off the steering wheel, flattened it, and tilted it up and down. *Maybe yes. Maybe no.* "It's your story. Remember?"

She did, though she wasn't all that keen on reliving one of the scariest nights of her life. She remembered running down the hillside, the beast racing behind her, and then tumbling into the creek to find . . . She closed her mind to the thought of Destiny's body submerged in the water, pale hair floating around her face. . . .

"He wants you to be a part of it. The star."

The light changed and he hit the gas, tearing around a corner and speeding along the road. She turned her face as they whipped past Emmett Tufts's black Mustang. Two miles later, they pulled into the Wilderness Motel, a two-story U-shaped building. Out front, near the awning that covered the space by the front doors, stood a nine-foot-tall wooden sculpture of Big Foot. The creature seemed to be walking toward the front door, looking over his shoulder as if to see if he was being watched, but definitely heading inside the Wilderness.

Fitting, Bianca thought, and probably the reason Sphinx had chosen this motel out of a half dozen in the area. A text came in and she checked her phone. Maddie. Well, well, her "friend" hadn't contacted her in a while.

Vigil Friday night for Destiny. 7 p.m. First Christian. Main St. Everyone's going. Wanna come with?

Bianca texted back: OK

Honestly, she didn't know how she felt about it.

Have u heard from Lindsay?

It was kind of an odd question, as Bianca didn't know Lindsay that well. They'd spent years together in school but had never been close. No. Why?

Her mom called looking for her. Asked if anyone had seen her since last night.

She's missing?

I guess. Her car too. Gotta go.

Bianca stared at the phone. It had to be a mistake. Lindsay was probably just with a friend or a boyfriend or something. Her mom was probably panicking for no reason. Right?

But she had the same weird feeling that she'd experienced the other night, right after the dream, that something malevolent was happening.

"What the hell is she doing here?" Lucky asked, almost to himself, bringing Bianca back to the here and now.

"Who?" she asked just as she spotted Michelle's Cadillac parked in the shade of a solitary pine. "Oh."

"Yeah, 'oh.'" His good mood vanished as he drove under an awning at the front entrance and headed toward some empty parking spots on the far side of the building that were still relatively close to the front doors.

"Michelle's not supposed to be here?" Bianca asked.

He sent her a look. "She wanted to come, of

course. She loves all things Hollywood and has a thing for Sphinx, which is probably good. But I thought it was best if it was just you and me. There might have to be some negotiating, and I thought it best if I handled it." His lips pinched in irritation, something that didn't happen much when he was dealing with his wife, but happened a lot when he and Mom got into it.

Bianca checked the mirror on the visor and cringed a little at her image. She'd worn as much makeup as she could, but her face was bruised and her chin . . . crap, would it ever be the same?

Probably not. There was a good chance she'd have to use any money she made from this reality show for plastic surgery. And a car. She could see herself in a sporty little two-door rather than borrowing her mother's old SUV or catching rides with her older brother in his pathetic excuse of a pickup. A car would be really nice, and her face fixed. She smiled for the first time that day.

Lucky parked near a solitary pine tree in the lot, then snapped his keys from the ignition. "Okay, let's go!" He was out of the car in an instant and around the back, to help her climb out. Which was totally unnecessary.

Together, they walked across the lot to the front doors. Bianca still limped a little, but she thought it was more from the stupid splint than her injury and wished she could get rid of the thing.

As the sliding glass doors opened to the motel

lobby, she shook off her doubts. This was cool. It was all cool. What was she worrying about? To hell with what Mom thought. She was going to sign the contract, and her dad, as her parent, would sign as well, so it would be legal.

Mom wouldn't like it, but that was just too damned bad. It was her life and she was going to star in Barclay Sphinx's reality show.

If Kywin Bell had been reticent to talk to the cops, Pescoli thought, his brother was downright inapproachable and rude. "What the hell are you cops doin' here?" Kip demanded. Then, "Wow, are you pregnant or what?"

"You're the first person who's noticed," Pescoli said dryly.

"Really?"

"No."

He stared at her a moment, then went back to stacking paint cans on shelves in the windowless room at the back of A&B Painting and Supplies, a paint store housed in a long, squat strip mall only a few blocks from the sheriff's office. A&B was at the far end of the building, its only neighbor a shoe repair store.

A plump woman with short white hair spiked around an apple-cheeked face and a name tag that read ARLENE, presumably the "A" of A&B, was helping a customer with paint chip choices when Alvarez and Pescoli ID'd themselves to her. She immediately excused herself, leaving the customer with several swatches in shades ranging from apricot to brilliant orange, and escorted the cops to this, a windowless "climate-controlled" room where all six foot five inches of Kip Bell was arranging plastic tubs and paint cans.

Kip, like his brother, took after his father, Frank, a real lowlife whom Pescoli had escorted to jail several times, the last for knocking around his ex-wife, Wilda, and shoving her into a wall. Though they were long divorced and Wilda remarried, they still had contact because of the kids and, like as not, when Frank and Wilda got together, things were going to get ugly. Wilda was large for a woman, tall and strong, and Frank was taller and heavier yet. Kip's hair was a dark blond, a little longer, at least on top, than his brother's, and he had several inches and over fifty pounds on Kywin.

"We just need to ask you some questions," Alvarez said as Arlene retreated.

Kip took a glance at Pescoli's belly. "Shouldn't you be like packin' for the hospital or somethin'?"

Her smile was ice. "Or somethin'. Y'know, Kip, less than a year ago you were charged with dealing. Opioids, I believe. Those are killers, y' know, and I think anyone who sells that crap should be put away for life."

"Hey, I'm working here. This is legit. I'm clean, too. What kind of shakedown is this?"

Alvarez gave her a questioning look, too, but Pescoli knew from experience that she needed to be the alpha dog right from the start if she wanted anything from Kip Bell.

"I need some questions answered," she stated flatly.

"What questions? Uh. Wait. The murdered girl. The friend of Kywin's. That's what this is about."

"You knew her, too."

"Her name, maybe."

Pescoli glanced down at his shoes, scuffed black leather and extremely large, possibly a size or so bigger than his brother's work boots.

"You were seen at parties with her."

His eyes narrowed, then slid to the side. "Someone's lying," he said, and went back to arranging the cans, matching numbers and color dots, lining them up on heavy-duty metal shelves.

Pescoli felt he was the one who was lying. "Some people called your brother her protector."

"Kywin? Like he could 'protect' anything." He stopped what he was doing and, towering over them, asked, "Was there something specific you wanted to ask me? Cuz, if not, I got work to do here. Arlene and Bruce, they don't like me loafin' around, y'know?"

Bruce. The "B" in A&B Painting and Supplies.

"Okay. Let's start with the last time you saw Destiny Montclaire."

"I barely knew her!"

"That's established." Pescoli waited, her expression hard.

He finally exhaled heavily. "I dunno. Maybe . . . maybe that night at the Midway? Lots of kids were there."

"A week ago Friday," she said.

"Yeah . . ." From there, Pescoli asked him the same questions she'd asked Kywin and his answers were nearly identical to his brother's, as if they'd rehearsed their story. He didn't know who would want to hurt Destiny, who had slept with her and could be the father of her unborn child or anything much about her. "She got around," he admitted finally. "Lots of guys, you know . . ."

"Had sex with her."

"Yeah. As I said, I didn't know her. All of the guys in my brother's group did. They're the ones who bragged about bagging her."

"Give me a few names."

"Ask Kywin. He's the one who knew her, and that's his crowd."

"How about him? Did he sleep with her?" Alvarez asked.

"Probably. Hey, I really don't know. Look, I'm only hanging out with all of 'em cuz it's summer. I'm a sophomore at UNLV. This job, here, at A&B, I got it when I was in high school and Arlene lets me fill in during the summer. They're busy, y'know, with the good weather. That's all I know."

"Where were you last weekend? Your brother was up at Reservoir Point," Pescoli said. Bell was a huge man, physically capable of snapping a small woman's neck, and surely able, should he don an ape/Sasquatch suit, of scaring the bejeezus out of anyone who came across him on a shadowy evening or a dark night. Including her daughter.

"Man, you really don't give up. I worked here, late, then hung out with friends."

"Who?"

"I dunno. Let's see. My bro, of course."

"Sure."

"And Tophman and the rest. We ended up at Austin Reece's place. His dad has it all set up. Awesome man cave with a huge TV, bar, pool table. Couches and recliners everywhere and then, outside, off the deck, a kick-ass pool." He gave Pescoli a cold stare. "I didn't leave in the middle of the night and go to Reservoir Point."

"What time did you go home?"

"The next morning. Left around six, came home, showered, then went to work again. Had to be there by seven." He sent them both a belligerent, defiant look this time. "Check with the other guys if you don't believe me."

"We will," Pescoli assured him.

Alvarez added. "And come down to the station. We'll need your DNA."

"Shit, I told you I didn't even know her."

"Then you've got nothing to worry about," Alvarez said.

"You damned cops. Always tryin' to bust my balls."

"Just do it," Pescoli advised and after a few more questions, they left.

"Prince of a guy," Alvarez said on the way out.

"You should meet his father."

Once inside the sweltering car, Alvarez pulled out of the long, squat building's parking lot and rolled down the window. "They're all going to alibi each other for both weekends," she said.

"Let 'em. I still want to talk to Austin Reece in person, at his place."

"He's lawyered up. His father, being an attorney, refused to let him talk to us without legal counsel present."

"Well, let's drop in and find out. I'd love to see this awesome 'man cave.' Gee, if Santana wanted one of those things when we'd been building the house, I think I would have shot him."

Alvarez snorted as the baby gave a sudden, big kick. Pescoli sucked in a breath, then tried to call Bianca, but her daughter didn't pick up. Nor did she respond to a text. Pescoli frowned, but told herself not to borrow trouble. Maybe Bianca was sleeping or taking one of her marathon showers, though she wasn't supposed to get the cast wet.

"Problems?" Alvarez asked.

"Don't know. Probably not." She called the station and told Zoller to let her know when either of the Bell boys came in and offered up DNA samples. Clicking off, she asked, "Who do you think the father of Destiny's baby is?" as she stuffed her phone into a pocket.

"Maybe whoever she met after she left Donny. So far, Donny seems to be the last person to see her. And he admits they fought. Maybe she told him about the baby, and he had no way of knowing that it wasn't his, right? She might not have known. So they get into it. He sees red, strangles and shakes her so hard he snaps her neck and kills her."

Pescoli turned the scenario over in her mind. It was possible. "Or he was in a black rage that she was seeing someone else."

"Or, it was someone else, the real baby daddy. Someone who was jealous or had another bone to pick with her. Something that didn't have anything to do with the fact that she was pregnant." She paused. "Or, it could have been completely random."

It didn't seem that the attack was the result of the girl being in the wrong place at the wrong time. "Doesn't feel that way," Pescoli said, squinting through the windshield. "It feels like it was done by someone she knows."

"Someone strong as . . ."

Big Foot? "Don't say it," Pescoli warned.

". . . an ox."

"I have to think the baby was the reason. We don't have any other motive for someone to kill her."

"No obvious motive," Alvarez agreed as she wheeled into the parking lot of Northern General Hospital. "But then maybe we're being blinded by the obvious. Maybe there's something else. Another reason someone wanted her dead."

Pescoli's cell phone rang, and she answered, even though she didn't recognize the number of the incoming call. "Detective Pescoli."

"Regan?" a frantic woman's voice asked. "This is Darlie Cronin. Remember me?" Without waiting for a reply, she ran on, the words tumbling faster and faster, one after the other. "I'm Lindsay's mother, Lindsay Cronin, a friend of Bianca's, and I work at the preschool and . . . I don't know what to do. She's missing. She was in her room last night when we went to bed, Roy and me, and then, and then, she didn't get up this morning, which sometimes happens. I mean, I didn't even check on her until around eleven or eleven-thirty, I think . . . what?"

She turned away from the phone for a second and had another muffled conversation before she said rapidly, "Roy says it was really almost noon and, and . . . I can't find her. Her car is gone. She's not answering her phone and I'm . . . I don't know what to do." She paused, gathered in a breath, then said a little more slowly. "After calling around, even the hospitals, I went to the station and filled out a missing persons report and the woman officer there was very nice but . . . but I don't think it's enough. I'm . . . we, Roy and I . . . oh, God, what if something's happened to her? To my baby?"

"Let's not jump to conclusions," Pescoli said, remembering the woman as being smart and kind, even-tempered, her only fault being that she was a little over-indulgent with her kids, an older boy and Lindsay. Darlie had always turned a blind eye to her daughter's faults, but then, that wasn't so unusual. "Why don't you start over?"

"Okay, okay."

Alvarez kept driving and Pescoli put the phone on speaker, so they both could hear.

Her voice quivering, Darlie filled in the blanks: Lindsay was missing, had been since last night. Though Lindsay had left in her car, in Darlie's opinion, her daughter had either been abducted or something horrible had happened to her. "The worrisome thing is she didn't take any clothes, and her iPad and makeup and everything is all still here. So if she left of her own accord, she planned to come back, but she's not answering her phone and . . . and the window was open. Someone could have come in, taken her at gun or knifepoint, or . . . oh, my God," she crumbled then, breaking into sobs.

Pescoli asked briskly, "What's your address?"
Darlie rattled it off.

"Okay, stay put," Pescoli said, dread seeping into her heart. "We're on our way."

CHAPTER 19

Barclay Sphinx was waiting at a round table in a meeting room off the lobby of the motel. Three window shades were open to a spectacular view of the parking lot, where shafts of sunlight were bouncing off the single row of cars parked next to the fenced-off swimming pool.

Dressed in a black T-shirt and another jacket and jeans, he wasn't alone. Not only was Michelle seated in one of the chairs but also two men and a woman, Fiona, whom she'd been introduced to at the meeting the night before.

Michelle was beaming, her makeup fresh, her sleeveless white dress hugging her curves, her hair twisted into some kind of braid that reminded Bianca of Elsa in *Frozen*. How long she'd been there, Bianca didn't know, but she was seated right next to Sphinx.

"There they are now," she said as Lucky held the door open for her.

"Bianca!" Sphinx said, getting to his feet and reaching out to grab her hand. His handshake was firm and warm, his smile wide, his little soul patch perfect in his otherwise clean-shaven face. "So glad you could come. Your dad and step-mom tell me that you're in for the pilot of *Big Foot Territory: Montana!* Perfect!" He waved her to a chair next to him, and Lucky sat one over. Fiona Carpenter moved to sit across from Bianca. The other two guys filled a couple of the remaining chairs.

Everyone had a small laptop on the table in front of them. And, again, there was a spread of food—three trays filled with a variety of cold meats and cheeses, breads, and sliced fruit and vegetables, with dips and butter-filled bowls scattered nearby. In the center of the display were two pots of coffee—regular and decaf—and some bottles of water.

"Help yourself," Sphinx said when he caught Bianca eyeing the pineapple spears and straw-berries dipped in chocolate. "Fi, get her a plate, would you? And for the dad—Luke, right?" At Lucky's nod, Sphinx continued, "Get him some-thing, too." Fiona promptly began filling two small paper plates. "I apologize," Sphinx said, and glanced at Michelle. "As I already told Michelle here, I have to leave tonight. I'm working on a new series about ghost towns in Oregon, so I'm swinging down to Darby Gulch and won't be back here for a couple of days. At that time, we'll begin filming, just as I outlined at the meeting last night. I'd want you to star in the first episode for certain, possibly the second depending upon how long I can string out the story line of the murdered girl."

Napkins and a variety of the refreshments were set in front of Lucky and Bianca. "Anything to drink?" Fi asked.

Bianca settled on a water, and Lucky poured himself a cup of coffee. Sphinx barely missed a beat as he continued, "The production crew will arrive tomorrow, legal's working to get everything set up, someone will be a liaison between us and the police department. I was hoping that your ex"—he looked over the tops of his glasses to Luke—"would be that person, but I got a real resistant vibe off her last night."

"I'll talk to her," Luke said, picking up the suggestion. "She'll probably come along."

"Excellent. Her insight and the whole cop angle would be great. And the gritty, tough-as-nails pregnant cop angle would really connect with some of our viewers. Yeah, I like it," he said, rubbing his soul patch as he thought, his eyes narrowing on some inner vision. "I like it a lot."

"The baby is due soon," Bianca pointed out.

"Well, we'll be pushing this fast. As early as the end of this week, or the weekend. The sooner the better." He was thinking out loud and said to Fi, "Take notes."

"Always do," she replied, typing on the laptop in front of her.

"Let's get the whole town involved in this, yes? Some sort of celebration." He fluttered his fingers, caught up in his vision. "Something like Big Foot Daze. How fast could we put that together? We'd need a little run time for publicity, but we could get the town involved, have a celebration."

"That'll take some time," Fiona warned him.

"Maybe, maybe not. We'll talk to the press. There's a local newspaper guy who wants an interview, Manny Something or Other."

"Manny Douglas. Got him on file. Just sent his info to your phone," Fi said.

"We can print our own flyers. Maybe Bianca could do a radio or TV interview or two—?" He glanced at Bianca, who didn't know what to say.

"We could make that work," Lucky said, nodding and grinning.

Michelle, too, was smiling.

"We'll get the mayor involved. You've got her name?" Sphinx asked.

"Right here," Fiona replied, glancing at her computer screen. "Carolina Justison."

"I'll need that number."

"Just sent it to your phone."

"Good. Include the cop's, Bianca's mother, and the sheriff's number as well."

"I did."

"God, love ya, Fi," he said.

"Sure, sure."

"Mom won't like it," Bianca said, earning her a reproving look from Dad.

"I said I'd take care of it," Lucky reminded her a bit tightly.

"Good, good. And even if she's not a believer, which I sense she's not, we can make that work, too. It'll add a little tension to the story line." He glanced at Bianca. "I'm loving this. All we need to get started is a contract." With a nod to Fi, he said, "I'll pass the baton to my assistant and she can get through all the legal stuff. You'll be paid, of course, as will all of the extras, people from the club last night, I'm thinking. Like those two or three guys who were mixing it up at the end of the meeting?"

"Ivor Hicks and Fred Nesmith?" Luke asked.

"Sure. Or guys like them. Local color. We need passionate people, very . . . rural, almost backwoodsy. Authentic. People that would be fascinating to our demographics, so no accountant or insurance salesman types, if you know what I mean. We want to see the raw side of Montana, the real gun-totin' cowboys and hunters and maybe some anti-government folks. Fi will take over, and when we've nailed down the contract, we'll talk story line and character development."

"Character development?" Luke asked.

"I'd like to work out Bianca's character."

She said, "Uh . . . I'm me."

"Of course, of course, but maybe a . . . more

condensed version of you, if you will, a stronger, more potent version." He turned his gaze from Bianca to his assistant. "Fi why don't you . . . ?"

Fiona smoothly segued into the point woman, directing them all to look at their computer screens. She laid out everything. All explained neatly and concisely.

And in the end, Bianca and Lucky signed.

She was, Michelle insisted, on her way to being a star.

Bianca wasn't sure about that, but she did know that, when she got home and admitted to her mother what she'd done, there would be hell to pay.

The Cronins hadn't seen or heard from their daughter since the night before.

"Normally, I wouldn't worry," Darlie said as she sat on the edge of a worn couch next to her husband. Pescoli and Alvarez were in chairs on the far side of an oval coffee table. "But this is so not like Lindsay." Darlie folded her hands over her lap, then refolded them nervously. Petite and blond, she wore a skirt and lacy top and kept glancing at her husband, a round man with a paunch, thinning brown hair, and a clipped mustache. Today he hadn't shaved, and silvery stubble covered his jaw and chin. He was in jeans and a T-shirt and he stared, for the most part, at the floor.

She handed Pescoli a neatly typed list of Lindsay's friends. She swore she knew of no one who would want to hurt her daughter. At that statement, she reached silently to her side, and her husband's large hand clasped over her outstretched palm.

"I keep telling myself she'll come home, that her phone is out of battery or turned off or lost or whatever, but . . ." She swallowed hard, the cords of her neck straining as she thought of the direst of consequences. Clearing her throat, she said, "We just want her back. We've called her brother. He's studying at Boise State, and Malcolm offered to come home, but we didn't see any reason for that; not unless he hears from her."

After taking her statement, they all walked through her room, saw the open window and the pillows bumping up under the covers.

"This is how you found the bed?" Pescoli asked.

Darlie nodded. "I know. It looks like she left of her own accord."

Hell yeah, it did. Pescoli remembered pulling this same trick herself and then, as a mother of teens, finding a similar bed with a fake body composed of pillows when Jeremy had sneaked out to meet his girlfriend, Heidi Brewster, when they'd both been in high school. "I'd say so," Pescoli said. She checked the window, found it unlatched, slightly open, as if whoever might have sneaked out of this room had used it for escape and left it open just enough in case she had to hoist herself back in the same way.

"No footprints in the flowerbed," Darlie said from the doorway of the small room with its circular rag rug, hand-me-down desk, and twin bed covered in a striped duvet. "I checked."

"Maybe this was the backup plan, to return if she got locked out or didn't want to make too much noise coming back in."

"That's the point," Darlie said, her voice cracking. "She never came back." Roy, standing next to her, placed a big arm over her shaking shoulders.

"Even if she did sneak out, she thought she was coming back."

Roy whispered, "Shh . . . it's okay, honey,"

She threw off his arm. "It's not okay, Roy. You know it's not okay!" Dabbing at her eyes where mascara was starting to run, she said to Pescoli, "Just find her, okay. Find my baby!"

Alvarez and Pescoli returned to the car. For whatever reason, Lindsay Cronin had waited until her parents were in bed, then sneaked out. They'd been right; there were no footprints in the mulch of the flower bed, no indication that anyone had climbed in or out of the window. Pescoli called the station and gave Zoller Lindsay's phone number so that records could be requested, as well as a description and the license plate of her Ford Focus for a BOLO—be on the lookout.

"I hope they're wrong about her," Pescoli said.

"Maybe she has a wild streak her parents don't know about and she's sleeping it off somewhere, not realizing her phone is turned off."

"Or without battery," Alvarez said. "What teenager has their phone off?"

Pescoli grunted and the baby kicked again. "We have to stop for lunch before we do anything else. I'm starved."

A few minutes later, they pulled into Wild Wills, a restaurant in the lower section of town on the river, one of Pescoli's favorite haunts.

Inside the front door, they passed by "Grizz," a huge stuffed Grizzly Bear that always wore a perpetual bared-tooth snarl and glass eyes and was outfitted by the staff for the season or holiday. Today he was wearing a pink polka-dot bikini with a matching floppy beach hat.

Pescoli noted the parasol tucked under one of his forelegs and a martini glass with a fake fruity drink tied to one of the huge, furry creature's paws. Someone had even painted his claws a flamingo pink, and to keep with the theme, a pair of plastic flamingos stood next to him, one sporting a bow tie, the other a choker necklace.

"I have this eerie feeling that all the bears in the county are plotting their revenge for this kind of humiliation, that they'll pull a *Planet of the Apes* on us and take over. Put us in cages, make us do all their dirty work and do lab tests on us."

"That's only if the rats join them."

Which made Pescoli think again about the creature that had been chasing Bianca.

What had Farnsby said when she'd asked if the "monster" could have been a bear? *"You see any claws?"*

Even painted dark pink, Grizz's claws looked deadly. Long, curved, sharp, and, today, tinted raspberry.

So what had chased her daughter?

Not a Sasquatch. No matter what members of the BFBs thought.

They moved into the spacious dining room with booths lining the walls and tables placed over the old plank floors. Overhead, wagon-wheel chandeliers had been suspended from a twenty-foot ceiling. On the walls, stuffed heads of animals, long dead, had been mounted, so that it appeared a variety of the creatures native to the area were staring down at the patrons as they dined. Bison, moose, bighorn sheep, deer, and elk, were present, along with a full-sized cougar, porcupines, and a beaver. On one wall, over the slowly spinning pie display, geese, pheasants, and ducks flew toward the exposed beams of the ceiling.

Alvarez cast her gaze at the once-living creatures that had become wall decorations. Above them, the huge head of a bison loomed, glassy eyes staring sightlessly. "They do more to squelch your appetite rather than enhance it."

"Sandy says the customers love 'em. Especially the tourists."

"Hmmm."

Alvarez ordered an Asian chicken salad with iced herbal tea, and Pescoli chose a turkey pot pie with a side of fries and sparkling water. The place was crowded, most tables occupied, the waiters moving quickly from one four-top to the next. Alvarez and Pescoli discussed the case, and by the time the food came, Pescoli thought she might faint. She dug in eagerly, making short work of everything on her plate, including the slice of orange that was supposed to be the garnish. Then, while Alvarez was still picking at her salad, Pescoli ordered a piece of peach crumble with ice cream. "You only live once," she said to Alvarez when the dessert came, piled with vanilla ice cream, a dab of whipped cream, and a drizzle of peach syrup.

"You're eating for two."

"What I'd really like is a Diet Coke, cigarette, and a beer . . . not in any order. Oh, yeah, and a corned beef sandwich, but I've got to wait until the baby's born."

"Maybe you could throw in some sushi, too."

Pescoli took a bite of ice cream and shook her head. "No raw fish for this girl, pregnant or not."

"Don't know what you're missing."

"Don't know and really don't care."

As she finished her dessert, they discussed the

case and the new wrinkle of Lindsay Cronin's disappearance. Disturbing, yes. But connected? Hard to say.

Alvarez's phone made a little bubbling noise. She looked at it, got a quick message, and nodded. To Pescoli, she said, "They got the records for Destiny's phone. Zoller's already going over the texts and calls, comparing them to her social media accounts, and the statements from everyone who knew her."

"Maybe we'll get something."

"Let's hope."

By the time Pescoli scraped off every last bite, she felt satisfied, her blood sugar restored to order, the baby no longer kicking. They paid the bill and drove directly to Northwest General, the hospital where Destiny Montclaire and Simone Delaney volunteered, the very hospital in which, months earlier, Dan Grayson had died. Neither Alvarez or Pescoli said anything about it, but it was as if his ghost were there between them.

Grimmer than they had been, each lost in her own thoughts, they didn't speak as they made their way to the cafeteria where Destiny had once worked part-time as an unpaid volunteer. No one within the kitchen staff had a bad thing to say about her. She was friendly and efficient, punctual and responsible, if at times quiet. Never did her supervisor worry that she would be late or not show up. She'd helped the cooks at the busiest times of the day, was always available to clean tables.

From the cafeteria, Alvarez and Pescoli made their way to the children's ward. Destiny had transferred to the children's wing about six months earlier. Here, they were told, she read stories or played with the kids or, once again, helped clean up.

No one in either food services or the children's ward had any idea who would want to harm her. Everyone was upset that she'd been killed and completely at a loss as to who would do anything so vile. To a person, they claimed no one had seen her since her last shift, which had happened two days before she went missing. Also, no one had known she was pregnant.

Alvarez and Pescoli ended up with a big fat zero in the information department until they were on their way out, when Pescoli checked with the personnel director and learned Simone was currently working.

Perfect.

Here was the chance to speak with Simone without Mary-Beth hovering over her and offering up answers rather than letting her daughter talk. They found Simone in the soiled-linen room, where she was dutifully pushing a full cart of dirty bed linens to an area near closed oversized garage doors, big enough for a truck to pull through. After the bin was in position, she rolled an empty bin under one of the huge chutes that opened from the ceiling.

She was dressed in scrubs, her hair tied into pigtails, her makeup toned down from the previous Saturday night, an ID card with her picture on a lanyard swinging from her neck. She saw the cops and sighed. "My mom said not to answer any questions."

Pescoli was impressed, in spite of herself, a the hard work Simone was doing. "Let me guess, she wants you to have a lawyer present."

She lifted a shoulder. "Yeah, but I don't really care what she says."

"We could wait until you go home and talk to you with your mom or dad or a lawyer, if that's what you want."

"Just ask me what you want to ask me."

"You and Destiny Montclaire were both volunteers here at the hospital," Alvarez said. "Were you friends, too?"

"We got along, but . . ." Simone shrugged, then rolled her eyes when, in a whoosh, a wad of bedding fell from one of the three chutes and landed in an empty bin. "Fun, huh?" she said, eyeing the soiled sheets. "My mom forced me to work here, well, volunteer. I don't get paid," she admitted. "Says it'll look good on my college applications."

"Did you hang out with Destiny?"

"Nah. We didn't even have shifts that overlapped. I'd see her around sometimes and once . . . no, twice, we ate together. That's when she was working with the kids, maybe a couple of months ago. Before that, when she worked in the cafeteria, it was crazy busy for her. We never even talked."

"Did you know she was pregnant?" Alvarez asked.

A shake of her head, pigtails swinging. "I don't think she told anybody, did she?" When they didn't respond, she added, "Anyway, I never heard about it until after she died. Like I said, we weren't close."

"Who was close to her?" Again, Alvarez.

"You mean besides Donny? I don't know. I think Kywin Bell had a thing for her and maybe"—she squished up her nose as if she were really thinking hard—"Emmett Tufts? Or Alex O'Hara? But maybe not. Sometimes those guys would look at her the way guys do when they think a girl is hot, but then they're all so horny they look at everyone that way. Come on. My shift's over. I have to lock up." She headed for the door and they followed after her. Once they'd passed into the hall, she locked the room behind them.

"What about girlfriends?" Pescoli questioned as they walked toward the elevator. "Who was her bestie?"

"I don't even know if she had one. I saw her

with Lara a couple of times. And . . . oh, maybe Maddie, because, you know, if the guys were looking at Destiny, then Maddie wanted to make sure they saw her, too."

"What about Lindsay Cronin?"

"I guess." She frowned. "I heard she was missing. Her mom called earlier."

"Have you seen her?"

"Not since the other night. At the Big Foot thing."

"What about texting or talking to her?"

"Same as everyone else, I guess. She's on group texts, but no, not since that meeting. We like hung out, yeah, but more in school, y'know. In summer we all kinda do our own thing unless there's a party or we hang out at the river or whatever."

She rang for the elevator and the doors opened. They all entered, and Simone said, "God, I hate this job." As the doors whispered shut and they started upward, Simone folded her arms across her chest and slumped against a polished wall. "You think it's really gonna help me get into Harvard or Yale or Stanford or UCLA? Stacking sheets and counting cotton balls? I don't think the people who are recruiting for college really give a rat's ass about how neatly I can organize pillowcases." The elevator car arrived with ding. An orderly pushing an elderly woman in a wheelchair waited until they stepped outside, then rolled his charge inside.

As they headed toward reception, afternoon light was streaming in from wide windows near the front entrance. Simone yanked the lanyard over her head, stuffed it into a pocket of her scrubs and withdrew a set of keys, then said, "Look I really gotta go. I don't know anything else."

"If you think of something, call us."

"Sure." She didn't say it with conviction, but she did add, "I think my mom just wants me to be busy this summer, that's what I think. So that I stay out of trouble." She headed for the exterior doors.

Alvarez checked her messages as she and Pescoli followed Simone outside. At the Subaru, she was still scrolling through them. "Guess what?" she finally said, looking up.

"I couldn't begin to," Pescoli muttered as she levered herself into the passenger seat.

"Zoller texted me. The night Destiny Montclaire disappeared, she called and texted Donny Justison. But he wasn't the only one. In separate texts, she also contacted Kywin Bell and Lindsay Cronin."

CHAPTER 20

They caught up with Kywin Bell just hopping out of a battered Dodge truck in the driveway of his father's house. The truck had been jacked up, the wheels oversized, the tailgate missing.

He saw the two cops approach. A scowl curved across his unshaven jaw. "I talked to you already," he said, retrieving a beat-up lunch pail from the truck's interior, then slamming the door shut.

"We just have a few more questions," Alvarez said.

"Well, I'm all outta answers. You already nearly cost me my job, so I'm done." He started for the house, a single-story post-war bungalow that was in need of more than just paint. The porch sagged, the shingles of the roof were curling and cracked, the gutters rusting.

"You're not quite done," said Pescoli.

Swatting at a bee, he spun around just before reaching the listing porch, lips compressed, nostrils flaring. "What is it with you cops, huh? Never satisfied. Always nagging. Just cuz my old man did time doesn't mean I had anything to do with . . . with *anything!*"

A scrawny gray cat that had been sunning itself on the porch got up quickly and slunk behind a couple of metal chairs. With a quick look over its shoulder and a swish of its tail, the feline slid off the porch to hide in a clump of dry weeds. Kywin reached for the dilapidated screen door as Alvarez said, "Destiny texted you on the last night she was seen alive."

"What?" He dropped his hands and stared at them in shock. Shaking his head, he reached into his jean pocket for a crumpled pack of cigarettes.

"I never got no text." He found a lighter, lit up, then blew smoke out of the side of his mouth in a fast stream.

"We have records from the cell company," Alvarez told him. "The text is there."

"They're wrong. I didn't get a text from her."

He was so sure of himself, Pescoli started to wonder a bit as he left his cigarette clamped in the corner of his mouth and dug in another pocket, located his cell phone and checked the screen, pressing buttons deftly before finding what he was looking for. "There," he said, holding the phone, face out, to the cops.

Shading the screen with one hand, Pescoli studied the phone. A tiny head shot of Destiny appeared beside a thread of texts, which included another picture, a selfie of her in a pink bikini at a swimming hole by the river. Her head was cocked to one side, her eyes dancing mischievously, her grin a little seductive. The attached message read: Swimming @Cougar Springs. Join me after work? She'd ended it with an emoticon of a smiley face wearing sunglasses. There were no more texts.

Pescoli pointed out, "You could have deleted any message you got from her."

"I didn't! For shit's sake, I told you, that's the last message I got from her."

Alvarez scrolled up. "She texted you just about every day, sometimes more than once."

"Yeah." He took a long drag from his cig. "Your point is . . . ?"

"So, didn't you think it was strange that she just stopped?"

"She's a chick. Y'know. They're all weird. Sometimes all in your grill, then they get pissed or into something or someone else and they, like, disappear." He reached for his phone. "Give it back. Some of that stuff is private." Then, not waiting, snatched it out of Alvarez's fingers. "Should never have let you see it."

"It proves nothing, Kywin," Pescoli said.

"I'm tellin' ya: I didn't get any text that night. I didn't delete any texts. I didn't hear from her after she sent me the last one you just seen." He held up the phone, shaking it.

"You didn't respond."

"No. I was busy. I was at work when she texted, then with the guys later that night. I already told you this." He took a final puff on his cigarette, then jabbed it into a cracked ceramic pot filled with sand and soil, where other dead butts had collected. "I gotta go."

Pescoli asked, "Have you talked to Lindsay Cronin?"

"What?" His eyebrows slammed together.

"Lindsay," she repeated. "Have you seen her?"

"I saw her at the party up at the point. When *Bianca* found Destiny. You know we were all there."

Alvarez asked, "You heard she's missing?"

"Simone said something about it." Rubbing the back of his neck, he said, "I don't know anything about her being gone." A pause, then his expression changed to incredulity. "Jesus, don't tell me you think I had something to do with that, too."

Pescoli said, "We don't know what happened to her, yet, but she got a message from Destiny, too. Sent about thirty seconds after she sent one to you."

Gone was the dismissive attitude. "Did Lindsay get hers?"

"We don't know," Alvarez said.

"Well, I didn't. I've told you over and over. I don't know anything about what happened to Des."

Pescoli pushed him. "What about Lindsay?"

"Are you deaf? Or just stupid? I had nothing to do with whatever happened to either one of them. I don't even like Lindsay. For Christ's sake, I'm done talkin' with you. *Done.* So get off my property and don't come back without a warrant!"

He grabbed the handle of the rusted screen door, yanked it hard enough that Pescoli thought it might come off its hinges, then stomped inside, the door banging behind him.

They were about to leave when a Chevy Suburban rolled into the driveway to park behind Kywin's truck.

Uh-oh. Pescoli braced herself as Franklin Bell,

nearly three hundred pounds of him, cut the engine and stepped into the yard. A trucker's cap shaded eyes already covered by mirrored aviator glasses, his jeans were dusty, his black T-shirt gray with Sheetrock dust. Franklin was a surly man who drank too much, and when he did, more often than not, he let his fists do his talking, and they never said anything good. His ex-wife, Wilda, could tell that story.

"What the hell are you doin' here?" he said, his lips curling into a snarl.

"Franklin," Pescoli greeted him flatly. "We needed to talk to your son about the disappearance of Lindsay Cronin."

"I thought her name was Destiny. And they found her." One sausage-like finger poked in Pescoli's direction. "Your kid found her."

"That's right. Destiny Montclaire was the victim of homicide and now Lindsay Cronin's gone missing."

"Damn." His lips folded in on themselves. "You think one of my boys had somethin' to do with it? That why you're here?" His gaze sliced from Kywin's truck to the house. "Just because I've had my trouble with you all don't mean my kids are . . ." He stared down at Pescoli. "Don't put this on my boys. You can pick on me all you want, but you leave Kywin and Kip alone."

A kick of adrenaline charged through Pescoli's blood. Franklin Bell was violent and unpredictable, but she said calmly, "Kywin got a text from the girl who was killed, Destiny Montclaire, on the night she died, then he lied about it. Still is lying. And now another girl he knows is missing."

"We're following up," Alvarez said.

"Lots of kids knew them girls." A muscle in his heavy jaw bulged, and within the tangle of his beard his mouth became a firm, hard line. "Don't you make this a witch hunt, y'hear? Don't you go blamin' Kywin for somethin' he didn't do. Now, get the hell off my property."

He stomped into the house much like Kywin had minutes before, slamming the door behind him. Pescoli and Alvarez headed to the Subaru.

"Kywin Bell is lying," Alvarez said.

"He and everyone else associated with this case." Pescoli glared at the little house where Franklin and his two sons lived. "Teenagers: they all lie. And Kywin knows he's in trouble. We've got proof."

"All we've got is that she texted him and he lied about getting the text. Nothing more."

"Yet," she said as Alvarez started the engine and they rolled away from the house, "it's just the tip of the iceberg. Those kids know more than they're telling, or at least some of them do. We just have to dig deeper."

By the time Pescoli got home, it was after nine. The dogs greeted her and she found Santana, freshly showered, long-neck bottle of beer in hand, stretched out on the couch in the family room. He was watching TV—some old Clint Eastwood movie that she should know the name of, but couldn't remember. God, the beer looked inviting.

He clicked off the television and met her in the kitchen, where she was opening the refrigerator and staring glumly at the interior. "I could make you a double margarita," he said and kissed her above her ear. She slid him a glance. He clarified, "A virgin."

"Always so thoughtful."

His grin was sexy. "I try."

"Try harder." Snagging a bottle of Perrier from the top shelf, she let the door close. "Bianca home? Or is she out being a movie star?"

"Make that 'reality TV star.' It's a few steps down from being an A-lister on the red carpet, I think." He took a swallow from his bottle. "But she's up in her room. Jeremy is out."

"With who?"

"He doesn't tell me and I don't ask. He's old enough to come and go as he pleases."

"Fine stepfather you turned out to be." She kicked off her shoes and ignored the fact that her feet were swollen. Yeah, being pregnant was just a barrel of laughs. "And don't tell me you try, okay?" She was joking, but it fell flat.

"You okay?" He was serious now, eyes assessing her.

"When am I ever 'okay'?"

"Point taken."

Leaning against the counter near the sink, she opened her bottle and took a drink. "Another girl's missing." She then went on to tell him about her day and the interview with Kywin Bell. She closed her eyes, rotating her neck, hoping to release the tension she'd felt ever since learning Lindsay Cronin was missing. "I can't help but think her disappearance is linked to Destiny Montclaire's. God, I hope we find her alive."

"But you're not betting on it."

"No. Her phone's gone dark. Turned off. Can't be GPS tracked because it's off. No one can reach her, and we haven't found her car. No one's seen her. We double-checked with friends, family, and the local hospitals, which the parents had already done . . . and . . . nothing. We've caught a couple of kids lying. . . . They know something but are hell-bent on keeping it on the down low. Oh, hell. I think I'd better go talk to Bianca."

"You think she knows something?"

"No, but the truth is, I don't know."

She headed up the stairs and found Bianca, leg propped on a pillow, watching reruns of *Big Foot Territory: Oregon!* on her iPad while simultaneously texting her friends. A frozen bag of peas lay atop her ankle.

"You heard about Lindsay?" her mother asked.

Bianca moved higher on the pillows as her

mother sat on the edge of the bed. "Everyone's talking about it. My phone's blowing up."

"Anyone know anything?"

"No." Bianca paused the action on the screen of her device, where two men with long hair and rifles were stealthily walking through a mountain wilderness. "Everyone's asking about her, but no one has any information. They're all saying that her parents think she snuck out, took her car, and didn't come back."

Pescoli nodded. "That's about the gist of it. Any ideas? Would she go off to meet a boyfriend?"

Bianca lifted her shoulders. "She really didn't have a boyfriend, was, you know, just part of the group."

"She didn't date?"

"She hooked up with Austin a couple of times, I think, but that was a while back. It never became anything. I think she likes him because he's rich and his dad helped him get into some big Ivy League college." She glanced back at the screen to the frozen image. "She really wants to go away to a four-year school, like her brother did. But he got some kind of athletic scholarship and her folks told her they really can't afford for both of them to go away to school or something. They want her to live at home for a while until Malcolm graduates, and she thinks that's crap."

"But she gets along with her folks."

"Yeah, oh, yeah, I think so."

Two more texts had chimed in during their conversation and Bianca glanced at her phone.

"If you hear anything, let me know, okay?"

Bianca nodded, glanced at the phone. She chewed on her lip and looked tense.

"You okay?" Pescoli asked, sensing more.

"Sure." No enthusiasm.

She prodded. "So how's the ankle?"

"It still hurts."

Pescoli started to get up but paused. "Are you sure about this—?" She motioned to the tablet and the frozen footage of the television show.

"Yeah, Mom, I'm sure," Bianca snapped, suddenly defensive. "I know you don't like it, think it's a 'crock' and a 'fake' and whatever else, but I think it's interesting and fun and might be, like Michelle says, a start of my acting career." She jutted out her chin, her eyes focused on her mother's face, almost daring her to engage in a fight.

"I think it's a mistake."

"I *know.*"

Pescoli wanted to go off the rails on the show, Barclay Sphinx, the whole preposterousness of the situation. She was tired of pretending she understood. "There is no Big Foot."

"Doesn't matter, does it?" Bianca countered as she hit the button on her iPad to start the program going again. "Because there is going to be a TV show about it."

"And that's what matters?"

"Exactly."

There was no use arguing. Her daughter was as stubborn as she was, and when Bianca set her mind, there was no changing it. So arguments about integrity or what was "real" in reality TV were going to fall on deaf ears. "Just let me know if you hear anything about Destiny or Lindsay, okay?"

But Bianca had already tuned in to the apparently fascinating story line of *Big Foot Territory: Oregon!*

So what was next, Pescoli wondered with an inward sigh, after Sphinx's new series on Sasquatch? Something like *The Real Housewives of Grizzly Falls*?

She made a strangled sound and padded downstairs to the den and Santana.

Alone in her room, her ankle throbbing, Bianca was bummed.

Nothing seemed to be going right.

Destiny's murder was always right there. Everyone was still talking about it, and there was even a vigil scheduled for later tonight.

Bianca wondered what had happened to her. Why had she been killed and left or dumped in the stream? It was unnerving. She glanced out the window to the fading sunlight. She couldn't help but think she might know the killer. Wasn't that what Mom thought, kept hinting at?

Worse yet, now Lindsay had disappeared. Had she really been kidnapped as some people thought? Or had she just taken off, tired of her parents butting into her life?

Why hadn't she contacted anybody?

She'd gone completely dark, not responding to calls, texts, instant messages, or anything to do with social media. All of which was *not* like Lindsay. Bianca bit her lip and studied the bedspread, not seeing the pattern for the turmoil in her mind. Could Lindsay's disappearance be a publicity stunt? Maybe she'd dropped out of sight to shine the light on herself a little more, as she hadn't been part of the core group picked for the filming of the reality show. She'd been disappointed, and there was a chance she might do something overtly dramatic to make Barclay Sphinx notice her. Was that it?

Stupidly, she'd posed these very questions to Lara, Maddie, and Simone, and they'd jumped all over the idea, sure that Lindsay would turn up and all of the attention from the media and Barclay Sphinx and his production company would shine on her.

Simone had texted, I wouldn't put it past her.

Maddie's response was, Maybe. She was pissed that she wasn't picked for filming tho this is extreme.

Lara's reply said it all: I think Lindsay would

do just about anything to get away from this town and her parents.

But would she really? Lindsay was kind of a pain, but disappearing for the sake of publicity, ripping out her parents' hearts, causing all her friends and family to freak out?

Bianca tried to push her thoughts on Destiny and Lindsay aside. She had more than enough to worry about as it was. Somehow, with this damned ankle, she had to get through the vigil, and then psych herself up for the filming of the pilot later in the night.

She'd learned that the script had changed quite a bit from Barclay Sphinx's original concept. The party of kids at Reservoir Point was no longer a large group but had been winnowed down to eight, four boys and four girls who'd come to the woods to drink, do a little weed, hang out around a campfire, and make out. That part wasn't that great, Bianca thought, hastily slapped together, but the kids involved, who had all been to the original party, were stoked to be a part of the project. Lara Haas, Maddie, and Simone were all beside themselves to have been chosen. They'd been paired with Austin, Emmett, Kywin, and TJ and had a few lame lines between them— the kind of things adults imagined kids would say to each other. "Man, this is bad-ass weed," or "Wanna go to the car so we can be alone?" That kind of dialogue. A few people the producer thought were essential would be in the peripheral area away from a campfire. They would only be shown smoking or drinking in a shot that panned the "crowd." The script also called for several members of the Big Foot Believers to be in the woods as well. They were supposedly hunting for a Sasquatch and had frightened one of the beasts, which, in turn, then chased Bianca. Or something like that. Barclay insisted the scenes were going to be "fluid" and "works in progress."

The changing of the party scene was okay, Bianca thought, as she glanced at her laptop, but there was another major alteration as well. The story line in this episode wouldn't swirl around Bianca as she'd originally been told. Her experience with Big Foot was just the starting point, an "energetic" and "exciting" way to begin the season —a teaser. Also, the central plot of the episode wouldn't concentrate on the murder—the finding of the body was just another dramatic point that was intended to grab the viewers' interest.

Nor was the focus of the series about Bianca, or what had happened to Destiny Rose Montclaire. No, the "integrity" of the plot surrounded two feuding families of Big Foot enthusiasts whom Barclay Sphinx had handpicked. That bit of information had caused a bit of a grumble with Carlton Jeffe and the local Big Foot Believers because, as it turned out, the actors chosen to be the series regulars resided somewhere north of

Missoula, and it also happened that they—two couples with children—had originally pitched the idea of *Big Foot Territory: Montana!* to Sphinx months ago when his *Big Foot Territory: Oregon!* had first aired and showed signs of promise. So, essentially, not only were the feuding couples the brains behind the show, but the stars as well.

One of the series originators was actually a writer who had come up with several episodes. However, none of the ideas for the series had been as attention grabbing as Bianca's story of being chased by a Big Foot and her subsequent discovery of the dead body of a classmate, so that was their big hook.

And they were rushing everything into production, Barclay had explained, to capture the public's interest in the murder of Destiny Rose Montclaire. Which, according to her mother, was just using the tragedy for his own gain.

The upshot was the whole preproduction had been squeezed. Taking the pitched ideas and scripts, reworking them to fit with Bianca's experience, and filming as quickly as could be done.

So, as it turned out, Bianca saw, the only reason the show was going to be filmed around Grizzly Falls was because of the murder, the actual real life-and-death tie to the area. And there was something just not right about that—something slimy and almost predatory about it.

Though her dad and Michelle had assured her the trailer at the end of the episode and the reward would help Destiny's family, the whole idea left a bad taste in her mouth.

Michelle was disappointed that her role might not be continued beyond episode one, and possibly two, but she still saw opportunity. After all, Sphinx had practically promised them that their "backstory" would still be woven into the main plot of the feuding Big Foot families. She seemed to think there was a strong chance that she and Bianca would be on camera again. Not so the other kids and extras. The jury was still out on Carlton Jeffe, Lex Farnsby, and Fred Nesmith of the Big Foot Believers. They would all appear in episode one, but that might be the end of their involvement, which was a case for more grumbling.

A chime indicated another text had come in.

She lifted the phone, stared at the screen, then sucked in a sharp breath.

The message was from Lindsay Cronin and said simply:

I'm not coming back.

CHAPTER 21

"We got the same text," the Cronins reported when Pescoli stopped by their house on the way to the vigil for Destiny Rose Montclaire. Darlie was sniffling against her husband again as they stood in the open doorway, Pescoli in the shade of the porch's overhang. When Bianca had received the text from Lindsay, Pescoli had reacted quickly, calling the department and filling in Zoller as well as Alvarez. Now, she was facing Lindsay's parents.

Darlie appeared to shiver despite the heat, and a cardigan sweater had been tossed over her shirt. Roy, though round, had seemed to shrink a bit, as if his plaid shirt were suddenly too big. They looked as if they'd aged a decade in a few days. Their worry was extreme, their fear palpable.

Pescoli felt for them. "I understand there was a group text, but I was hoping there was more."

"No," Roy said, frowning.

"I called back immediately," his wife said. "To Lindsay. The text came and I speed-dialed Lindsay. No answer. Then I texted and called and texted and called, leaving message after message, begging her to respond, but she didn't." Her eyes were flat, her cheeks red from weeping. "Why would she do this to us?"

"She wouldn't, hon," her husband assured her. "Not our Lindsay." His jaw tightened and he squeezed his wife close.

Pescoli nodded. They were living a parent's worst nightmare.

A dry breeze scuttled leaves and bark dust across the porch and plucked at Pescoli's hair. Clearing her throat, Darlie reached into the pocket of her sweater, pulled out a Kleenex, and dabbed at the corner of her eyes. "We called Malcolm. He's on his way back here from Boise now, should be here any minute. We hoped he'd heard something more, but he didn't."

"Got the same text as the rest of us." Roy scowled darkly. "It's like it went out to every damned person on her contact list on her phone. You know what I think, Detective?"

"What?"

"I think that whoever took her sent out that group text so everybody would back off. He knows we're lookin' for her, that we won't stop 'til we find her and he's panickin'. Tryin' to throw us off. Tryin' to make us think she's fine, maybe angry . . . alive and fine."

Pescoli nodded; she'd had the same idea. "It's an angle we're exploring."

"I don't give a rat's ass about angles and exploring or anything else. I just want my girl back." He was angry, his lips pursed, but his chin wobbled a little, giving away his fear. His wife tried to say something, but the effort was too great and she ended up just sighing and squeezing out more tears.

"It's what we want, too, Roy," Pescoli said. "And we're putting all of our resources into finding her."

"You'd better, by golly."

With that, she left feeling worse than she had before. She'd hoped Lindsay's parents would have heard more from her, but like Roy, she was very suspicious that the text had come from Lindsay's abductor . . . or her killer. . . .

Nope. She wouldn't think that way. Not yet. But as she climbed behind the wheel of her Jeep, adjusting the seat back a little farther to accommodate her ever-widening girth, she couldn't help but imagine Lindsay Cronin's face superimposed on the corpse of Destiny Rose Montclaire.

Would they find Lindsay, strangled, her body submerged in one of the dozens of mountain streams near Grizzly Falls?

"Damn it all to hell," she muttered, starting the car and easing into traffic. After receiving the text, Bianca had checked with all of her friends and sure enough, they'd received copies of the message: I'm not coming back, but nothing more. Like Lindsay's parents, several had tried to reach out to the girl, by texting or calling or using social media, but there had been no response, at least none that Pescoli knew of.

So why send the text?

To make people believe Lindsay was alive and letting everyone know she was leaving for good? That didn't make any sense. But then, nothing did.

On her way to the vigil, she called Alvarez at the station. So far, Lindsay's car hadn't been located, nor had she used her debit card on her bank account, and the only activity on her phone was the one very recent text.

She drummed her fingers on the steering wheel. This case disturbed her at an emotional level, the kids involved being in Bianca's circle of friends. Was that it? Were they being targeted because they knew something?

Frowning, she drove to a stop sign and waited for a thirty-something woman pushing a stroller. Backed by the lowering sun, her profile in silhouette, the mother was distracted, phone in the hand as she pushed the stroller, her concentration on the screen.

Pescoli squinted, was reminded of her own kids as little ones, thought about the baby about to be born and the coming years, first smiles, giggles, tentative steps, running and swimming, heading off to preschool before she knew it. Just like Jeremy and Bianca . . .

The baby kicked and she was reminded that the birth was imminent, happening soon. In the next week she'd be going on maternity leave. But could she? While these cases weren't solved?

"You'll have to wait," she told her unborn child as she drove toward the church. She was rewarded with more little kicks.

Another tough little kid, she thought, as willful as her first two. She'd silently blamed Jeremy and Bianca's fathers for all their stubborn, headstrong traits, but now, if baby number three proved as mulish as her other two, she might have to take another hard look at herself.

For some reason, everyone seemed to think that Bianca would know what had happened to Lindsay. Just because her mom was a cop and investigating the case didn't mean she was privy to any new information, yet her friends had all seemed to elevate her to the position of Information Central, even though she knew nothing.

"Come on," Maddie had wheedled in a phone call while Bianca was sorting through her closet, wondering what was appropriate to wear to a vigil. "You must know something. Your mom's all over this."

"Even if she did know something, she wouldn't tell me." Maddie had argued some more, but Bianca had finally hung up and, after a fruitless search for something perfect, closed the closet door, figuring jeans, a black top, and zero jewelry would be good enough.

Then Lara had texted: Where the hell is she? You think maybe this is one of her high drama stunts to gain attention? It would be just like her! Tell your mom not to be fooled!

While she was zipping up a pair of boots, Rod Devlin private messaged her: I'm worried about Linds. What if something happened to her? What's your mom say?

And on and on. Making her more nervous than she was before, and that was pretty nervous. She still had the uncanny sensation that she was being watched. Wherever she went, she had this *feeling* that someone was observing her and waiting. For what? She couldn't guess. Nor did she know who it was or even if he existed. Maybe she was making it all up, her mind going a little crazy after finding Destiny's body. She probably should see a shrink.

Or maybe everyone else should just leave her alone. All of her acquaintances, from Austin Reece to Bryant Tophman and Simone Delaney, were all over her. Bianca was beginning to think the whole group was a bunch of morons. Even Seneca Martinez, who had been her friend since before they'd started school, left her a text: I'm really worried about Linds. In fact, I'm weirded out by everything that's going on. Your mom will catch whoever did this, tho'. Right? And soon?

Bianca sure as hell hoped so. She touched up her lip gloss, decided her messy bun was good enough, and headed downstairs in her ungainly brace. She didn't like the pressure and she hated the dreams that haunted her sleep. Nagging nightmares where the players changed. Sometimes she was with kids from school, other times she was in a group of the Big Foot Believers, and once she was even at the old preschool, Good Feelings. But the kids weren't toddlers any longer. They were teenagers who smoked and drank and swore and had sex while the preschool teacher, Miss Love, freaked out and tried to put them all in time-outs, where they continued their bad behavior.

She'd woken up from that one with a headache. The dream had receded, but it had left her with a vivid image of making out with Austin Reece, which totally grossed her out. In the dream, she'd really been into the make-out session, turned on to the point of considering sex with him.

As if that would ever happen.

Ugh!

If *that* was what was in her subconscious, her brain was a very scary place.

Hoping to have a one-on-one with Austin Reece, Alvarez drove to his parents' home, a huge, sprawling stone house in a gated community that bordered the one private country club in Grizzly Falls. She'd gotten through the gate by showing her ID to a guard, who called and warned whoever was at the Reece home that she was coming.

She'd met Austin's father in the ornate, two-story foyer. Stiff backed, thick hair prematurely gray, wearing rimless glasses and a polo shirt and pressed slacks, Bernard Reece allowed her inside but didn't move from the marbled main hallway. He stated firmly that he would not allow his son to be interviewed unless he or another attorney was present during the questioning.

"I think I've made it crystal clear that Austin isn't going to speak with you or anyone else from your department alone. I know how this works."

There was no arguing. She tried. Got nowhere. "Then bring him into the station tomorrow. Early," she suggested and kept her tone even, her gaze direct. "Sit in."

"I have an appointment early in the morning. Nine o'clock."

"Not a problem. I'm up early. Let's make it seven."

His lips flattened a bit. "I'll be busy. As I am now."

"Then don't come. But I'll be there, and if Austin doesn't show up, it won't be good. As you said, you 'know how this works.' "

His eyes flashed for a second. Then one side of his mouth lifted as if he were amused. "A threat?" he said, before holding up a hand to cut off any response. "No, don't tell me: a promise. Just like on television."

"Yeah, that's right. We're just like the TV cops." She sent him a hard stare. "Tomorrow."

She drove away wondering what Bernard Reece was hiding. What did he know about his kid that made him so wary? Was it because he was a lawyer and, as such, was inherently suspicious, or was there more to the story? Did he suspect that his Ivy League–bound boy was in the kind of trouble that would alter the course of his life, turn all those gilded dreams to rubble?

She thought about Reece all the way to Missoula, where she located Veronica Palermo's apartment building three blocks off campus. The parking lot was dusty, the asphalt crumbling in places, lines for spaces having long faded. L-shaped and flat-roofed, the two stories of the Campus Court Apartments were painted a peeling gunmetal gray. Along each level ran covered porches where a few old aluminum deck chairs, coolers, and wooden crates used as tables had been set on the concrete around the doorways.

Alvarez parked near a fenced area that was intended to hide the garbage bins, but the broken gate and the Dumpster with its open lid and trash mounding to the point of overflowing gave the secret away.

Donny Justison's college friend's apartment was located on the second level. Alvarez climbed the chipped concrete steps, knocked on the door, and heard a flurry of footsteps. Seconds later, the door opened, and a girl of about nineteen stood in frayed jean shorts and a pink tank top that showed off black bra straps. Her auburn hair was wet and she was wearing no makeup.

"I'm looking for Veronica Palmero."

"I'm her. Who're you?"

Alvarez introduced herself and showed her badge. Veronica carefully looked at her ID, determined she was legit, and led her inside a flat that smelled of lingering cigarette smoke mingled with the distinct odor of marijuana. Dirty dishes were stacked on the counters and piled in the sink, and clothes, including a big pair of men's shorts, were scattered over a cheap brown carpet. "Look I don't have much time," Veronica said. "I've got to get dressed for work."

"This won't take long. I just have a few questions about Destiny Montclaire. I know you already spoke to a deputy, but I'd like to clear up a few things."

"That bitch?" She waved Alvarez inside and took a seat, cross-legged, on a worn gray couch. "I already told that deputy guy who came here all I know, which is nothing. I never even met the chick."

"I just need to clarify a few things."

"Go ahead and sit down, but this has gotta be short." She pointed to a chair that looked as if something had recently been spilled upon it, and instead sat on a mustard-colored ottoman.

Alvarez remained standing. "You're living here alone?"

"For now. Jessica—my roommate, Jessica Tanaka?—she went home for the summer. Works for her dad, but I stayed on to keep this place. I work and am taking two classes this summer."

"And you know Donny Justison?"

She gave Alvarez the "duh" look. "He's only my boyfriend."

"So, you're close."

She crossed her fingers and held them up for Alvarez to inspect. "We're like this. We tell each other everything," she said as a scrawny tabby cat trotted from the hallway and hopped onto the back of the couch. Veronica stroked it and then waxed euphoric about Donny, the mayor's son, the athlete, the "sweetest guy on the planet, and I mean it." She gladly answered questions about Donald Justison Junior, and admitted that they were "deeply involved," and "in love," and "would probably get married."

"Really?"

"Oh, sure. We're soul mates," she said, nodding her head sagely. "But not 'til after we graduate, though. My folks would kill me if I didn't finish up with my degree first."

"You called Destiny Rose Montclaire a bitch."

"Because she was one." Again, the bobblehead nod. "I hate to talk bad about the dead, y'know, but she was like the worst." She glanced at a fish tank mounted on a small table near an older television. "Oh." She scrambled to her feet, grabbed a can of fish food sitting on the TV, opened it, and tossed a handful of fish food into the water. A dozen tetras flashed to the surface, the water roiling. "How are you, guys?" she said to the fish. "Sorry. I know Mommy's gone and Aunt Ronnie forgot." She actually made fish faces into the smudged glass.

Secretly Alvarez wondered how she would ever graduate. She asked, "How?"

"Huh?" Veronica glanced over her shoulder.

"How was Destiny Montclaire the worst?"

"Everybody knew it. Destiny was always calling and texting and messaging Donny. Bitching him out, you know. No wonder he broke up with her. She, like, couldn't get it that it was O-V-E-R."

"Did you know that he met her on the day she went missing, before her body was found?"

She couldn't suppress a telltale jerk of surprise. "He was with me that day."

Alvarez paused. "Do you know what day that was?"

"Uh-huh. That Friday. Donny was—we were together—" She snapped closed the lid of the fish food.

Everything about the girl said she was lying. "Did you know she was pregnant?"

"The baby wasn't his. You know that. Donny told me he gave up his DNA and you guys tested him and that baby wasn't his." She said it as if the fact that he wasn't the father of Destiny's baby absolved him from any sin, including the fact that he'd likely been cheating on each of them with the other. She set the small can back on the table and scowled, but any further questions Alvarez asked didn't produce any more information.

Even before Veronica had started lying, Alvarez had realized Veronica wouldn't be much help in ferreting out the truth. She was just too much in love with Donny, and she didn't seem to think that lying to the police was a problem, no matter how many times Alvarez tried to impress upon her the importance of the truth.

No, Veronica would defend Donny to the death and provide alibis whether they were true or not. But Donny Justison knew more than he was saying, Alvarez was sure of it. He'd already lied to them; she felt it in her bones.

Now you're sounding like Pescoli. You need proof, not gut feelings.

Somehow, some way, she was going to get it, she thought as she drove out of town. Her muscles were tight, her frustration level in the stratosphere, and to top it all off, she got stuck behind a tractor pulling along the road at fifteen miles an hour.

"Really?" she said and after a sharp curve, spied a straightaway and hit the gas. She flew around the farmer, who, in a ball cap, eyes on the road ahead, took the time to wave as she sped past.

Once the farmer was in her rearview, she hit the button to open the sun roof, rolled down the windows, and ripped off the band holding her hair away from her face so that the wind could rip through it.

She considered the case, all the angles, all the suspects. She had circled around over everything again and had just arrived at the outskirts of town when her phone rang. With a glance at the screen, she saw it was Sage Zoller and answered.

"Alvarez."

"It's Zoller," the junior detective said. "The lab did an analysis on the bit of rubber found under the victim's fingernails. Latex. Most likely from a glove, the type used in hospitals."

"That's what we thought."

"No DNA could be found on it."

"Damn." That had been the hope, a slim one, but a hope.

"I've been checking around. The glove is pretty common and its usage widespread. The gloves can be found in hospitals and just about anywhere else you'd want to look. Stores in town sell them and we're checking that, but along with the hospitals, they're used in clinics and vet clinics and are sold commercially to anyone who wants to keep their hands sterile. Farmers for examining animals, or people who clean houses or whatever. And, of course, you can get them online. We're checking local outlets to see if any were purchased recently, but that's probably not going to be all that effective. Anyone who visited a hospital room or a clinic where they were having an exam could have snagged a pair."

"So no good news?"

"Only that the company that makes them color codes them by size. This particular glove, dark purple, is a large, so probably a male. A big male."

"Which just confirms what we already know." They'd already determined it would take a person of some strength to strangle the girl.

"I'm still looking for inconsistencies in the statements of all the kids at the party and Destiny Rose's circle of family and friends. Double-checking her phone and social media information, her email and texts. So far, nothing."

"All right. See if you can find anything linking her to Lindsay Cronin. We know they were in the same class and hung out together peripherally, but I wonder if there's another connection, one that's not so obvious."

"I'll see if I can come up with anything."

"Good. Me, too." Alvarez clicked off, feeling more frustrated than ever. Lindsay Cronin and Destiny Rose Montclaire, what was the connection?

There had to be a way to crack the case, she told herself as she closed the sun roof and managed to pull her hair back and bind it again. She just had to figure out how.

CHAPTER 22

Pescoli shifted from one foot to the other. From a small knoll near the parking lot, she observed the crowd that had gathered at the First Methodist Church.

With a steeply pitched roof, tall steeple, and tracery windows, the church was straight out of America, circa 1850. Tonight, the grounds around it were filled with townspeople who had come for the candlelight vigil for Destiny Rose Montclaire. Somewhere in this throng, Pescoli suspected, was the killer. And perhaps Donny Justison, Lindsay Cronin, and Kywin Bell knew who.

They weren't hedging their bets though; several policemen were in the crowd, some with their families, others with small cameras or their phones, taking pictures and videos of the crowd.

Destiny's parents were near the steps, Helene softly crying, dabbing at her eyes with a wadded tissue, Glenn's arm around her as he stood, dry-eyed, almost defiant. A couple of other adults, close friends or family members, Pescoli guessed, huddled around them.

The Cronins stood off to one side, both dry-eyed, both white-faced, most likely worrying that they would be attending another vigil soon, one for their own daughter. A man in his twenties stood next to them. Short and stocky, buzz-cut blond hair, and grim expression, he looked enough like Roy for Pescoli to assume he was the older boy, Lindsay's brother, Malcolm.

But there was a little ray of hope since Lindsay's phone was still working and, at least temporarily, it had turned on and *someone* had sent a message that might be able to be tracked, though she wasn't betting that the caller was Lindsay. Zoller and the techies at the station were working with the cell phone company and trying to track down where that latest signal had come from. The trouble was, even if it pinged on a tower, the range here was huge, the exact location impossible to pinpoint unless the phone was on, the GPS working. Lindsay's cell phone records were on the way, so they would soon discover who the last person she'd contacted before she'd disappeared was.

As she scanned the crowd that had gathered to honor Destiny Rose Montclaire, Pescoli wondered how Destiny's murder and Lindsay's disappearance were linked. It seemed moronic to her to think they were totally separate events.

Most of the kids who'd been caught at Reservoir Point nearly a week earlier were in attendance. They appeared appropriately somber, probably because not only were they standing near each other, but their parents were there, too. They all filled the lawn that stretched from the church to the parsonage. Donny Justison stood next to the O'Hara brothers, Alex and TJ, and Rod Devlin and Austin Reece rounded out the crew. Maddie Averill, along with Lara Haas, Selena Martinez, and Simone Delaney, was nearby, and even Bianca had elected to hang out with the group, all of whom were dressed in dark colors, grays and navy blue, black and brown. Not one of them smiled. No one played with their cell phones except to use the small lighted screens as candles.

The only friend missing was Lindsay Cronin.

As Pescoli watched, Maddie inched closer to TJ and Lara, seeming to be looking for someone in the crowd. Maddie whispered something to Bianca, but their conversation was hushed and brief.

Pescoli recognized Maddie Averill's parents, and Mary-Beth Delaney. The Tufts stood nearby: Richtor was positioned behind his wife, Marjory, his hands on her shoulders, his silver goatee a telltale sign of the disparity in their ages, as she was at least twenty years younger than he, maybe more, as Jeremy had known her in school. Richtor was also a good six inches taller than his wife. Marjory was petite with a curvy figure. She could easily have been mistaken for one of Richtor's children. His two sons, Emmett and Preston, were nearby, a few feet from their father and Marjory, while their mother, Terri, stood at a distance from them, on the far side of the church, unable to ignore her ex and his new wife. Her eyes darted in Marjory's direction even when she was whispering to Billie O'Hara, Alex and TJ's mother. Like her former husband, Terri was trim, even muscular, judging by the width of her shoulders. She was also tall, pushing six feet, though she was wearing flats. Her features were sharp and tight, large eyes and a pointed nose that she'd passed on to both of her sons. Her lips were compressed tightly, and if ever there was hatred in them, it was now directed at her ex-husband's young wife, quickly disguised as she looked away. Clearly she hadn't gotten over the fact that she'd been thrown over for another woman who had been little more than a girl at the time. Her frown became an icy smile of satis-faction as her gaze focused on Marjory, as if she knew something no one else did.

Huh. Pescoli regarded her thoughtfully, then turned her attention to Billie O'Hara. Alex and TJ's mother was dressed in black running gear with a gray tunic thrown over her yoga pants. She was the shorter of the two women, an athlete, compact and probably still competing in triathlons. Her hair was so black it shone whenever light hit it and was now scraped tightly away from her face to a small knot twisted atop her head. Over-sized gold hoops swung from her earlobes, and they danced as she whispered to Terri and chuckled, as if the two were sharing a private joke. She and Terri both sent sideways looks toward Richtor and his current wife—something going on there that Pescoli wondered about.

But they were only part of the mourners. It seemed that half the town was here, paying their respects.

Pescoli shifted a little for a better view of the Bell brothers, who were front and center, hard to miss. Kip was taller than most in the crowd and separated from his brother, Kywin, by his mother, Wilda Wyze, who seemed to have come to the service with her sons. They didn't exactly tower over her as Wilda was an Amazon of a woman, one who, in her youth, had won a couple of local body-building competitions. Neither the boys' father, Franklin Bell, nor Greg Wyze, Wilda's second husband, was with the family tonight. Greg, nearing fifty, was the manager of an independent grocery store. His hours varied so he could be working tonight. He could also have stayed home to care for the younger children, two girls ten years or so younger than Wilda's older boys. It was also likely he didn't know his step-sons' circle of friends well enough to feel he should attend the vigil.

In Franklin's case, he was probably sitting at the end stool at the Elbow Room, a hole-in-the-wall bar that was situated in the older section of town near the river and rumored to be his favorite watering hole.

Kywin shot a glance Pescoli's way, his face

a mask of distrust. When she met his eyes, he looked quickly away, taking a step behind his older brother, as if using Kip as a shield. All the while, Wilda glowered, a sense of unease emanating off her, and she spoke to no one that Pescoli could see, just kept an eagle eye on her grown sons, both of whom, in Pescoli's opinion, were thugs. They knew more than they were saying about Destiny's death and Lindsay Cronin's disappearance; Pescoli was sure of it. She just couldn't prove that they were involved, or knew who was.

As she studied the families and friends and acquaintances of Destiny Rose Montclaire, Pescoli couldn't help but wonder about the relationship dynamics of teenagers on the verge of adulthood, most of whom had known each other since preschool, and now, if not involved, were at least touched by the murder of one of their own and the disappearance of another.

A soft breeze blew across the churchyard, rustling the branches of the pine and aspen. Candles flickered, a cause for concern with the dry conditions. Though the grass surrounding the church was thick and recently watered, the areas abutting it were dusty and tinder dry.

She spied Santana standing with Jeremy, not too far from Bianca. Santana caught her eye, gave a quick little nod, then let her be. They'd had the discussion: he'd be with the kids tonight, she'd be on the job.

Reverend Tophman led the service. Dressed in black aside from a white clerical collar, the minister stood on the porch leading to the vestibule of the church. He was an unassuming-looking man, starting to bald, his gray hair military cut, his physique thin from years of running, an open Bible in one hand. With his other hand, he made gestures as he spoke. His wife, Janie, stood off to one side, two steps below him and next to their son Bryant, whom Pescoli had met a time or two and interviewed recently. Bryant hadn't been outwardly rude, like the Bell brothers, but he'd been reticent and glum, avoided eye contact by staring at the floor of the interview room, while Pescoli had tried to pry information out of him. The reverend and his wife had attended the interview, allowing their son to talk, encouraging him to speak the truth, but, in Pescoli's opinion, they represented a visible physical barrier that hadn't allowed Bryant the chance to open up.

Rounder than her husband, with a cap of graying curls, apple cheeks and a perpetual smile, wearing a simple print dress, Janie watched her husband preach in obvious adoration, as if she were a wallflower of a school girl and the most popular boy in school—maybe the quarterback of the football team—had just asked her to dance. Janie Tophman still appeared lost in puppy love with her husband of thirty-odd years.

The reverend spoke calmly, in a soothing voice.

He was beloved by his congregation, a pillar of the community, and was always front and center at many charitable events. He'd been the preacher at First Methodist for over fifteen years, raised his kids here, and never been relocated by the church, which was a bit unusual, but maybe reflected his deep ties to the community.

The Tophmans were both vocal about their boy being a "good son, a good Christian boy," nearly echoing the very words that Mary-Beth Delaney had used to describe her daughter, Simone: "a good girl."

Maybe, Pescoli thought, staring at the sullen kid. Or, maybe not. Rather than pray when his father suggested they all bow their heads in prayer, Bryant Tophman, wide-eyed, studied the toes of his black cowboy boots.

"Our children have been taught the way of the Lord," Janie Tophman had said to Pescoli after the interview at the station, when they'd been walking out past Joelle Fisher's desk. Pescoli remembered the conversation clearly, even though she'd been trying to avoid Joelle, who was still going on and on about a baby shower. "Our older children have proved that to be true," Janie said as she brushed a nonexistent piece of lint from the bodice of her dress.

"Now, Mother, there's no reason to brag," the reverend had responded with a soft, amused chuckle.

"I'm just saying," Janie had gone on as they walked through the doors. "Both Barbara Jane and Boyd are upstanding members of their community. Married. Children. Boyd followed in his father's footsteps into the ministry and has his own congregation down in Boise. Barbara is a stay-at-home mom who homeschools." Janie had beamed with pride, her chest swelling. The older children were at least a dozen years ahead of Bryant, so Pescoli thought he might have been an "oops," but she'd never say as much, especially considering her current condition.

Even so, she'd been left with the feeling that Bryant was very efficiently pulling the wool over his parents' adoring eyes.

"See anything?" Alvarez asked in a whisper as she crossed the patchy parking lot and joined Pescoli.

"The usual. Same kids that were at Reservoir Point to start with. It's like déjà vu all over again," she said quietly, "and then there's the production crew. Barclay Sphinx's crowd." She hitched her chin to a spot on another rise, where cameras were rolling and Fiona Carpenter was buzzing around, trying to look somber, but clearly more interested in camera angles and lighting. Lucky was planted near her, standing with his hands together, never letting any member of the crew out of his sight for long. Michelle, for once, wasn't at his side.

"Not the press?"

"They're here." Pescoli motioned toward a guy with a shoulder cam, and what appeared to be a female reporter standing closer to the church, near a laurel hedge running alongside the building. Manny Douglas was in the congregation, front and center, listening raptly to the reverend's speech and probably recording every word. And, as expected, Sheriff Cooper Blackwater was standing near the edge of the mourners, his hawkish features tight, lips compressed, gaze sliding over each person in the congregation.

"How were things in Missoula?"

"Veronica Palermo thinks Donny Justison is a god. If he needs an alibi, she's going to provide it."

"Great," Pescoli muttered sardonically.

"Yeah."

As the sermon wore on, Pescoli caught sight of Michelle hurrying from the street, where she'd obviously just parked her car. She was in heels and a short dress, her gaze searching the throng. She spied Luke and waved, then quickly started weaving through the packed mourners toward him.

"We've got ourselves a three-ring circus under the guise of being a vigil for Destiny Rose," Pescoli said dryly.

For the better part of a week, Pescoli had been doing a slow, steady burn. It had started the night she'd returned home and Bianca had admitted that she had agreed, through Lucky's urging, and with his parental permission, to do the damned reality show. Later tonight, they'd begin filming while the rest of the town, under Mayor Justison's guidance, was preparing for Big Foot Daze, which had come to be through a quickly convened meeting of the city council where Sphinx had spoken and agreed to host the celebration over Labor Day. That would be pushing things, as it was already August, but the mayor had been thrilled and declared, through an article in the *Mountain Reporter,* that the event would help the economy, create jobs, and put Grizzly Falls on the map.

For what? Pescoli thought. *Big Foot Capital of Montana?* Already, she was seeing signs that it was happening. A few statues of the creature that had been tucked away collecting dust were now front and center in storefronts.

The hype was already beginning.

And Pescoli hated it.

Despite her ex-husband's pleas and Barclay Sphinx's interest in her "story line" and "character development," Pescoli had avoided meeting with the producer. She'd stepped away from Bianca being involved only because her daughter had been adamant, and Lucky had supported her a hundred and fifty percent. Pescoli had even bitten her tongue when she'd wondered what was in it for Lucky. She wanted no part of it for herself, though. Let Bianca deal with her father on this one.

Fortunately, Sphinx had been out of town for a few days, so all Pescoli had to do to ignore him was refuse his calls and not return them. Easy deal. She was too damned busy. Not only did she hear the clock ticking toward her ever looming delivery date, but as the days passed, she felt frustrated and stymied in the homicide investigation.

Not that she wanted Bianca involved at all.

"Maybe you've gotta let go a little, just let this happen," Santana had told her a few days earlier. "Roll with it."

They'd been standing in the kitchen, he with a beer, she with a damned sparkling water, as they'd tried to find something from the refrigerator to put together for dinner. The dogs, hopeful a crumb could fall their way, had been milling at their feet.

"Roll with it?" Pescoli had repeated as she'd pulled out a third of an extra-large pizza left over from the night before. "That's your suggestion?" She dropped the pizza, still in its oversized cardboard box and smelling of garlic, onions, and cheese, onto the counter.

"I don't see how you can fight it."

"Pretty sure I can."

"But is it worth it? You've got a big case to work out and, like it or not, the baby's coming." He touched her on the belly and she slapped his hand away. She was spoiling for a fight, irritated to the back teeth at his attitude about Bianca, Big Foot, and especially her ex.

He didn't say anything, but his eyes told her how far she'd stepped over the line.

"Sorry," she said shortly, shutting the refrigerator door. "I don't mean to be such a bitch, but damn it, all this Big Foot reality show crap is bugging the hell out of me. The production crew is here, there's talk of 'Big Foot Daze,' and the town's buzzing like an angry wasp. Tourists rolling in. Gawkers. People drawn to the spectacle. And the first scene that they're shooting for Sphinx's reality series? They're filming *right after* the candlelight vigil Friday night! Can you believe that? It's all crazy-making, that's what it is, but yeah, as you pointed out, I've got a murder investigation to handle."

His gaze dropped pointedly to her stomach.

"I know, the baby. I'm sorry." She picked up his hand, drew it to her, and held it close over her protruding belly. "I can't wait for him to get here and to be done with this 'high risk' pregnancy, all because I'm pushing forty." That pissed her off, too. Along with a myriad of other things.

"Him?"

"Or her? Whatever he/she is." Pescoli leaned into him. "It's just that the timing isn't great."

"When is it ever?"

He pulled her in close and she closed her eyes and drank in the smell of him. Even when she was at her worst, he managed to still love her. It was humbling, and she vowed to stop being such a bitch.

"It'll be over soon."

No, no, it wouldn't. Yeah, she wouldn't be pregnant any longer, but the journey of raising a child would just be beginning. Santana didn't really understand it, not deep in his gut like she did in hers. He'd never had a child before and had come into her life when her kids were in high school. But he'd learn.

As if he'd read her thoughts, he kissed her forehead and said, "It'll be fun. An adventure."

She'd managed to choke out a laugh, and he'd reached around her, flipped open the box, and found a piece of cold pepperoni.

"I know. 'Course I know, Santana. I'm only afraid he . . . or *she* . . . will be as bad-ass as you are and then what the hell are we gonna do?"

She still didn't know.

Now, as Michelle hurried to Lucky's side, standing on her tiptoes and giving him a light kiss on the cheek, Pescoli turned her attention back to the rest of the throng, those mourners who had come to listen to Tophman go on and on. She noticed Lara Haas, edging through the crowd to talk to Emmett Tufts and his brother, Preston. Marjory, slipping away from her husband's protective grip for a second, said a word or two to Lara and the Tufts brothers, her stepsons.

Preston, a few years older than Emmett, spoke to both girls while Emmett, who had two or three inches and twenty or thirty pounds on his older brother, kept looking over his shoulder at his father, who came up, caught his wife's hand, and gave it a tight squeeze.

A little tension there.

She realized both Preston and Emmett kept sneaking glances at Marjory, as well as Terri and Billie. The whole scene hit Pescoli the wrong way—like they were all guilty of some collusion—but she told herself she was being overly suspicious. Not everyone in this crowd was involved in murder or abduction.

Catching movement in the parking lot, she saw Fred Nesmith pull up in a Chevy Silverado. Edie, the authoritarian cashier at the meeting, and two men with flowing gray beards climbed out of the king cab, their boots crunching on the gravel as they alighted. Nesmith reached into his pocket. The pickup's headlights blinked and it gave a sharp beep as it locked.

Within seconds, a black Lexus rolled into the lot, Barclay Sphinx at the wheel, Jeffe in the passenger seat. They parked and caught up to the others; then the entire entourage of members from the club joined the congregation.

Pescoli noticed that Barclay moved through

the crowd to settle in next to the Montclaires. Destiny's father nodded to the producer while the minister, if he noticed any commotion, didn't so much as stumble over a word. In his smooth tone, Reverend Tophman continued to preach to the people who'd come to pay their respects.

There appeared to be some kind of silent conversation going on between Glenn Montclaire and Barclay Sphinx. She raised an eyebrow at Alvarez, who had caught the producer's arrival as well.

"He's already set up a reward, ten grand for help in finding and convicting Destiny's killer," Alvarez whispered. "I just got a text from Blackwater. It happened late this afternoon. Sphinx called the Montclaires, then set it up through the mayor, who gave the word to Blackwater. He wasn't happy that Sphinx hadn't come to him directly."

Pescoli was irked, as well. The investigation had barely gotten going, and though she encouraged the public's help, the mention of a reward always brought out the crazies and the desperate, all of which the sheriff's office would have to wade through.

"Sphinx wanted to hold a press conference about it," Alvarez added.

"I bet."

"The sheriff is balking."

"Really?" Pescoli found that hard to believe.

"He thinks we should handle any press conference."

"For once, I agree."

"The mayor doesn't see it that way."

Pescoli hazarded a glance at Carolina Justison, who was sliding through the crowd, aiming for a position near Sphinx.

And all the while, Reverend Tophman kept talking about Destiny Rose Montclaire going home to God.

"Let us pray," he intoned again, smiling beatifically. Pescoli bowed her head, but she watched the group, faces lit by the unsteady light of candles or images of candles via cell phone apps, all devoutly praying or wanting to appear that way.

CHAPTER 23

"Detective!"

Regan was walking to her vehicle after the service when she heard Barclay Sphinx's voice calling for her. Every muscle in her back tightened and she reluctantly turned to see him jogging toward her. She just didn't trust the guy and had trouble keeping her expression neutral. Several people were also hurrying after him—Carlton Jeffe, Ivor Hicks, and Luke were all making their way through knots of people as they tried to catch up with the producer. Michelle, incredibly agile in her four-inch heels, managed to stay with them. The good news was that Bianca wasn't part of the entourage.

"Be a part of my show, Detective Pescoli," Barclay said, offering up an engaging grin in the thin illumination from a street lamp. "Change your mind. Join us."

"We've already been through this."

"Your daughter has agreed to be the star. And you're aware filming starts tonight." He glanced at his watch. "The on-site crew is already setting up at Reservoir Point. The rest of us are heading up there now. All you have to do is come."

"Thank you, no. I'm out." She saw that he was about to launch into more arguments and staved them off with, "I don't believe Big Foot exists, and I don't like how you're exploiting this town and Destiny Montclaire's death, all for ratings. And now another girl is missing. So, no."

"Exploiting? Oh. No. No. We're not exploiting anyone. What girl's missing?"

"Lindsay Cronin."

Her name didn't seem to register with him as he placed a splayed hand over his chest. "I'm trying to help the investigation."

"And how's that?"

"With all the publicity we're generating. Just take the trailer after the show . . ."

Pescoli seethed. Any publicity for the case, even if it proved beneficial, was created to win over mass appeal, create a buzz and add up to helping ratings for his new show. The underlying reason for Sphinx's involvement was that dead, murdered girls made for interesting TV. It was all about money.

"This could help Destiny's family and—" He was going on, but Pescoli cut him off.

"The trailer and everything else you do can be done without my input. Ask the sheriff."

"I have. Sheriff Blackwater's agreed to be a part of it."

"Oh." Of course. Just when she was beginning to have a smidgen of faith in the sheriff, his true colors came to light.

"But he's not Bianca's mother," Sphinx pointed out. "He doesn't have that emotional connection with her, so it's a whole different thing. Touches a different emotion for the viewer." Again, he flashed his engaging grin, as if Barclay Sphinx really believed he could somehow charm her into being a part of his reality show.

"Find a stand-in," she suggested.

"Michelle has agreed to do the part," he said, watching her reaction.

Pescoli's heart dropped. *Michelle?* She wanted to argue about Michelle not being old enough, or smart enough or anything enough to be Bianca's biological mother, but held it back with an effort. "Good," she said tightly. "Then you're set. If you'll excuse me."

She climbed into her Jeep and engaged the engine, hitting the gas and reversing before driving out of the lot. As she paused to check the street, she glanced in her rearview mirror and spied Sphinx looking dumbfounded while Michelle, who had caught up with him, was positively radiant.

What was it she'd told Bianca? That this part in *Big Foot Territory: Montana!* was just the beginning? That Bianca was on her way to being a star? Well, now, it seemed it was Michelle's big break, too.

"Have at it," she said aloud.

She was about to pull away when she saw two boys, one of the Bell brothers—Kywin, she thought—move next to Bryant Tophman, who had escaped from his mother and father as they spoke with other mourners. The two men—because they sure didn't look like teens, both big and muscular —slapped hands and then turned from each other, Tophman stuffing something furtively into the front pocket of his jeans while Bell disappeared through the dispersing crowd.

In her career as a cop, she'd seen more than her share of drug deals go down, from street hoodlums and prostitutes to white-collar workers and doctors, or kids and a friend's parent or older sibling, so she recognized the quick, secretive action, but it was more than a little bold right here in a damned candlelight vigil with parents, friends, and the cops around. What kind of idiots were they?

Kids, she told herself. *With the bodies of men and the brains of children. Boys who think they're invincible and way smarter than they are.*

So, if those dunderheads were hiding something about Destiny Montclaire's death or Lindsay Cronin's disappearance, they were bound to screw up, and she was going to catch them.

She only hoped it happened before someone else died.

The forest around Reservoir Point was nearly dark.

Eerie.

A sliver of moon rising through the wispy clouds.

It was much like the night Bianca had been running for her life, certain a monster was chasing her down the mountain, bearing down on her, its hot, horrid breath at her back. She could remember the feelings. The terror. Calling up those raw emotions for this, her big scene recreating the moment "Big Foot" chased her into the canyon, was easy.

The crew had set up at the top of the very trail she'd run down almost a week earlier. There were lights in play, enough to pick up the action, but dim enough to make it obvious to the viewers that it was night.

Bianca closed her eyes. Gathered herself.

Tapped into her raw emotions of terror and pain as she waited at the top of the trail, wedged between two huge boulders, standing on her mark, ready to race down the hillside.

She was pumped. Adrenaline raced through her bloodstream and her heart was pounding, her nerves tight.

Get this right. Do it!

She'd read the loose script, and Barclay Sphinx had talked to her about what he wanted from each scene.

For this one, she was supposed to run through the woods as if she were scared out of her mind, to keep looking over her shoulder and to show panic, fear, and pain. All she had to do was remember how she'd felt that night and she was there. The cameraman—a bearded guy named Rob—would basically be playing the part of the monster chasing her, the lens Big Foot's eye, so she'd have reason to turn her face and really emote. Showing pain shouldn't be a problem. Running on her ankle was certain to ensure a level of agony. Even now, while she was just waiting, it throbbed. She gritted her teeth. Her doctor would freak if he knew she was doing this, but she didn't care. Poised for flight, she rotated the kinks from her neck, then swatted at a mosquito that buzzed near her head.

She'd been told that since Rob would be following her, she was supposed to look like she was running fast and hard, when, in essence, she would be slowly jogging so he could keep up without jostling the camera too much and they could get good, clear footage that wasn't too jerky.

Other camera operators would catch the action as she headed downhill, one midway and the other at the bottom of the incline when she pitched headlong into the creek, where the "dead body"—really little more than a life-sized doll—was in place beneath the water. It didn't look real with its fake hair and painted eyes, but she had been assured it would appear genuine in the film. And it could be doctored, made to look more real through computer-generated imagery, post filming. The images of it would be grainy and distorted, so the viewers would only get a glimpse before the camera cut away; most of the horror was left to the viewers' imaginations.

Sphinx had explained to Bianca that there would be several takes of her run down the hillside and all the footage would be reviewed, edited, and spliced together to make the filming appear seamless and "real."

Mentally she'd turned a corner by pushing back her doubts about Barclay Sphinx's motives. She told herself they didn't matter, that the filming tonight was the first step to achieving her goals of becoming a star, even though she was a little disappointed in the script as the story line surrounding this episode of the series was only minimally about her.

Still, she was one step closer to Hollywood.

"Okay, everybody. Places!" a disembodied voice called from somewhere behind her, and then, "Action!"

She took off. Jogging headlong down the path, breathing more loudly than she needed to, looking over her shoulder, hoping that raw panic was evident on her face. She remembered frantically racing down this very path, the twists, the turns, the sheer terror of the monster chasing her, and oh, yeah, the pain! She winced as she passed the second camera, maybe overplaying it as she hobbled, but the pain was real enough, each step downhill sending a jab of agony through her ankle.

She heard the cameraman behind her, pretended it was the monster she'd seen the week before, and kept glancing fearfully behind, reminding herself the red light blinking on the shoulder cam was that gold eye of whatever creature had torn after her through these stands of hemlock and pine.

She heard the creek before she saw it, noticed the camerawoman on the bank, and headed straight for the stream, which rushed and cascaded more loudly than it had before, as the crew was piping in more water from a truck situated upstream, out of view of the cameras.

For effect, Bianca was panting loudly as she

passed the camerawoman on the fly. She recognized her mark, the edge of the stream where the water eddied and pooled, saw the exact spot where she was supposed to trip over an exposed root and fall with a little scream into the water.

Almost there!

From the corner of her eye, she caught a glimpse of the mannequin, lying just under the surface, half hidden in the dark pool and tethered by an invisible bit of fishing line. Everything was in its place.

Now!

Her toe hit the root and she pitched herself forward, her arms flying out as she screamed for effect and hit the cold rush of water. Uncomfortable, but not terrible. God, she hoped it looked as if she'd stumbled. She submerged and focused on the doll.

The mannequin stared back.

Eye sockets were blackened. The lower half of the face was only a skull, as if something had eaten away the tissue.

This wasn't the doll! The mannequin! This thing in the water was *real*. A dead woman! With rotting flesh flaking from stark white bone, pale hair floating around a face without eyes, rotting flesh hanging by sinews, a gossamer dress wafting in the current.

Bianca shot to the surface and shrieked for all she was worth, her scream echoing through the canyon. She scrambled wildly away, splashing water, slipping on the bank, trying to get away from the horror of the dead girl's face, the terror that seized her throat. Coughing and sputtering, she staggered to her feet. Pain screamed up her ankle. She fell, slid back toward the water and the wretched, rotting corpse. "Oh, God. Oh, God. Oh, God!"

Heart thundering, she flailed backward, scuttling frantically backward up the bank, eyes stretched wide, her body soaked, her fear real.

Then, like a bolt of lightning, it hit her. The production crew and Barclay Effin' Sphinx had *played* her.

"What the hell did you do?" she cried.

"Cut! Cut!" a voice called loudly, then Mel, a production assistant who'd been beyond the scope of the lights, ran forward. "You're okay," she said. Small, athletic, hair cropped close to her head, she grabbed hold of Bianca's arm.

Bianca yanked her arm back. "I'm definitely not fine! You put that horrid thing in there. You made me think there was a real girl down there." She pointed a shaking finger at the stream. "What the hell is that?"

"Don't worry. It's not real. Hey, can I get a towel over here?" she called to someone behind her.

"I *know* it's not real." *Now*, Bianca silently added, *I know it's not real* now.

Mel admitted, "We switched out the mannequins."

"But that's all wrong . . . I mean you were going to fix it in post-production. CGI or whatever."

"We wanted to get your real gut reaction. Your horror." Someone gave Mel a terry-cloth hand towel, which she passed over to Bianca. "And it worked," she said as Bianca swiped the dripping water from her face. "Your expression was perfect. We wanted to see that terror, that fear, to get it all in one take, and you were fantastic!"

"I was scammed. I want to talk to Barclay."

"It was his idea to change things up and surprise you, make it real to enhance your performance."

Bianca was burned. Who did these people think they were? Obviously, despite anything else he'd said, Barclay Sphinx didn't have faith that she could act, could pull off the scene on her own. God, she was *pissed*. Tossing her hair to one side of her face, she wrapped her hand around the strands and squeezed, wringing out the water, feeling like a fool, or worse yet, a naive teenager who'd just been shown how foolish she was.

Crap!

Mel said, "The point is, it's done. Unless something shows up in editing, we're good here."

Bianca was pressing the towel to her face.

"Oh, watch that. Don't dry yourself off too much. We need you wet for the next scene."

Bianca wasn't sure she wanted to do any more scenes. She was starting to believe that her mother was right about the whole damned show.

"You got any more 'surprises' for me?" she snarled.

"That only works once." Mel flashed an encouraging smile.

Bianca tossed a look to the creek, where the hideous, lifelike mannequin lay beneath the surface of the water, the blond hair still wafting in the current.

Her face burned with embarrassment, and she had the absurd feeling she was about to cry.

"Now come on," Mel said. "Let's get moving. Back to the parking lot. We want to wrap up that scene with you talking to your mom about what happened."

Bianca reined in her emotions with an effort. "She's not my mother," she muttered, following after the woman to the gravel-strewn area where the party scenes had been filmed. The campfire, though gas-fueled and controlled, was still burning, a couple of rocks and a few sleeping bags scattered around it, while farther back, out of the camera's sweep, were all of the equipment and vehicles—cranes, light poles, trucks and the like—and people clustered and waiting. Beyond the perimeter of the set, there were other vehicles, curious bystanders hoping for a glimpse of the filming, reporters thinking they might catch a story, as this was, after all, the scene of a recent murder.

"Take five," Mel told her, waving toward an

empty chair. "And you can put your ankle brace back on. We won't film you any lower than your waist, so it won't show." She started to walk away, then turned and added, "But don't dry off, okay? The next scene will be you, here." She twirled her finger to include the parking area, where three pickups and a couple of sedans were parked around the perimeter of the lot, about ten feet from the campfire pit. "That's the scene with your mom, the woman cop."

That was another thing that bothered Bianca. Michelle being cast as not only her mom, but a policewoman, a detective. They had her dressed in slacks, a blouse and jacket, her hair clipped behind her head, a fake gun mounted on her belt, boots with significant heels, not at all like her mother's, which was probably good. But acting as if Michelle were her real mom, that would be tough. Michelle was okay and all, and really cool usually . . . but . . . she just wasn't her mother.

While waiting for the scene to be set up, Bianca grabbed a bottle of water from a cart, cracked the cap, and took a long swallow just as Maddie and Lara approached.

Eyes shining, Maddie said, "Is this the coolest or what?" She was taking in all of the action, watching the new scene being set up with one eye on Teej, who was joking around with Austin on the far side of the campfire.

"I guess."

Mel was heading to Teej and Austin, directing them to sit next to the campfire.

Her gaze never leaving Teej, Maddie said to Bianca, "I can't believe your mom didn't want to be a part of it."

"She doesn't believe all this stuff about Big Foot. Thinks it's all a lot of hype."

"So?" Lara asked. "I mean, when does something like *television* come to Grizzly Frickin' Falls. *Never.*"

Bianca said shortly, "Mom's busy."

"Oh, well, yeah, with the investigation," Lara said.

For a second, Maddie and Lara both tried to look sad, almost as if on cue acting like they cared about Destiny. It kinda made Bianca sick.

Maddie broke the uncomfortable silence. "I'm going to grab something to drink. They've got Diet Coke. You guys want anything?"

"That stuff'll kill you," Lara advised.

"Oh, right. When? In about a hundred years?" Maddie tossed her hair and headed toward the drink cart, and Lara turned back to Bianca.

"At least Michelle gets to play your mom in the series. Kinda keeps it in the family, and besides she's *so* cool. Sorry to say, but way cooler than your real mom."

Bianca pressed her lips together.

"She's hotter. Be better for the show," Lara went on. "I mean, no offense, your mom's *okay*, but she doesn't have the same 'it' factor that Michelle does. This is way better. She makes a better cop."

"*What?*"

"I mean TV cop. Oh, come on, you know I'm right."

Bianca glanced over at the area tagged for the next scene: Bianca's meeting with her cop mom. If the production crew had intended to make Michelle seem like Regan, they'd already got it wrong, Bianca thought. In heeled boots and a tight outfit Regan Pescoli wouldn't have been caught dead in, Michelle was deep in conversation with Barclay Sphinx. Her platinum hair, braided and falling over a shoulder, gleamed in the production lights as she, intent on what the producer was saying, leaned a hip against a Jeep that had been fitted with a light bar and a sheriff's department logo.

"See what I mean?" Lara said as Barclay even touched Michelle lightly on the shoulder as he went through the scene with her.

Yeah, Bianca thought, *the television version of a female detective.* So why didn't it ring true? Why did it bug her so much?

Michelle looked fantastic, no question, but it wasn't right. Bianca took another swallow of water and caught Michelle raining a smile back at the producer, the kind of smile she usually reserved for Dad. It was weird. Unsettling. Bianca had always known Michelle was a flirt, the kind of woman who lit up around men, but this was different. Bianca sensed a deeper emotion running here.

"And your mom's sooo prego," Lara went on. "Like huge. She'd fill up the whole picture on a wide screen."

"She's going to have a baby," Bianca ground out.

"I'm just saying, she's not right," Lara sniffed.

Maddie returned, a sweating Diet Coke can in hand. "So has your mom figured out who killed her?" she asked Bianca as she cracked the top of the can open.

"What?" Bianca was pissed at Lara and everything else.

"Destiny. Does she know who did it? You said she doesn't think it was a Big Foot." She took a sip as a worker stretched an electrical cord around the perimeter of the next scene. "I mean, I don't either, but who would have done it? Who does she think?"

"I don't know," Bianca said, more annoyed than ever. She didn't want to discuss her mom's work or the case. "She's working on it."

"Does she think that the baby's father did it? Killed her?" Maddie asked. "I hear it wasn't Donny's."

"I don't know," Bianca snapped again. Her ankle throbbed, she was sure the makeup used to disguise the split on her lip wasn't working, the mosquitoes were driving her nuts, and the whole night was a big pain.

Maddie said, "Well, who do *you* think it was?"

"How would I know? For God sakes. That's what the homicide detectives are for."

"I was talking about the baby's father." Maddie took another drink from her can. "Who do you think he is?"

"Don't have a clue." Bianca was abrupt. "I didn't know her that well."

"Probably could be anybody," Lara said. "All the boys liked her. And they're all horny as hell." She nodded, her blond hair catching in the low light. "I know."

"Not all of them," Maddie said pointedly.

Lara laughed. "What? You think Teej wouldn't go for it, if she came on to him?"

"He wouldn't!"

A sly smile curved over Lara's full lips. "Why don't you go ask him?"

"Lara!" Maddie sputtered as Simone joined the group.

Lara turned to Simone. "What do you think? Would Teej have banged Destiny if he had the chance?"

"He's a guy, isn't he?" she replied with a shrug. "Hey, where did you get that?" she asked, pointing to Maddie's soda.

"You guys are sick!" Maddie spat. "Who knows who Destiny slept with, and who cares?"

"You were the one that brought it up," Lara reminded her. The mean undertone in her voice couldn't be missed.

"Teej wasn't interested in Destiny," Maddie said darkly.

"Think we hit a nerve?" Lara asked, and both she and Simone tittered. When Maddie looked like she was about to cry, Lara added, "Oh, come on. It has nothing to do with love or romance or any of that shit. It's about wanting to fuck. Guys —all guys—want it all the time. Why wouldn't he? Because Alex had already fucked her? So what? That would probably only make him want to do it more. Kind of a brother competition or sibling rivalry thing. You can't take it personally."

"Teej isn't like that," Maddie said angrily.

"Uh-huh." Lara smirked.

"You are such a bitch, Lara. Such a bitch."

Lara laughed as Mel yelled over to the group. "Okay, places, everyone! Bianca? You and your mom. Over by the Jeep." Michelle straightened and took a couple of steps, getting in position for the correct camera angle that would include the sheriff's department vehicles and Bianca. Before she could answer, Mel looked over at Bianca and, from the pull of her eyebrows and tightening of her lips, it was obvious she was running out of patience. "Bianca? Today?"

Bianca hobbled to the Jeep and heard Simone snigger, "Break a leg," followed by giggling.

Idiots, she thought and had a fleeting thought that maybe, this time, her mother had been right. Maybe agreeing to be part of the production and recreating the discovery of the dead girl's body was a big, big mistake.

CHAPTER 24

She couldn't breathe!

Huge hands clasped over her throat, cutting off her air. Struggling, she tried to suck in any whisper of air, but it was impossible. The beast holding her wouldn't let go. And here, deep in the wilderness, no one could hear the struggle or her strangled attempts to cry out.

No. No. No!

This couldn't be happening!

She tried to scream, to kick, to scratch and rid herself of the manacles surrounding her throat, holding her fast. But her assailant was strong. So damned strong.

Help me, oh, please . . . someone help me.

But no one knew where she was, that she was in the forest at the hands of a maniac. *God, please . . .*

Her lungs felt as if they would explode, her eyes bulged.

Why would he do this? Why? Frantic, she fought, throwing her weight away from him, attempting to break his deadly hold, hoping to kick him hard in his shins or his nuts, wherever she could lash out. To no avail. Her blows found no mark, her stabs at breaking free only serving to make him increase his hold.

The pain in her lungs was excruciating. So much pressure and a blackness pulled at the edges of her consciousness, a darkness that was as alluring as it was deadly.

Don't give up! Keep fighting. Someone will come. You'll be saved! You can't die! Not like this, not when . . . the baby. Oh, God, the baby! She struggled harder, but her mind was dulled with pain, her movements sluggish and she knew she was on the verge of losing consciousness. If that happened, it would be over. She would surely die at his hands.

How had she gotten here?

Why had she trusted him?

She'd been so, so foolish.

The world spun crazily. Tops of trees seemed to skim the sky. The moon, pearlescent and shining in the darkness, the sounds of the night, the rush of wind and buzz of insects and whir of bat wings now silent beneath the thunder of her pulse beating in her ears, the fear that was consuming her, the infinite blackness crawling into her vision.

He was going to kill her!

She'd trusted him.

Stupidly.

And now he intended to cut off her air and hold her down. Strangle her until she passed out and . . .

She fought harder, her fingernails ripping at the backs of those steely hands, slicing into his . . . not skin, but something covering his hands. *Gloves!* The son of a bitch was wearing gloves. So that he could murder her and get away with it! Leave no trace of his damned DNA! No way! No friggin' way! Her thoughts were wild, the darkness in her peripheral vision closing in.

She twisted her neck, intent on biting his arm when she heard him take a deep breath. Then, as her burning lungs gave out and lightning bolts flashed behind her eyes, she felt an increased pressure on her throat. Harder, stronger, and . . . and . . . then the blackness around the edge of her vision swallowed her.

The call came in at two minutes after 5 a.m. It was still nearly dark, just the hint of dim light filtering through the open French doors as Pescoli fumbled for her phone. Groaning, she looked at the lit screen of her cell: Alvarez.

This was not going to be good news, she thought as the first cries of morning birds slipped inside on a soft breeze.

"Yeah?" she answered groggily, surfacing to realize that she was alone in the bed. She pushed herself into a sitting position and figured Santana had already gotten up, was maybe downstairs going over book work or getting ready for another day working not only this place but the Long ranch as well.

"We've got another one."

"Another what?" Pescoli asked, staring over the mound that had once been her trim abdomen to the view, through the open doors, of the lake. A hint of sunlight burst over the mountains to the east. "Dead body?"

"No."

For a second, Pescoli felt relief. "Then what?" she asked around a yawn.

"A girl scared out of her wits by Big Foot."

"What? No. Come on."

"Lara Haas claims she was chased by a huge, hairy monster up near Reservoir Point. The thing tried to strangle her, but she got away."

Pescoli rubbed her eyes with her free hand. "Wait a sec. This was when? After the filming of the reality series? Because Sphinx's production crew was up there most of the night, until the early morning." This wasn't adding up. Bianca had come in sometime around 3 a.m. Pescoli had heard the sounds of Michelle's car's idling engine as she'd dropped Bianca off, then the distinctive rumble of the garage door lifting and closing, a few soft woofs from the dogs, and finally the sound of footsteps on the stairs. Once she'd heard her daughter's bedroom door open and close, Pescoli had drifted off again. She considered Lara Haas. "Sounds like a hoax."

"Anything involving Big Foot sounds like a hoax, but I thought since this happened to Bianca last week, or at least something similar, you might want to check it out."

"Is she up there at Reservoir Point now?"

"No, she called nine-one-one. She's pretty beat up, I guess, and ended up at Northern General. I'm heading to the hospital now."

"But she was at the reservoir? Is that where the . . . beast . . . chased her?"

"Yeah."

"I thought the place was barricaded off because of the filming."

"It is," Alvarez said. "They slipped through the temporary fencing."

"They?"

"Alex O'Hara was with her."

Another member of the group who couldn't be trusted, at least in Pescoli's opinion. "Barclay Sphinx is gonna be pissed if anything is missing or broken."

"Unless there's real evidence of Big Foot. Then he'll be ecstatic. All that free publicity at another sighting."

"Makes you wonder, doesn't it?" she muttered. What if everything that was happening was a big publicity stunt? But no, there was homicide involved. As despicable as she found the producer, Pescoli didn't believe him capable of murder. Then again, she'd been wrong before.

"Yes," Alvarez agreed.

"It will be tough to believe it's a Sasquatch. Those creatures are not only camera and people shy, they're hairy and don't seem to shed, it seems. And though they presumably hunt and eat, they're so damned tidy, they don't leave any evidence of their kills, not a trace. Also, I guess they don't defecate, as no spoor can be found. And when they die, their carcasses must go through super rapid disintegration because their bones and teeth turn to dust in seconds flat. Unless maybe aliens come down and whisk the corpses back to an unknown planet in another solar system. Remind me to ask Ivor Hicks about that. He claims the reptilians under the leadership of a General Krytor or something took him away for a few hours to do experiments on him, if I remember correctly."

"I'm with ya. But even so, since Bianca claims she saw something like a Big Foot last week, and a girl's body was discovered . . ."

"Yeah, yeah, I know." All this talk of the mythical, overhyped beast was giving Pescoli a headache. "I'm on my way. I'll meet you at the hospital." After hanging up, she leaned back against the headboard for a second. What the hell was going on? Another Big Foot sighting landing a girl in the hospital? She couldn't help but wonder if it was all staged, just like the reality show, all part of some elaborate prank, or, as she'd thought before, a publicity stunt.

She pushed herself upright and rolled out of bed, then found her dreaded maternity pants and top, dressed hastily, unlocked the safe for her sidearm, and slipped it into her shoulder holster.

Down the hall, she passed the door to the small nursery. The door was ajar and she cast a glance inside. The crib was already pushed into one corner, a chest of drawers on the opposite wall. The room was painted a soft gray and nearly ready for its tiny, as yet unborn, occupant. A huge package of diapers was still wrapped in plastic, and on the changing table a fluffy, lop-eared bunny, a gift from one of Pescoli's sisters, peered at her.

It was hard to believe that within the next four weeks a new little person would call this room home.

Oh, man. She could hardly wait.

But she wasn't ready. Not yet.

She took a few more steps in the hallway only to stop at Bianca's door, where she peeked inside to find her daughter, her injured ankle elevated and resting on a pillow, one arm flung across her face, her curly hair a tangled mess, sleeping as if she were dead.

But she was safe.

Good. She felt a moment's relief and closed the door.

On the stairs she was met with the aroma of freshly brewed coffee. Following the scent, she maneuvered around the obstacles of three energetic dogs and found her husband at the single-cup espresso machine, where a travel cup, the latte still frothing, was waiting. "For you," he said, indicating the mug. He'd showered and was dressed in jeans, a T-shirt, and socks, his boots standing at attention near the back door. "Coffee. Well, kinda."

"You mean 'decaf'?"

"Yep. I heard your phone. Figured you'd be down." He handed her the cup.

"I think I need something stronger this morning, but thanks." She took an experimental sip. "You're too good to me."

"Never in doubt."

"And so humble."

"That's right. So what's up?"

"If you can believe it, there's been another Big Foot attack."

"I don't. Believe it."

"Me, neither. Call me a skeptic, but . . ." She took another swallow. "Mmm." Despite the lack of energy rush, the coffee was hot and helped get her early morning going.

He slid her a glance. "What happened?" he asked.

"Supposedly one of the girls who was up at Reservoir Point for the filming of that damned show was attacked. I guess all of Sphinx's cameras, and production people and lights and noise, didn't scare off these incredibly shy creatures. Turns out, maybe they were just waiting for the camera crew to show up."

He snorted.

"But the upshot is that another girl is in the hospital, so whatever chased her or attacked her is real. We just don't know what it is. I'm betting it's the same being that chased Bianca." She rotated the travel cup in a hand as she thought. "Whatever's happening is pissing me off."

"It won't be your problem in a few days," he reminded her.

"Yeah, what? Just because I'm gonna have a baby, I'm gonna bail on the investigation?"

"It'll slow you down."

"It's not like I'm having major surgery, or will be laid up forever." To his credit, he didn't push it. She knew she'd be off work for a while, that the first few weeks and months would be a blur of breast feeding, and nights without sleep, and diapers, and being so in love with the new little addition to the family that nothing else would seem to matter. She'd been through it before and was gladly doing it again. Just. Not. Yet.

"I'm heading to the hospital to visit the victim, Lara Haas," she told him.

"One of Bianca's friends. The blonde with . . ."

Was he really going to say, "The blonde with the tits?" but had thought better of it? *Men! So damned predictable. And really—so annoying.*

"With the incredible body?" she supplied as he let the sentence fade. "Yeah, that's the one. After I chat with her, I might head back to the reservoir. See what I can see. I guess I'll catch you later—with all that's going on, probably not until tonight. Thanks for the latte."

"I was going to say with the privileged attitude."

She squinted at him. "Uh-huh."

"That's what you said," he reminded, eyes full of mirth.

"Yeah." She set the cup in the sink and started to turn away, but he caught her wrist, pulled her back to face him and then kissed her as he hadn't kissed her in a long while. She'd expected a buss across the cheek, instead she got warm lips, big hands splayed across her back, and the slickness of his tongue running over the seam of her lips. Her resistance fled and she felt herself turning into molten butter. Her knees nearly gave out and erotic images of the two of them played through her mind. Santana, with a quick, intense glance, or the merest touch, could make her think of long hours of sexual foreplay and satisfaction. It was always erotic and sometimes, like now, frustrating.

"Not now," she said as he lifted his head.

"Later, then."

"A lot later. I'm pretty damned pregnant."

"And sexy as hell."

"Oh, man," she said as he released her. "You are *so* full of it."

"I know. But you two be careful out there." He looked at her protruding belly.

She was smiling as she walked through the family room. The dogs, ever hopeful for a ride, trailed after her and she left them, tails wagging, for Santana to deal with.

Minutes later, she was driving down the lane to the main road, the lake shimmering gold with the rising sun, stars fading as night turned to day. She rolled down her window, smelled the scents of dry grass and dust—summer—in the air and watched as the sun crested the hills. All the while, she tried to wrap her head around Lara Haas's claims. Obviously if the girl had been admitted to the hospital, she'd been injured.

Like Bianca.

What was Lara doing up at the reservoir?

Why had some "creature" chased after her?

Had it attacked?

It all sounded unbelievable. None of it made a whole lot of sense.

But neither had Bianca's story and it was very real.

The streets in town were quiet. She met only a few cars and trucks, people on their way to work, but she was uncomfortable behind the steering wheel and felt, again, the Braxton Hicks contractions that had been showing up periodically over the past few weeks. She told herself this wasn't her first rodeo, she knew all the signs, and that when real labor was imminent, she'd know it.

But it's been more than a few years since you were last pregnant. Your body has changed a lot.

"Oh, shut up," she growled and glanced at her reflection in the rearview mirror. "It's not happening, not yet." She had far too much to do before she could even think about maternity leave.

Once again, she turned her thoughts to the task at hand and the attack on Lara Haas. Was it too convenient? Some kind of setup, or publicity stunt? "You're a jaded, pregnant cop whose BS radar is always cranked too high," she told herself with another look in the mirror. "Or, maybe just a damned good detective. Let's go with that. Yeah, I like that better."

At Northern General, the lot was fairly empty, only a few vehicles parked near the front doors. She found an empty spot and headed inside, taking the elevator to the second floor, where she found the room occupied by Lara Haas.

A nurse was attending to her patient, taking vital signs, and Alvarez stood near the windows, turning when she heard Pescoli arrive.

Propped on the bed, the head of which was raised, Lara, devoid of makeup, looked more like a kid than ever, as if she were closer to fifteen than twenty. In a flash, Pescoli remembered her as a toddler at the preschool. She'd been pretty even then, round blue eyes, blond hair, pink cheeks and rosebud lips. Now, an IV dripped colorless fluid into her right arm while her left forearm was elevated, a padded splint holding her wrist and hand immobile. There were surface scratches on her face and arms, and a dark discoloration visible at her neckline.

Pescoli didn't say a word as the nurse, a prim woman in her fifties in scrubs and rimless glasses, took Lara's vitals, then, not particularly happy the cops were there, looked from Pescoli to Alvarez. "Does the doctor know you're here?"

"Don't know," Alvarez said.

"I'll check. Remember, the patient has been through a lot," she said, glaring at the detectives over the tops of her glasses. "We're still waiting on the results of some of her tests."

Alvarez gave a quick nod.

"Hmmm." The nurse started to exit, then took a closer look at Pescoli's baby bump. "You're near term."

"Yes, I am." Pescoli felt her feathers ruffled a bit.

The nurse's thin eyebrows arched knowingly. She looked about to say something more, but caught a warning in Pescoli's eyes and glanced back at the bed. "I'll be at the desk if you need anything," she said to Lara as she pointed to a remote call button attached to the rails of the hospital bed.

Lara smiled weakly. "Thanks."

"So how're you feeling?" Alvarez asked as the nurse exited.

"Pretty rough," she admitted, her lower lip quivering slightly. "My mom is out of town, but she's on her way back from Spokane right now."

"What about your dad?"

Her eyes slid to the side. "They're separated. He's in San Francisco. For a while. But Mom. She'll be here soon." She managed a brave little smile that faltered slightly, and she blinked back tears.

Pescoli felt a pang of empathy for Lara—she was, after all, just a teenager. How duplicitous could she be? Silently berating herself for her own jaded attitude, she said, "Why don't you tell us what happened?"

"It was just like Bianca," Lara said. Then she paused. "Wait a minute. Aren't you homicide cops?" Her blue eyes rounded. "No one died, did they? No one was killed. Right?" She appeared about to panic.

"Nothing like that," Alvarez said. "We just think what happened to you might be considered part of a wider investigation."

"Okay."

Pescoli asked, "Why were you up at Reservoir Point?"

"I lost my phone, earlier. When we were all up there, at the Point, filming, you know? Last night. I had it because I remember texting and then being told that all our phones had to be turned off. So I did. And we did our scenes, if you can call them that, I mean, I'm barely on screen at all and just in a group shot. But a bunch of us were there, around the fake campfire, sitting on logs. I think that's when my phone must've fallen out of my pocket and I didn't notice since I wasn't supposed to use it."

"Then what?" Alvarez asked, when she paused.

"After the filming, we all left and Alex and I went to the Midway Diner. That's when I noticed it was gone. I was freaked, you know? I mean, I can. Not. Live. Not without my phone, so Alex and I, we went up there looking for it."

"In the dark?" Pescoli asked.

"Yeah, everyone was gone. It was weird being up there with all that equipment in the dark, but I had to get it back, so we went through the barricade and started looking. The trouble was that, since it was turned off, we couldn't call it. I'd hoped that I hadn't turned it off, and we would be able to hear it or see it in the dark because it would light up when we called, but nah. That didn't work."

Pescoli took over questioning. "So then . . . after you couldn't find the phone, what happened?"

"We looked all around the campfire area and it

wasn't there. I remembered going up the trail a bit, to watch Bianca's big scene where the Big Foot is chasing her down the mountain, so Alex and I checked there, and that's when . . . that's when . . . we could maybe hear it. I thought it would be okay, because Alex was going to call it and it would light up and ring, so really, the dark works best. Well, kinda."

"But it was turned off."

"Yeah." She nodded, the back of her head sliding against her pillow. "That was the problem."

"So, what happened?"

"Alex started dialing the phone and we didn't hear anything, see anything, for a while. He used his flashlight app, and we looked for it all around where we were during the filming, but we just couldn't find it."

Her eyes were wide, and if she was lying, Pescoli couldn't see it. Still, a serious niggle of doubt crept through her mind. This was all just too damned bizarre.

Lara, then, went on in minute detail about walking through the woods and searching for the phone. They had been about to give up when, using the flashlight app on Alex's phone, they'd found it, right where she'd been standing, out of the camera's sight line by the creek.

"Then Alex took off for a minute to take a leak in the woods."

"Aren't there Porta Potties up there for the filming? For the cast and crew?"

"Yeah, yeah. But he's a guy and it's their thing, I think, to pee outside. The Porta Potties really aren't all that great. So anyway, I'm standing there, waiting, wondering how long it can take him when I get this weird feeling that someone's watching me."

"Alex?" Pescoli asked.

"No, no . . . I knew it wasn't him. He was pissing and—"

Pescoli cut in, "How did you know it wasn't—?"

"I just knew, okay. So I tell myself it's nothing, when I hear something. A kind of rustling in the dry brush and it freaks me out a little because of what's been going on, and I didn't want to run into a cougar or a coyote or whatever, not even a squirrel or a snake . . . so I yell to Alex to hurry up, and this rustling gets louder, kind of a crashing through the trees and then, oh, God, I hear breathing." Lara was gazing out the window now, into her story. "So I started moving, y'know, trying to get away, but I'm a little mixed up in the darkness, I got a little lost. I don't know, but I think I went the wrong way. I was scared and confused. But I started running, because I kept thinking about the bears and maybe wolves and Big Foot . . . and I remember thinking about what happened to Bianca . . . and Destiny . . . and then there was this . . . *growl*. Real low. Real scary. So now I'm running and screaming. Yelling for Alex and then all of a sudden"—she started shaking her head as if denying her own words—"I *saw* it, whatever it was, a big shadowy thing, coming right at me! I screamed and turned, tried to run back the way I came, but I was scared out of my mind, and I got off the trail and there were berry vines and branches scraping at me and at some point I fell, and I put my hand out to catch myself and pulled some muscles in my arm and . . . oh, God, it *came after me.* I couldn't get away. It grabbed me from behind and started choking me and I couldn't breathe, couldn't get away." She was nearly hyperventilating.

"But you did," Pescoli encouraged. "You got away."

"But only because Alex started yelling and it heard him and dropped me. Boom! Right on my ass. Then it took off like a shot, running so fast into the woods and in seconds it disappeared! Just like that. It just vanished!" she said, as if she'd witnessed a magic trick, or more likely, a miracle. Her gaze moved from to Pescoli, then to Alvarez. "It . . . it could have killed me," she whispered, her good hand to her throat, the IV tubing stretching.

"And you're sure this was a monster? A . . . Sasquatch?" Pescoli asked.

"Yes! Yes! I mean . . . I think so. I didn't *see* it, not its face, but it was huge and fast and strong and hairy and smelled and . . ." She shivered, almost on cue. "I've never been so scared in my life." She started sniffling, but Pescoli didn't see any tears forming.

"Could you have mistaken the creature for a big man?" Pescoli said. "Maybe one in some kind of ape suit?"

Lara gasped. "You don't believe me? But . . . you think Bianca saw one?" She glared at Pescoli. Sitting up taller in the bed, she said, "It was there, damn it! Probably that same huge creature that chased Bianca. You're just lucky we're both alive!"

On hurried footsteps the nurse returned, her face a mask of quiet rage. "I think you should go now," she said to the cops. "Ms. Haas needs her rest."

When Pescoli didn't immediately head for the door, the nurse said, "I don't care who you are, Detectives, I want you out. Now." Her chin jutted, daring them to breach her authority, but Pescoli was done. They'd gotten all they needed from Lara Haas, and if nothing else, the splint on her wrist and the bruising surrounding her neck convinced Pescoli there was a certifiable homicidal maniac on the loose.

Man? Beast? Mythical creature?

Ten to one, the killer was human.

CHAPTER 25

As they walked down the hallway of Northern General, Pescoli cast a look over her shoulder to Lara's room. "Her injuries seem minor, so why is she spending the night in the hospital?"

"I asked that before you came," Alvarez said. "She's slightly concussed and they want to watch her. No broken bones, but some minor contusions and abrasions. I think they might have released her earlier, but she's a minor and her parents aren't around. They're probably being cautious. Don't want a lawsuit."

"Is the whole country lawsuit happy?" Pescoli groused as they passed an orderly pushing a rattling cart in the other direction. "Almost every witness we've interviewed has asked about lawyering up. As if they're all in it together."

Alvarez raised an eyebrow. "You think?"

"No, I don't think, but this whole case has taken on a weird, carnival aspect, and that's not good, not when we've got a homicide to solve. Big Foot fever aside, a girl is dead."

The corridor opened to a waiting area with a wide bank of windows and a few scattered chairs and couches arranged around small tables, with a few potted plants.

Pescoli spied Manny Douglas, who had cornered

Alex O'Hara near a potted palm tree. Alex's hands were stuffed into the front pockets of dusty jeans, and he was obviously looking for a way to get out of a conversation with the reporter.

Pescoli's mood went from bad to worse.

". . . you really think it was a Big Foot?" Manny was saying. As usual, he was dressed in khakis and a flannel shirt. "And this was what time again?"

"Excuse us," Pescoli said, directing her gaze at the reporter. "If you don't mind, we'd like to talk to Mr. O'Hara for a few minutes."

Manny pulled a face but didn't argue. Instead, he said, "And, I'd like to talk to the two of you." He had a pocket recorder on a short table, the magazines that had been fanned across its top pushed to one side. Also, he'd been taking notes on a small spiral notebook. He offered the detectives that cat-that-ate-the-canary grin Pescoli detested.

"Not now."

"I just want an update on the Montclaire murder. The victim was pregnant. That's already been reported." He paused, taking in Pescoli's condition. She didn't comment, nor, thankfully, did he. "So, I know you've been taking DNA samples. Do you know who the father of the baby is?"

Almost imperceptibly Alex O'Hara stiffened, his jaw tightening despite the fact that he was struggling to keep his expression neutral.

"Not yet," Pescoli said, "but we're getting closer." She added the last more for Alex's information than the reporter's, to see his reaction, and he seemed to blanch a little beneath his olive skin. "We're comparing DNA of the fetus with some of the suspects."

"Who are—?" Manny asked, pen poised as he stared at Pescoli as if she'd lost her mind. For years, she'd kept him at arm's length, refusing to give him any insight or information on the cases she worked, and now, at last, she was offering up information.

"I can't say," she said, still watching the older O'Hara brother, "but we're narrowing the field. Shouldn't be long now."

Had Alex O'Hara's Adam's apple bobbed a bit? She wondered just how intimately he'd known Destiny Rose. He'd admitted she was an acquaintance—his friend Donny Justison's girlfriend— but he'd acted as if they really hadn't hung out much, or something like that. She'd have to double-check.

"How long before you know?" Manny asked.

"We're still working on it. Look, we're done here, Manny. You know the drill. If you want any more information, you, like the rest of the press, will have to go through the regular channels."

Manny whined, "I've got a deadline."

"Don't we all?" she said, thinking about how the clock was ticking and they weren't getting any closer to solving the murder. "Talk to the PIO."

"The public information officer—the new guy, Drummond? He won't tell me anything."

"Not my problem," she said and had a sudden thought. "Then call the sheriff."

Let Blackwater handle it. Before Douglas could argue further, she said to Alex O'Hara. "We need to talk to you." A glance to the reporter. "Alone."

Manny Douglas held out his hands and backed away, across the expanse of the waiting room, found a chair, sat down, and pretended interest in his cell phone, though Pescoli figured he was trying to overhear the conversation. An elderly couple occupied two other chairs and they, too, had shown interest in the conversation—she, pausing in her knitting; he, not turning a page of the magazine he'd been staring at.

"There's an alcove on the other side of the elevators," Alvarez suggested and led the way to a small area with a couple of chairs and a floor-to-ceiling window that overlooked the parking lot.

"Over here," Pescoli said, indicating a grouping of chairs around a circular coffee table strewn with dog-eared magazines. As they all took a seat, she said, "Tell us how you ended up at Reservoir Point."

"I was helping Lara," he said, obviously nervous, his swagger gone, his confidence shaken. "She lost her phone and thought she left it up there. . . ." He launched into the same story they'd heard from Lara. Point for point, his telling of the events of the night before was consistent with what she'd said, any variation slight enough not to matter. Either he was telling the truth, or they'd worked out and rehearsed their tale well. Had they had enough time? It seemed unlikely.

"You saw the person or thing who attacked her?" Alvarez clarified.

"I just heard it running away. I was yelling and screaming, and it went crashing off through the forest. Like it was scared of me."

Pescoli said, "So you can show us where this all happened? If we took you up there, to Reservoir Point."

Alex met her gaze. Was there a challenge in his eyes? "Sure," he said, and whatever confidence he'd lost earlier had returned.

"Then let's go." Pescoli was already on her feet and heading out the door.

They drove to Reservoir Point in separate vehicles. Pescoli was the first to arrive, with Alex O'Hara in a truck right behind her and Alvarez in her Subaru bringing up the rear. She didn't doubt for a second that Manny Douglas would be on their heels.

When they arrived, she found they weren't alone. Beyond a barricade of cones and temporary fencing, the first members of the production crew were on the scene, already cradling paper cups of coffee, smoking cigarettes, talking and stringing electrical wires.

"This is off limits." A petite, athletic woman who was bristling with authority approached and introduced herself as Melanie Kline. She acted as if she wanted to kick them off the site, until Pescoli introduced herself and Alvarez, then produced their badges.

"Pescoli?" Mel repeated, as she made the connection. "Bianca's mother. The cop." She glanced over at Alvarez, sizing her up. Probably wondering how she could fit a pretty Hispanic woman into the cast. To Pescoli, she said, "What happened?"

"Another girl was attacked up here. Lara Haas."

"What? Attacked? By who? No." She looked stricken as she shook her head. "Is she okay?"

"Will be. She's still in the hospital. We're not certain who was behind it." She shot a look to Alex, silently reminding him to keep his thoughts to himself. No need to stir up the rogue Big Foot theory any more than it already was. Yet.

"For the love of God."

A crow flew overhead, flapping into the branches of a tall pine, cawing loudly. Mel didn't seem to notice. For a second, she was lost in thought. Then, after drawing in a long breath, she said, "Wow. When did this happen?"

"Early this morning."

"Up here?"

"According to her. And Mr. O'Hara here." Mel's gaze finally fell on Alex. She scraped a hand through her hair and bit her lip. "Alex, yes, we've met. You're in the group scenes and Lara, oh my God." She took in a long breath. "She's part of the cast. Jesus, and we were here late."

"It was after production had shut down for the night." Alvarez, too, glanced at Alex, who was nodding his agreement just as a cell phone chirped, and Mel reached deep into the pocket of her cargo pants, removed the phone, glanced at the screen, pushed a button, and dropped it again. Several members of the crew had stopped their work and conversations to drift closer.

"This shouldn't take long," Alvarez said as more vehicles arrived, one with Manny Douglas at the wheel.

"I can't have you messing up our equipment or our sets," Mel said, very serious, once again the woman in charge. "We'll help of course, accommodate you, but this is very expensive equipment and we're on a tight schedule. There's already trouble on another project, and Mr. Sphinx is planning to leave for Oregon again, later this afternoon, maybe tonight."

The show about ghosts in Darby Gulch. Another intellectual masterpiece.

Mel paused. Shook her head. "Another attack. Wow." Then, back in the moment, "We're already setting up for tonight. We're filming again. Try not to disturb anything. Seriously. Barclay—Mr. Sphinx, he won't be happy."

Not my problem, Pescoli thought and didn't believe it anyway. Sphinx seemed like a publicity hound to her and was always looking for some way to get attention and promote his project, so she'd bet he'd turn Lara's misfortune into his own advantage. Hadn't he done just that with Destiny Montclaire's death? "This is public property," she said, stepping in. "And a continuing homicide investigation. We have the authority to be here, as my partner said, and we should be done quickly." To Alex, she added, "Try to avoid the equipment and set—unless the attack occurred there—and show us where the attack happened."

The conversation was over. She was already striding past two guys in watch caps sipping coffee and Mel, who was extracting her mobile phone from her pocket again, no doubt contacting Sphinx.

Fine. Bring it on.

Alex took the lead, striding up the trail where shafts of morning sunlight filtered through the branches overhead to dapple the ground. Alvarez was close behind. Pescoli fought and failed to keep up. She wasn't one of those pregnant women who ran miles, or did yoga or any kind of weight training or aerobics. She'd taken care of herself except for gaining a few extra pounds, but now her lack of exercise regimen and approaching due date were catching up with her. The only good news was that, as she lagged behind, she heard bossy little Mel give Manny Douglas his marching orders off the site. Hearing the reporter smarmily discharged was satisfying, and brought a smile to her face.

Breathing hard, she trekked up part of the dusty trail that curved around the banks of the creek. The water was a small trickle at this point, cutting through the thickets of pine, hemlock, and aspen, sunlight dappling the ripples that twisted into shadow again. It was still early, not quite eight o'clock, and already she thought the day would be a scorcher, the August sun unforgiving.

She felt a twinge deep inside. Cursing the damned Braxton Hicks contractions, she paused to catch her breath and noted that there were hundreds of footprints in the dust of the path. Even the dry weeds and low-lying brush that flanked the trail had been trampled by dozens of boots, sneakers, flip-flops, sandals, whatever. But she didn't see any huge, bare footprints, large enough to cause her to think that a Sasquatch had wandered past.

She moved along and caught up with Alvarez and Alex O'Hara at a spot where the trail was split, each side cutting around an old snag from a tree that had fallen long ago.

"It was about here," he was saying. "I saw her phone, just there." He pointed at a bleached, exposed root from the long-dead stump. "I handed it to her and then, while she was turning it on, I decided to take a piss, but I didn't want to do it in front of her, even in the dark, so I went up the hill, over here. . . ." He hiked up around a copse of pines and disappeared behind it. They followed.

"And?" Pescoli aid.

"Well, then I was kinda, y'know, midstream when I heard her scream."

"What did you do?" Alvarez said, eyeing him through her sunglasses.

"I yelled and finished, y'know. Quick as I could. I mean, I thought, *Oh, shit, what now?* Then I took off down the hill. . . ."

Alvarez wandered around the area behind trunks of the trees, bent down, picked up some dirt and sniffed it as she rubbed it through the tips of her fingers. "Smells like urine."

He looked scandalized. "I told ya."

"Okay, so then what?" she asked, straightening and dusting her hands.

"I found Lara. She was all messed up, and this . . . *thing* . . . was crashing through the forest. I had my phone—we'd used the flashlight app looking for Lara's cell—but I couldn't see him and even though I took a picture, it didn't show." He dug into the back pocket of his jeans and came up with the phone, showing that the last two pictures were the night-dark forest. As Alvarez slipped her sunglasses onto her head and squinted at the phone, Pescoli peered over her shoulder.

Nothing. Just blurry dark images of . . . who knew what?

"So then I called nine-one-one," he said. "She was hurt. I didn't know how bad. The cops and EMTs and even someone from the fire department came. They took her to the hospital in an ambulance, and I followed, to be sure she was okay." When they didn't say anything, he added, "And that was it. I've been at the hospital since then."

They asked a few more questions, got no more information, then searched the hillside for any kinds of clues and came up empty, nothing that either confirmed or denied Alex and Lara's story.

Once they'd returned to the staging area of the set, Pescoli was sweating, her stomach rumbling. Sure enough, Manny Douglas was still hanging out just beyond the periphery of the set, and he wasn't the only reporter who had arrived. A white television news van emblazoned with the red and blue logo for a local station had pulled up on the far side of the barricade. Nearby, positioned in front of a huge boulder, a trim newswoman with layered auburn hair and a smile of perfect white teeth was holding a microphone and speaking to Barclay Sphinx while a cameraman stood to one side recording the interview.

That was fast.

Unshaven, in a turtleneck, jacket, and jeans,

Barclay was saying ". . . such a scare. Yes. I feel fortunate that Miss Haas is all right."

"Is she a member of the *Big Foot Territory: Montana!* cast?" the reporter asked.

"Yes, yes." Barclay was nodding, stroking his soul patch, his eyes thoughtful behind his glasses. "A good little actress."

"What part does she play?"

"In the first episode, she's one of a group of local kids we hired to kind of recreate what happened at the first sighting, but I'm still working through the upcoming scripts, so who knows?" He gave a smile. "I like to use as much local talent as possible."

His assessment of the situation, while echoing what he'd said at the Big Foot Believers meeting, wasn't what was actually happening with the series, at least not according to Bianca. She'd been under the impression that the continuing plot line was going to swirl around feuding families from somewhere north of Missoula. Maybe Bianca had gotten it wrong, which Pescoli didn't believe, or maybe Sphinx had changed his mind again, or even maybe the producer was playing to the audience as these local reporters could stir up some buzz about the series, start the ball rolling, get some statewide, regional, even national coverage.

Time would tell, of course, but time was something she didn't have much of. Her cell phone jangled. She checked the screen. Sage Zoller. "Pescoli," she answered, still watching the producer work his audience.

"Thought you'd want to know. Nine-one-one got a call about a break in a guardrail. A road deputy went out to check and reported that it's broken, right on a curve of the road leading to Horsebrier Ridge, almost at the summit."

Oh, no. Pescoli's heart was ice.

"The deputy looked over the edge and thought he saw a car buried in the brush about a hundred feet down or so. We got an emergency crew out there, EMTs, firefighters, and a couple rappelled down the cliff. Turns out to be a Ford Focus, registered to Lindsay Cronin."

"Anyone inside?" she asked, dreading the answer.

"Yeah. One. Dead. Female. ID says it's her. Lindsay Cronin."

Pescoli fought the urge to throw up right here, at Reservoir Point, with a television camera rolling. "Let's go," she said to Alvarez, then to Alex. "I'll need a sample of your DNA ASAP, and I'll want one from your brother."

"What? We didn't do anything!"

She gave him a look that said she didn't believe him. "I'm going to get one from everyone who knew Destiny Montclaire, any boy she even said hello to. Tell your brother and get down to the station."

"I'm not gonna do it."

Pescoli turned on him. She was tired of all the arguments, the hiding behind lawyers, the petulance of it all. Now two girls were dead. Who knew how many more? Her stomach roiled and anger sped through her veins. "Then I'll go through the system. But that looks pretty bad that you're refusing, so think it over. You've got about twenty minutes. Then, if I haven't heard that you've voluntarily given up a sample, I'll get a court order and if you don't comply I'll throw your ass in jail and I'll force the issue. Got it?"

"Jesus, all I've done is try to help," he complained.

"Then you can help a little more." She flashed a cold-as-ice smile. "Just do it, Alex." And then she and Alvarez were striding back to the car. Thoughts of Lindsay Cronin crowded Pescoli's brain. An accident? In the middle of the night? After talking to Kywin Bell?

She remembered Lindsay as a preschooler, a shy little girl, but curious. Intelligent . . . and again, like with Lara Haas, that was a long while ago for Pescoli, who recalled Lindsay through her preschool days, and then later, when she and Bianca were in the primary grades of elementary school and on sports teams together—that was, until Bianca turned her attention away from anything remotely athletic.

And now Lindsay was dead.

She felt a numbness deep inside, a dark pain for the loss of such a young life, a girl on the brink of becoming a woman, who was not so unlike her own daughter. Maybe it was Pescoli's pregnancy, hormones going crazy so near the birth, or perhaps she was growing soft as she aged, or more probably because Lindsay's death, like Destiny's before her, hit so close to home.

Pescoli felt sucker-punched. For the love of God, maybe everyone around her was right; maybe she should turn in her damned badge and give up investigating homicides, when one human takes the life of another.

"What's going on?" Alvarez asked, snapping Pescoli back to the here and now. "Who called?"

"Zoller." She was at the Jeep and was in control again, pushing aside her emotions, trying to think rationally, like a cop. "Looks like we found Lindsay Cronin, in her car, at the bottom of Horsebrier Canyon."

"Oh, God." Alvarez expelled a heavy breath. Seeing Pescoli trying to lever herself behind the wheel, she ordered, "Come with me. I'll drive. Let's get on this." And with that, she headed to her Subaru.

CHAPTER 26

"I didn't do nothin'!" Kywin Bell said for about the fourth time since he'd been sitting across the table in the interview room. Sullen, with dark circles under his eyes, he slouched on the small of his back, long legs extended, muscular arms crossed over his chest, stretching his T-shirt. "I don't know why you hauled me down here."

Alvarez was having none of it.

"We found Lindsay Cronin's phone. She texted you to meet her up at Horsebrier Ridge." She shoved a piece of paper across the small table, which showed the conversation.

He skimmed down the messages. "This isn't me." He looked absolutely confused.

"It says it is. The number is yours. I double-checked."

"But I never got it." His mouth dropped open and he read over each text on the three pages. "All this is what she sent me, but I swear to God, I never seen this last one before." Frustrated, he shoved both hands through his hair. "I showed you my goddamned phone. And, *no*, I didn't delete any, okay? I never got the fuckin' message." He was furious, his jaw working. "I gave you a damned DNA sample. I don't know what you want from me. I didn't kill Destiny, and I don't know nothin' about Lindsay."

"Your phone works, but the two girls who died, who texted you on the night they each died, those messages didn't get through?" she demanded.

"Jesus! I never saw this before! Never. I swear to God. And the same with the one from Destiny."

He was lying. She could see in it his eyes, smell it in the sweat off his skin. He had a secret and was holding it close, yet he appeared shocked that the police had found the texts, that, perhaps, they'd ever existed.

"Then why was she texting you?"

"We were friends. That was it." His face clouded and he said, "You're setting me up, aren't ya? You goddamned cops are setting me up. You're harassing me, and trying to find someone to blame. You probably doctored the phones! This is a trick, right?" His eyes narrowed as if he'd latched on to the truth. "My old man told me how to handle you. He says you probably did something electronically to the phone, messed it up with that text from Destiny, that you've got somethin' out for my family. For him. So, I want a lawyer, okay? You get me one. I'm not sayin' nothing else."

"You're sure that's what you want to do?"

"Yep. So, unless you're going to hold me, or get the lawyer, I'm outta here." And with that, he walked, more like swaggered, out of the room.

Alvarez gritted her teeth. She didn't like him, but he was right and she hated to admit it. They didn't have enough to hold him, and there was something about his demeanor that she believed. He seemed so totally baffled by it all. And he had given up his DNA, as had his brother and a couple of other boys. Austin Reece, because of Lawyer-Daddy—who just happened to be dating the mayor, it seemed—refused to have his son give up a sample without a court order.

God, Bernard Reece was a sanctimonious bastard.

She left the room a little defeated, a little angry.

She'd hoped to shake a little more information out of Kywin Bell by bringing him down to the small, windowless room with the two-way observation mirror. He'd known he was being observed, had seen the cameras, and had never once slid away from his story that he was innocent, that he'd never gotten a text from Lindsay on the night she'd gone missing, and he'd actually seemed a bit emotional at the knowledge she was dead.

As Alvarez made her way to her office, avoiding a couple of uniformed deputies walking the opposite direction, she was oblivious to the sounds of the office, the murmur of conversation punctuated with laughter, the continual ring of desk phones or personalized ring tones of cell phones, the constant tread of footsteps, or clunk of printers and fax machines, the rattle of coffee cups and constant hum of the air-conditioning system. All were lost to her as she thought about the case.

Kywin had seemed genuinely startled when she'd given him the news about Lindsay Cronin. "No way!" he'd said, shaking his head, the edges of his mouth pulled into a frown as she'd sat him in the plastic chair he'd occupied during the interview. "You're just tryin' to mess with me." Unfortunately, that hadn't been true. She'd been on the ridge when the body had been removed from the wreckage. The little car had been mangled, crumpled metal and plastic as the Focus had apparently nose-dived over the railing.

Firemen had scaled the cliff with ropes, then, once in the chasm, had worked to get to the driver, who, pinned in her seat, was hanging upside down, seat belt still in place, her body as broken and twisted as the car.

Alvarez had looked into the body bag and felt her insides go cold. Questions that had haunted her about the victim for the past few days now pounded through her brain:

Why had she left in the middle of the night?

Where had she been going?

It appeared she'd thought she was meeting Kywin, but where?

What had happened?

Was the crash really the result of a single car accident?

What had made her lose control of the car?

Had she swerved to miss an oncoming vehicle? Or an animal?

Had she been forced off the road?

Had anyone been in the car at any time during her drive?

Did anyone else know where she was going?

And on and on. It all seemed so useless.

She'd driven Pescoli back to the reservoir to pick up her car. It was nearly noon, and the place was a beehive of activity. The crew was setting up for the coming night's shoot, and the word about another attack by Big Foot had been circulated to the press. There were two news vans, one from Missoula, another from Spokane.

"Looks like Grizzly Falls could be trending," Pescoli had observed, then said, "Oh, for the love of God, Lucky's here. What the hell?" She let out a long, slow breath as she eyed her ex, who was sipping water from a bottle and chatting up some of the grips. "He's just so into this thing, like because Bianca is involved in the whole reality thing, and now Michelle, too, he's somehow stumbled on a pot of gold."

"She's here, too," Alvarez said, spying Luke's current wife approaching him. "Uh-oh."

"What?" Pescoli's eyebrows drew together as Michelle, in shorts, a tight T-shirt, and strappy, high-heeled sandals, strode to Luke and said something sharply to him. His lips thinned and he snapped back.

Alvarez couldn't hear the words being tossed at each of them, but they were both angry, and pointedly so. Michelle had jabbed her finger at Luke's chest. He caught her wrist, pulled her around the trailer that had been parked on the property, and disappeared from sight.

"Trouble in paradise?" Pescoli shook her head. "Maybe that pot of gold isn't so gilded after all. They've been married for years, and I've never once seen them get into it, which says a lot about Michelle. Luke and I? We fought like cats and dogs from the get-go. Huh." She glanced at her watch. "I've got to go. I'll meet you back at the station."

A reporter had recognized her as she stepped out of Alvarez's Subaru. "Detective Pescoli? Can I have a word? Your daughter, she's in the show, right? And she was rumored to have been attacked by a Big Foot."

Alvarez saw her partner's back stiffen as she said a few quick words to the bird-like blonde and nearly dove into her Jeep this time. Hitting the gas, she reversed to a wide spot in the road and quickly turned around, leaving the reporter to watch the dust pluming behind her. Before she was seen, Alvarez took off as well. She didn't have the personal connection for an intriguing story about the filming that her partner did, but she was a detective investigating the case, still trying to connect the dots between the two girls' deaths, and she'd been in a rush to interview Kywin Bell, the most likely of suspects, anyway.

Though Kywin had shut her down, there was still a long list of others who knew more than they were saying.

"My advice," Dr. Peeples said as Regan sat on the end of the examination table in the clinic, "is that you consider starting your maternity leave soon. You're partially effaced, about thirty percent, and that baby's coming." Ramona Peeples, a slender African-American woman, had been Regan's OB-GYN for the past ten years. Her offices were attached to Northern General Hospital and now, standing in a white lab coat worn over slacks and a magenta blouse, she was staring hard at her patient.

"I know," Pescoli agreed, anxious to get out of the small examination room. Pictures of babies hung on the beige walls, and other than the padded table on which she was now seated, there was only a rolling cart and cupboards, a counter with a glistening sink.

"Before you start coming up with excuses, all very valid, I'm certain, think about your health and the baby's," Peeples advised. "I know all about the cases you're investigating, so I understand that your job is very high stress. Hence the elevation in your blood pressure."

"Slight elevation," Pescoli said, "Your own words, '*slight* elevation.' "

"But worth noting. Especially given your age."

"My age? Geez, it's not like I'm ancient. I'm not even forty."

"But soon," the doctor said, eyeing her chart. "In less than a year. And watch your salt intake." She held a clipboard over her chest. "It's just a little while longer, and I don't like to take any chances."

"Okay, me neither."

The doctor gave her a small smile. "Consider hanging up your holster, Detective, just for a little while. Some of the world's problems might wait, even if you're not on the job. I'll see you next week."

With that, she was out the door and Pescoli reached for her clothes. The world's problems might wait, but she wasn't so certain about her investigations, here in Grizzly Falls. And she was tired of people acting like she had one foot in the grave just because she was pregnant. With all the tests she'd gone through due to her age making her condition a "high risk" pregnancy, she'd been told that the baby was healthy, was gaining weight, and should be here right on time.

"Don't rush things," she said, touching her protruding belly, "but your father and I can't wait to meet you." She smiled, then added, "I really can't say the same for your brother and sister, though, but I'm betting they'll come around." She caught sight of herself in the mirror, a hugely pregnant person talking to herself. That probably wasn't so strange, but not exactly the image she wanted to portray as she ignored everyone's advice that she start taking her maternity leave. "We'd better keep these little chats to ourselves," she advised her unborn child as she began to dress. "Otherwise people might think I'm nuts and you'll end up being born in an asylum. Not the way you want to come into the world."

Dressed, she headed into the hallway, where she spied other pregnant women being helped by people in the clinic. Every woman with a baby bump seemed to be at least ten years younger than she, some more like twenty, though she reasoned she was just being super sensitive after getting the word from her doctor. But she was fine. That's all that mattered.

Outside, she slipped on a pair of sunglasses. The blasting sun was heating the asphalt of the parking lot that stretched from the clinics to the doors of Northern General, where, in a few weeks, she'd deliver the baby. On her way to her Jeep, Pescoli noticed a news van taking up two spaces near the main doors. The same reporter whom she'd seen earlier at Reservoir Point was interviewing Barclay Sphinx, who was standing front and center, his back to the building, a handful of onlookers gathered under the overhang of the main doors, watching.

What the hell is that all about?

The crowd parted a little as Lara Haas, seated in a wheelchair, was pushed outside by an orderly. Sphinx motioned to a small woman, who produced a huge bouquet of flowers and balloons, which she gave to him and he, in turn, bestowed upon Lara. She was still wearing the splint, but managed to gather up the posies and, squinting a little, her smile as bright as the damned Montana sun, spoke both to the producer and the reporter. No longer was she without makeup. In the intervening hours since this morning, when Pescoli and Alvarez had interviewed her, Lara Haas had found her blush, lip gloss, mascara, and foundation, at the very least. And she'd worked on her hair, which, shining and shimmering with blond streaks, curled softly around her neck and shoulders. Gone was the hospital gown, replaced by white shorts and a pink T-shirt with a deep V neckline that offered a view of her cleavage. It also showed off the ring of bruises at her neck.

The whole scene smacked of being staged, and that little niggle of suspicion she'd felt earlier in Lara's hospital room grew. Something about Lara's encounter with Big Foot and her injuries was way off.

The doors opened again, and this time Lara's parents, Arletta and Nelson, headed outside, each carrying some of Lara's belongings or other vases of flowers. If ever there were a mother/daughter resemblance, it was visited on the Haas women. Both were blond, buxom, and beautiful, though Lara, possibly because of Nelson's genes, was a few inches taller than her tiny mother. In pressed chinos and a white dress shirt unbuttoned at the neck, Nelson was built like a runner, lanky and slim, thinning reddish hair brushed to disguise a growing bald spot.

Hadn't Lara said her parents had split?

Now, perhaps brought together by their daughter's trauma, they seemed friendly enough, surely more than cordial, as they tended to Lara, talked to the reporter and Sphinx. Then, after about five minutes, all left together in the same sporty white Mercedes.

"Show's over," she said as she unlocked her Jeep and levered herself into the warm interior. "Highlights at eleven."

She headed into the office, where she found, on her desk, a new ceramic mug decorated with a huge brown footprint and the words: BIG FOOT DAZE, GRIZZLY FALLS, MONTANA.

"Oh, for God's sake." She set her things onto her chair. The effervescent tempo of Joelle's high heels clicked toward her door, and the secretary popped her head into the office. She was dressed in beige and brown, and sure enough, her earrings actually were dangling footprints.

"Don't tell me," Pescoli said.

But she did. "We're already starting the celebration for Big Foot Daze. Mayor Justison wanted every public employee to have a cup to display on their desks, to promote the upcoming celebration."

Pescoli hoisted the mug as if it were a beer stein. "We can't get another detective on staff or an improved heating system, but this is in the budget?"

She looked afraid that Pescoli might actually hurl it. "Publicity, you know. Now, detective, I've talked to some of the other officers and staff members, and we'd all like to do a little something for the new baby."

Pescoli was suddenly tired. "I know. I appreciate it. But I don't need, nor do I want a shower."

"I got that message. Loud and clear." Her lips pinched a little, and Pescoli saw that she'd not only disappointed the woman, but hurt her. Oh, geez. "So"—she cleared her throat—"we all got together and . . . well, here." She handed Pescoli a card from the pocket of her dress. Pescoli took it and opened the envelope. There was a cute little card inside with a rocking horse on the front, signed by everyone in the department, and a gift certificate to a baby store in Missoula. Touched, she found it hard to come up with the right thing to say. "Thank you, Joelle. You know, I don't mean to be such a bitch about the shower, but it's just . . . just not my thing." Impossible to explain to a woman who lived in perpetual party mode.

Joelle brightened. "Well, don't be surprised if you're inundated with food once that little person arrives. I'm organizing a meal chain."

"A what?"

"Kind of like a prayer chain in church, you'll see. Everyone brings something on a different day, gets a look at the baby, should be interesting. I wonder what Deputy Watershed will be bringing." She looked thoughtful. "He likes to hunt, you know. Brags about eating all kinds of wildlife. I'll contain him. No eel or beaver or bear or God-knows-what." She gave a mock shudder. "I might put him on for a bottle of wine, but oh, then he'd bring some of that homemade stuff that he makes himself. Have you ever heard of dandelion wine? It's like his and Frank Nesmith's favorite, I swear. Well, don't you worry, I'm handling it!"

"Really, Joelle, I don't think you'll need to—"

But she found herself talking to dead air as Joelle had slipped back into the hallway and clipped away, the click of her heels fading as she headed toward the front office of the station.

Pescoli had just checked her email and made a couple of calls when Alvarez appeared, phone in hand. "Take a look at this," she said, and handed Pescoli her phone, which was connected to the website for a local TV station. Along the bottom of the small screen, a running news ticker read: BREAKING NEWS: BIG FOOT SIGHTING. CREATURE THAT APPEARS TO BE A SASQUATCH SHOWN ON DRONE FOOTAGE NEAR GRIZZLY FALLS, MONTANA.

"Drone footage?" Pescoli asked as she watched what appeared to be a large ape-like creature hurrying into the undergrowth.

"Apparently several members of the Big Foot Believers own drones. This film was taken by Carlton Jeffe, and it's very high-tech, of course."

"Of course." She stared at the screen. The drone, flying high over the forest, moved downward, circling the area trying to catch a better view, but the creature, for the most part, was in shadow or hidden completely by a canopy of branches, only appearing where the foliage was less dense. Yes, the animal, standing on two legs, walking quickly, seemed large, but Pescoli's perspective was off. A Big Foot? Nah.

Alvarez said, "Jeffe does have a permit to own a drone. I checked."

She watched the replay again. "Where was this taken? And when?"

"Today, a few hours ago, and it's in a canyon only about half a mile to Reservoir Point, as the drone flies."

"Or the Big Foot lumbers," Pescoli said dryly. "It's a guy in an ape suit. A big guy. Has to be."

She pointed to the screen. "So, how does this have anything to do with Lindsay Cronin's car crash? Or is it unrelated?" She didn't believe it. Two friends who died in separate incidents? The first, certainly the victim of homicide, the second, one of the last people who was contacted by Destiny Rose Montclaire before her death, in a single car crash.

And Kywin Bell had been close to both girls.

"I got a preliminary autopsy report on Lindsay Cronin. Looks like she died in the crash. Ribs punctured a lung, head trauma, broken bones. Even though she was wearing a seat belt, the car was crushed, just crumpled in on her."

"Don't tell me she was pregnant."

"No."

"Anyone told her parents yet?"

"Two deputies gave the Cronins the news. They're destroyed, of course, the older brother quiet, kind of keeping it all in. Roy, her father, called me and came in and ID'd the body."

"Not the mother?"

"Darlie declined."

"I don't blame her. That would be rough. Beyond rough." As she sat at her desk, nearly ready to give birth to her third child, a cute little card propped up near her computer, anticipation growing to welcome a new family member, she felt a bit humbled that she had this embarrassment of riches when the Cronins had just lost their only daughter.

CHAPTER 27

The three detectives hashed it out in a back room often used for meetings or, if they needed one, a task force. The windows were mounted high, just enough to let in the late afternoon light, two whiteboards were pressed against one wall, and there were several laptop computers on the large table at which Pescoli and Alvarez sat, listening to Detective Sage Zoller, as she went over the information in the Montclaire case. As she talked, information appeared on their screens.

"So, here's what we know," she said. "There are rumors that Destiny had several boyfriends and used one against the other. But, Donald Justison Junior is not the father of her child."

"That doesn't rule him out as a suspect," Alvarez said. "In fact, that might have been his motive to kill her, that she cheated on him."

"Who is the father?" Pescoli asked. The room was hot and stuffy; the air conditioner, which kept some parts of the building as cold as ice, was unable to filter any of that cool air here. An oscillating fan standing in a corner did little more than move the hot air around, ruffling papers on the table.

"Unknown. We've ruled out Bryant Tophman, Rod Devlin, Emmett Tufts, and TJ O'Hara as the baby daddy," Sage admitted. "None of them are a match."

"Again, it doesn't mean they weren't involved," Pescoli argued.

Zoller nodded. "So far, Austin Reece has refused to give a sample and his father is blocking it every way."

Alvarez growled, "I'm getting a court order. That kid is going to get swabbed."

"Good," Pescoli said, shifting in the chair. Sitting for long periods of time was difficult, and she'd been up for what seemed like years.

Zoller continued, "Alex O'Hara and the Bell brothers' samples are being processed, should be back from the lab tonight or early tomorrow morning."

Pescoli grunted. "What else?"

"The lab has no other physical evidence other than the bit of latex under the victim's nails. It's assumed she was fighting her attacker off as he strangled her and she managed to pierce the latex."

"No easy feat," Alvarez observed. "That stuff is made so that it won't rupture. That's the whole idea."

Pescoli fanned herself with her file folder. "So we got lucky."

Zoller didn't look convinced. "We already know those gloves can be found everywhere, from hospitals to labs, to your local construction sites.

Anyone could pick up a pack. . . . We're checking recent orders from various outlets, but that'll take some time."

"What about alibis?" Pescoli said.

"As for the statements of the people interviewed, they're all over the map, as you can see," Sage said. "Most of them have alibis, but some are each other's."

Alvarez was sliding through the statements, all of which were highlighted. "So the Bell brothers were with each other."

Sage nodded. "And other kids in and out of their group, too. No one's admitting to meeting up with Destiny."

"Except for Donny Justison," Alvarez said.

"Yeah, and he's lying about it. First, Veronica Palmero gives him an alibi he didn't use, and then he says that he didn't meet Destiny in the woods. That she came by his house. Either way, he's a liar."

They'd already thought that she might have been killed somewhere else and brought to the creek, but had no proof. Nothing was coming together.

"Do we have statements for any of her other acquaintances, people who knew her and weren't at the party on the night she was found?" Pescoli asked Sage.

"Yep. Cousins, old boyfriends, her family. Everyone is accounted for. And as far as we can tell, she didn't have any kind of secret life. No one would profit from her death. She had no money and there wasn't an insurance policy on her."

"So the last person, aside from the killer, to see Destiny Montclaire alive was Donny Justison," Alvarez said.

Pescoli added, "Unless he is the killer."

"Uh-huh." Alvarez rubbed the back of her neck. "And the people she texted that night were Lindsay Cronin and Kywin Bell."

"That's right," Zoller said. "Now Lindsay Cronin's dead and Kywin claims he never got the text."

Pescoli said, "Just like he never got the text from Lindsay Cronin. Someone's lying."

"No. Not just someone. The whole lot of them," Alvarez said shortly. "If you scroll through these statements, they're like Swiss cheese, filled with holes. But yeah, Kywin's definitely hiding something. I know he's lying, I can feel it, but his reaction to the missing texts seemed genuine. He insists he's never seen them before."

"An act," Pescoli said. "Just like his old man." She leaned back in the chair, trying to get comfortable. It was impossible.

"There's an interesting thing, though," Sage said. "It might be nothing, but I went over the phone and text records of Kywin Bell. Nothing." She brought the phone records up on screen. "But when you compare them to his brother's? Kip's. Take a look." She split the screen and both records came up. "If you notice, Destiny called Kip as well. They knew each other, obviously, but more than that, she seemed to pocket-dial him a lot. Those are the short conversations, or non-conversations, that only lasted a second or two."

Pescoli leaned closer to the screen.

"I tend to pocket-dial the same couple of people," Zoller went on. "It happens. But what's noteworthy is that on the dates of the missing texts, take a look, there's a quick call to Kip that didn't last for even two seconds. They didn't connect, so I thought originally that she'd hit the wrong number by accident, or pocket-dialed him . . . but what if she didn't?"

"You mean it was what? A signal?" Pescoli felt a sizzle of excitement.

"So that he would get a message on his brother's phone?" Alvarez was thinking aloud, her thoughts in sync with Pescoli's.

Zoller said, "She pocket-dialed him a lot, so I didn't think anything of it at first. But maybe those times when he didn't pick up were some-how a signal back so then she didn't text Kywin."

"Why?" Pescoli asked.

Alvarez posed, "Because she was seeing Kip on the side and was supposed to be dating Kywin?"

"No one says Kywin was involved with her,"

Pescoli pointed out. "Destiny Rose Montclaire, yes. But Lindsay?"

"Let's ask him," Alvarez said.

They tossed the idea around some more. Then Pescoli stood and stretched for a second. "Sorry," she said. "I can only sit in one position so long." She settled into her chair again and asked Zoller, "What do we know about Lindsay Cronin's accident?"

"The accident reconstruction crew spent hours at Horsebrier Ridge. They think she swerved, as if to avoid something, or as if something was in the car and forced her to turn sharply. She lost control and went through the guardrail. There was no indication that she was actually run off the road, but that's still a possibility. It seems unlikely at her age that she would have had a heart attack or anything debilitating. She didn't have any medical history of anything like seizures."

"But she could have dropped her cell phone and reached for it. Something like that," Alvarez said. "Or a malfunction of the vehicle."

"It's possible," Zoller agreed. "Once they get the car out of the canyon and go over the mechanics."

Pescoli grumbled, "So we really don't know anything more except it's a helluva coincidence." The baby kicked and she shifted in her chair again.

"Not really, but on a side note, I found some pictures of the missing Big Foot costume." The picture came up on the screen. "It's not been located, but here's what it looks like." Sure enough, an image of a man in a shaggy ape suit appeared. "It's the same color as the one in Carlton Jeffe's film, unfortunately." Zoller seemed a little disturbed. "I was hoping there would be differences, so that there would be less doubt that the creature is real."

"You think Jeffe and the Big Foot Believers created this film, that it's a hoax?" Alvarez asked.

"Oh, no. I don't think Carlton would be involved in that. He's sincere. But there are others . . ." She lifted a hand from her computer mouse and waggled it back and forth. "I'm not so sure."

"You got names?" Pescoli asked.

"All of the kids you suspect in the murders could have taken the suit. For the Bell brothers, Alex O'Hara, Donny Justison, Bryant Tophman, and the rest of them, including Marjory Tuft's stepsons, it's all just a fun time for them to get together and go out in the woods and hunt a Sasquatch. They hang out with Ivor Hicks and Fred Nesmith—nutcases—and secretly laugh at them and play the whole game. Any one of them could have taken the costume. Or not . . ." She clicked another button on her computer and said, "I checked with costume stores as far away as Spokane and Boise, even Salt Lake. None rented any Sasquatch costumes in the last couple of months, but now, with the upcoming reality show, there's more interest."

"Great," Pescoli said.

"This next page," Zoller continued, "is a list of all the materials used to make the missing costume. All man-made. Any fibers located at any of the scenes will be compared."

"Good." Pescoli squirmed in her chair again. "This is progress," she said, but they still had no answers.

They talked some more, got no further, decided to take a break. Pescoli's back was beginning to ache, and she'd had several texts from Bianca asking about when she was coming home. Bianca was at the house by herself as Santana and Jeremy were also working late, rounding up a couple of steers that had gotten out of a hole in the fence line at the Long ranch.

On my way, she typed and headed out, first calling in a to-go order at Wild Wills, then driving to the lower section of town, where, already, banners announcing Big Foot Daze had been strung across Main Street near the court-house. It was amazing how quickly the town had adopted the holiday and gotten it together. All propelled by Mayor Justison, who, it seemed, when she was so inclined, could move mountains, and find a Sasquatch or two in the process.

She parked in a no-parking zone as the lot and

streets were full. If she actually got a ticket, she'd deal with it, and she wouldn't be inside long enough to get her Jeep towed.

Heading into the restaurant, she passed Grizz, who, it appeared, had also gotten into the spirit of Big Foot Daze as he'd given up his bikini to don an ape mask, just as if he were pretending to be Sasquatch. In her current mood, Pescoli actually missed the swim attire.

The whole town had gone nuts, she thought, embracing the newfound holiday celebration and the damned reality show somehow while conveniently pushing the tragedies of the two girls' deaths to the background. The doors to the restaurant opened, and Terri Tufts, Wilda Wyze, and Billie O'Hara walked in. They started for the bar when Wilda caught sight of Pescoli.

"Just a minute," she said to her friends. Then she turned to loom over Pescoli. She wasn't a short woman, but Wilda, the ex-bodybuilder, currently in black skinny jeans and a bat-wing T-shirt, had to be over six feet. With a hawkish nose, and eyes glinting with suppressed fury, she reminded Pescoli of a huge crow. "I heard you and your partner have been harassing my sons."

"Just asking questions."

"I know about you cops. It's because of their damned father." As she mentioned Franklin Bell, her entire face puckered, as if she'd just sucked on a lemon. "But they're not like that worthless piece of crap. And they look out for each other. Have each other's back. They're good boys."

How many times had she heard that phrase during this investigation? Every parent wanting to impress upon her that their kids were "good."

"They knew the victim," she said. "Both of your sons. Two girls are dead and each of them contacted Kywin."

"Along with others."

"Who live with an ex-con."

"My boys are practically adults." Again, the tight-lipped expression. "I'd have them live with me, but I've got Greg and the girls—" She caught herself making excuses and said, "You can't blame my sons for their father's sins. I know that you busted Franklin a couple of times and that you hate him, well, fine. That's . . . that's your job, and the son of a bitch deserved it."

"You pressed charges," Pescoli reminded her.

"And I would again! He beat the crap out of me, wanted to kill me. I said he deserved it, didn't I? He should be locked up for life!" Her color had risen. She was really working herself up, and Pescoli thought, with her size and musculature, she could still probably give her ex a run for his money when they got into it. "But Kip and Kywin, they're not Frank."

"Hey!" Billie O'Hara touched her friend on the arm. "Let it go. She's been at my boys, too. Regan's just doing her job."

428

Wilda sent a withering glance at her shorter friend. "But she's zeroed in on mine."

"Don't think that's true," Billie argued, gold hoop earrings catching the light as she shook her head. "I just don't get why you aren't all over Donny Justison. He was the boyfriend, right? And she broke up with him, I heard. He's got a temper, that one."

"But he's the mayor's son." Terri Tufts joined the party. Added her two cents. "And she's involved with Bernard Reece, so Donny, like Austin, has got a built-in attorney."

"We're looking at everyone," Pescoli said.

"Well, just look at everyone equally," Wilda advised, agitated. "My kids are innocent!"

Wilda seemed particularly upset, and Pescoli wondered if she knew something she wasn't telling, too. She decided to press her. "Kip and Kywin know something, Wilda. I intend to find out what it is, and if they're involved in the death of Destiny Rose Montclaire or Lindsay Cronin, I'm going to nail them."

Her lips tightened. "I'm warning you. Back off, Regan. They each proved they weren't the father of that girl's baby, so leave them the hell alone."

"I'm going where this investigation takes me, and if it takes me to Kip and Kywin, and I find out they're complicit—"

"Did you hear me? You're barking up the wrong damned tree. My sons are innocent!"

"Maybe if they stopped hiding things, we'd get to the truth."

"You miserable—"

"Hey—" Billie cut Wilda off. "Let's go into the bar. Get a drink. Forget this."

Pescoli said, "Good idea. You don't want to get in the way of a homicide investigation." She was looking pointedly at the Bell brothers' mother, and Wilda got the message.

"You've always been a bitch, Pescoli."

Pescoli's ire rose. "But a convenient bitch, right? When you needed me? When Frank was beating the living crap out of you in front of your boys?"

Wilda threw off Billie's grip and hurled herself at Pescoli, grabbing her by her neck.

Despite her bulk, Pescoli moved quickly, took hold of the woman's right wrist, and turned it back on itself.

Wilda shrieked and, with her free hand, slashed at Pescoli's cheek, raking her nails across the skin, drawing blood.

Pescoli pushed a little harder on the arm and Wilda's knees buckled as she fell against Grizz, her cheek pressed into his hairy belly, the heavy bear rocking unsteadily.

Pescoli didn't let go.

"Stop!" Wilda cried. "Stop! Stop!"

"Hey!" a sharp voice yelled.

From the corner of her eye, Pescoli saw Sandy,

the owner, carrying two large bags as she and the hostess raced into the entryway.

"What the hell's going on here!" Sandy demanded, dropping the bags. "For the love of God, Detective!"

Wilda whimpered and Pescoli yanked on her arm a little harder, tweaking those ripped muscles. "You don't really want to attack a police officer," she advised into the other woman's ear. "Especially a pregnant one whose hormones are way out of sync."

The big woman howled in pain.

"Stop it!" Billie cried.

"That's right. Enough!" Sandy said, and Pescoli, breathing hard, released her grip and took a step back, allowing Wilda to climb unsteadily to her feet.

"You're crazy!" Wilda cried, rubbing her arm and glaring at Pescoli. "Fucking Looney Toons. I'll have you up on charges."

"Good thinking," Pescoli snapped. "Use that excuse after you attack a *pregnant* police officer."

"You're a freak, Pescoli!" Wilda yelled. "Frank said you were and . . . and for once that SOB was right!" She looked as if she wanted to spit on her, and Pescoli glared at her, silently saying, *Go ahead and try.*

"Enough," Billie declared. "Come on, Wilda. I'll buy you that drink. A double margarita."

Terri, who'd been silent and staring at the fight in horror, cleared her throat. "It's still happy hour, right, Sandy?"

"Sure, sure," the owner said, obviously just glad the fight was over.

Terri glanced down at Pescoli's pregnancy bump. "You're due soon. Real soon. Shouldn't you be on maternity leave?"

Man, she was tired of hearing that, but before she could respond, Terri added, "Seems to be a lot of that going around."

"What?" she asked.

"Pregnancy." And for just a second, Pescoli thought she saw a glimmer of satisfaction in the twist of Terri's lips—the smug look of someone who knows something—a secret. Make that a malicious secret.

"And why would that be a big deal?"

"I guess it's not," Terri said. "Usually. Unless your husband is shooting blanks."

"What? Pregnancy?" Pescoli asked, pulling back on her temper with an effort. There was a little glimmer of satisfaction in the twist of Terri's lips. "Who?"

"Someone whose husband is shooting blanks." She laughed then, a wicked little chuckle echoed by her friends. "Forget it," Terri said over her shoulder as they headed into the bar, but Wilda waited till her friends were out of earshot to add tautly, "I'm serious, Regan, you leave my boys

432

out of this mess." Then she followed after them through the open doorway to the bar.

Watching them go, Sandy said, "What the hell was that all about?"

Sandy picked up the dropped bags while, from behind a fringe of long bangs, she watched Pescoli nervously, as if she thought, as Wilda Wyze had charged, the detective was unstable.

"A misunderstanding," Pescoli said, accepting the takeout bags that Sandy offered. "Wilda doesn't seem to think I'm fit to do my job."

"And you just proved her point," Sandy said. "You nearly knocked down Grizz in the process."

"It would serve him right," Pescoli said. "What's with the Big Foot getup?"

"He's just getting into the spirit of the upcoming holiday."

"Please." She snorted.

"You're not into Big Foot Daze?" Sandy asked. "You know, it's going to be good for business. Rod Larimer came by and he's rented out the Bull and Bear for the next six weeks. The inn's booked solid. And I've got reservations coming in like crazy."

"So Mayor Justison and Barclay Sphinx and the Big Foot Believers are right. Sasquatch is good for the town."

"You got it," Sandy said as the phone rang and she grabbed it. Two couples were coming into the foyer and they oohed and aahed over the stuffed grizzly bear in his Sasquatch attire.

"Isn't that cute?" one of the women said, and Pescoli couldn't stand it another second. She thought she might actually be sick if one more person tried to tell her how great Big Foot was for the town. She headed outside and found her Jeep where she'd left it, no ticket in sight.

She climbed inside and glanced down the street. She noticed, along with the banners announcing the upcoming event, several carved wooden statues of Big Foot, both male and female, on display. How had that happened? Had the merchants found the statues tucked away in their basements collecting dust, or had they ordered them from the guy who did chainsaw art just out of town?

Whatever the case, Big Foot Daze was definitely happening. Like it or not.

At the end of the block, she turned onto the road leading across a set of train tracks before it wound along the face of Boxer Bluff, past the area of older homes where Mayor Justison lived, then higher still and past the sheriff's department on her way home. She caught a glimpse of her face in the mirror and saw the red tracks on her cheek where Wilda Wyze had attempted to scratch her eyes out.

The woman's temper had skyrocketed from zero to sixty in half a second. Yes, Pescoli had goaded her after Wilda's initial attack, but the woman's reaction was way out of line. She was over the top. Was she scared for her sons, afraid they were being railroaded, or was there more to her fury? Did she know something? A secret they were harboring? If the altercation had done anything, it had increased Pescoli's suspicions about the Bell brothers rather than allay them.

Lost in thought, she drove by rote, stopping for stoplights and ignoring the Braxton Hicks pangs that had started about the time she left the restaurant. All the while, she was going over the homicide investigation and, more specifically, replaying the scene with the women she'd just dealt with in the foyer of the restaurant. While Wilda had definitely been the aggressor, Billie O'Hara had played the part of peacekeeper. But what about Terri Tufts and her supercilious attitude, the same knowing smile she'd displayed on the night of the vigil? What had she said about Pescoli's pregnancy? *Seems to be a lot of that going around.* As if she were enjoying her own private and nasty joke.

Who was this husband shooting blanks?

She followed a minivan filled with kids and decorated with bumper stickers proclaiming I HEART JESUS as it buzzed along over the speed limit.

Pescoli was certain she was missing something, something important, something that was scratching at the back of her mind, something she couldn't quite reach. But the aroma of the food was distracting her. Her stomach rumbled, reminding her she hadn't eaten in hours.

At the house, she found Bianca downstairs on the couch, her ankle propped up on a pillow, Cisco and Sturgis curled up beside her, cell phone and iPad at hand, television tuned to the news. Her hair was wet and curly, as if she'd just gotten out of the shower, and she was dressed in pajama bottoms and a T-shirt. She glanced up as her mother arrived, but couldn't muster up a smile.

"Hey," Pescoli said to Bianca as the dogs bounced off the couch to come greet her.

"Hi." Bianca's voice was flat and she looked like she'd lost her best friend. "What happened to your face?"

"Long story," Pescoli said. "Why the long face?" She dropped the sacks onto the kitchen island, taking time to pet a madly barking and twirling Cisco. "Yeah, I love you, too," she said to the terrier, then scratched Sturgis's ears as the lab wagged his tail. When Bianca didn't answer, she said, "Got your texts. What's going on?"

"Nothing."

"Doesn't seem like nothing. Especially when you kept texting me about coming home."

Bianca lifted a shoulder. Then, as if she couldn't hold it in a minute longer, she faced her mother and blinked back tears. "I'm off the show," she said with more than a touch of anger. "Michelle called a little while ago. Barclay Sphinx is 'going in another direction.' " She cleared her throat. "Lara Haas is in and I'm out."

CHAPTER 28

Pescoli rounded the end of the sectional while the dogs milled around beneath the counter, where the food still in the bags was probably getting cold. She took a seat next to her daughter. "What do you mean 'Lara's in and you're out'?"

"Just that." Bianca flopped back on the couch. "Michelle called."

"What did she say?"

"She talked to Barclay. Like earlier today. And he . . . he's thinking about 'taking the show in another direction.' " Bianca made air quotes with her fingers.

"After filming just one episode?"

"I guess."

Pescoli thought the show was already scripted, at least loosely, and this didn't make a lot of sense. "What other direction?"

"A direction that doesn't include me. Or our family." Bianca sunk lower on the cushions, her lower lip protruding, disappointment emanating from her in waves.

"Is he going to play up the feuding families

angle?" Pescoli asked. Wasn't there something about that?

Sighing, Bianca plucked at a nonexistent piece of lint on the arm of the sectional. "I guess. But it's all because of Lara. She's the last one who saw Big Foot, and Barclay is all over that."

"*Thinks* she saw one."

"Doesn't matter. And then that Big Foot Believer guy, Carlton Jeffe, got a visual of a Big Foot on film with his drone . . . so it's probably the same one that chased Lara. She was already on the news talking about it. First at the hospital and then at her home with her mom and dad there." Cisco abandoned his position under the counter and hopped up onto the couch. Bianca absently stroked his rough coat.

"Okay, I see Lara's got the media attention right now. But I thought they had some kind of plot line sketched out."

"They did. Do. But after the pilot, where I'm the one who is chased by Big Foot, they're going to focus on Lara, even make her live with one of the feuding families or something. They're going to cut something into what we've already filmed, focus in on her at the campfire or whatever, so the viewers can connect with her or something. That's what Michelle said. Then they want her to re-create what happened to her, when she went back searching for her cell phone, like she lost it during the party scene. They'll make it fit in with the story and then follow her story line."

"And what happens to your character?"

Pushing a lock of wet hair from her face, she said, "Don't know. Michelle said she'd keep me posted."

"Michelle still on the show?"

"Yeah. Remember: She's the cop! She's *you*."

"I know, but if you're out, I thought they might get rid of your mother as well, come up with some other investigator, or something."

"Well, they didn't," she huffed, crossing her arms over her chest. "Michelle and Barclay are tight."

"Yeah?"

"Yeah. She said she went to some seminar he gave a few years ago, or something, and I think they've kept in touch ever since, though, I think she kept it kind of a secret, didn't want anyone to know."

This was news. "She knew him before he showed up here?"

"I think." Bianca nodded, her wet curls bouncing on her shoulders. "Well, kinda."

Huh, Pescoli thought, filing the information away. "Well, I wouldn't worry about it too much. If the reality show is in this much flux, if the episodes aren't set in stone, which seems to be the case, then just do your job, best as you can and maybe things will change again."

Bianca lifted a skeptical brow. "You've met

Lara, right?" she said sarcastically. "You know it's impossible to compete with her. At least for male attention. Just ask Maddie."

Pescoli remembered that Maddie had been in love with TJ O'Hara, but he, like most of the other boys around that age, was forever lusting after Lara. "So you think Barclay Sphinx isn't immune to her charms."

"If you mean her boobs? Then no. It's disgusting." Scowling, she said, "I don't want to talk about it anymore."

"Okay. I've got dinner. It might be getting cold, but burgers, fries, and a spinach salad." Bianca was forever trying different diets and every once in a while she was off meat, professing to be a vegetarian. But not always, so when Pescoli brought home takeout, she always hedged her bets.

"Are you going to tell me what happened to your face?" Bianca asked.

"Oh. Well, your mother got into a catfight."

"For real?"

"Apparently Wilda Wyze doesn't like how I'm treating her boys. You know, like they could be suspects."

"So she *fought* you?" Bianca was both incredulous and somewhat impressed. "Don't you carry a gun?"

"I usually don't need a sidearm to pick up takeout."

"So you just let her claw you?"

"Well, that's not really how it went down. She took offense to the fact that we've been questioning her sons."

"And she attacked you? Are you kidding me?"

"It was a . . . scuffle. She came at me, and I . . . convinced her to back off."

"You mean, like a fight? You're pregnant!"

"That is a fact. And Terri Tufts commented on it, too." Without explaining how physical the altercation actually became, she told Bianca about meeting the three women in the foyer of Wild Wills, the accusations and the fight.

"Wow." Bianca stared at the scratches on her mother's face. "I know Kywin's mother is kind of angry all the time, he says so, but wow." Bianca carefully touched her mother's face. "That's intense."

"I suppose I'll live. Without plastic surgery."

"Are you going to put her in jail?"

Pescoli shook her head. "I probably should, but nah. Wilda's got enough problems. Older kids who are borderline hoodlums, an ex who's a regular in prison, and two more girls she's trying to raise. Even though I wouldn't call her Mother of the Year, Wilda's trying and so, just because she's a hothead with talon-like nails, I'm going to give her a pass. This time. But if she comes at me again, I won't think twice about arresting her and putting her in jail."

"Good."

"But I'm okay." That much was true as far as her face was concerned, but she did feel a rolling pang in her mid-section, an increased pressure that gave her pause. It had to be another Braxton Hicks contraction, right? Her due date was still a few weeks off. Ignoring it, she said, "Do you know if those three are tight? Wilda Wyze and Terri Tufts and Billie O'Hara?"

"You'd know better than me. I mean, they all were when we were growing up, weren't they? The boys were in soccer and Little League and basketball, all kinds of sports, and on the same teams a lot of the time."

"Terri made a comment about my pregnancy, and said something like, 'It's going around these days,' " Pescoli revealed.

"Probably because Marjory is," Bianca said, "You know, Emmett and Preston's stepmom? She's not very far along. Doesn't show or anything. But I think Terri is pissed, anyway, Emmett said so."

"She didn't seem pissed."

"Then I don't know, but it's weird for everyone. Especially Emmett. He's kind of freaked out about it."

"Why?"

"Because he's going to have a baby brother or sister and he's like me. Almost grown." She let her gaze drop to her mother's abdomen. "I know you and Santana are all into it, and you should be, but for me and Jer, it's kind of . . . well, upsetting in a way. We don't like to think of you as . . ."

"Sexual?"

She made a face. "Yeah. And we know you and Santana . . . well, but did you have to go and get pregnant when you're, like, almost ready for retirement?"

"Retirement. Geez, Bianca, I'm not in the grave yet." Another pain was starting to swell inside her.

"Well, if it's weird for me, it's got to be super freaky for Emmett because he was going with Marjory when she hooked up with his dad."

"What?" Pescoli said, trying not to wince as the pain increased. "Emmett dated Marjory? They were a couple?"

"Yeah, for like three or four months, and then she went for the dad or he went for her. He was still married to Terri at the time. They got divorced and then Richtor and Marjory got married and now she's knocked up."

Husband shooting blanks . . .

Oh, God.

No. No reason to follow that line of thinking. Terri Tufts was a bitter ex, and bitter exes said a lot of bitter, untrue things.

But she did ask, "Is Mr. Tufts excited about the baby?" The pressure decreased slightly and she took a breath. *I cannot be going into labor. I. Can. Not.*

"I don't know."

Pescoli's cell phone chirped and she saw that Luke was on the line. Great. The last thing she needed was to deal with her ex, but ignoring Luke never seemed to work.

"Hi," she answered shortly.

"Have you heard?" he demanded, and she could tell that he was driving, could hear the rush of traffic noise in the background. And he was mad as hell; she recognized his fury in the timbre of his voice.

"Have I heard what?"

"About the show?" He was practically shouting. "That Bianca's out and that bimbo Lara Haas is in? That she claims she was attacked by a Big Foot? Jesus Christ, that has to be a setup!"

"A setup?"

"Are you playing dumb? Lara's attack was obviously staged. Fake!" Then, he must've turned his head away from the phone as his voice was suddenly muted, though she heard him yell, "Way to go, asshole. Cut me off, will ya?" Then his voice was stronger again, when he returned. "I'm driving."

"I figured."

Back on topic, his voice clear again, he said, "I don't believe for a second that she lost her phone up there at Reservoir Point when they were filming and then she didn't notice it for a couple of hours or so, long enough for the crew to shut down? No way. I'm telling you, that girl has been angling for a starring role in *Big Foot Territory: Montana!* from the get-go. She was targeting Bianca, trying to figure out how to become the star, and she did it." Again, his voice became muted, but she still heard, "Holy shit, asshole! Get off the road! That part belongs to Bianca! Hold on a sec. I've got to turn. Oh, shit!" She heard what sounded like the phone being dropped.

She wondered where he was heading in such a state, and a cold certainty settled in the pit of her stomach.

"That was Dad?" Bianca asked, twisting on the couch to look at her.

"Yeah, but I lost him. . . ." Her voice trailed off when headlights flashed through the trees as a vehicle came speeding down the lane. Lucky's vintage Chevy was kicking up a trail of dust. "Oh, wait." she said, clicking off the phone. "I think I just found him."

Oh, joy.

"Gotcha!" Alvarez muttered, double-checking the lab results. No doubt about it. Kywin Bell was the father of Destiny Rose Montclaire's unborn child. "You snakey, little lying bastard," she said as she grabbed her keys and sidearm from her locker, then headed into the warm Montana night.

Destiny Rose's self-appointed "protector," and one of the people Destiny had texted on the night she died, had been lying to everyone. All that complaining about being harassed by the police, and whining about wanting a lawyer was to cover his own lying ass.

"Too late," she said as she climbed into the warm interior of her Outback, rolled down the windows, backed out of her parking space, and drove out of the lot. The sun was hanging low in the sky, just about to settle over the western ridge of mountains, dusk quickly approaching. Squinting, she pulled her sunglasses from the console, slipped them over her eyes, and, at the traffic light, dialed Pescoli.

Her partner didn't pick up, so she left a quick voice mail about arresting Kywin Bell, then kept driving. It was finally all coming together. Kywin had been seeing Destiny behind Donny Justison's back, or maybe even to his knowledge as Donny and Destiny had broken up because of Veronica Palmero. Or for whatever reason. And oops, Destiny gets pregnant. Maybe she didn't even know which of the boys she'd slept with could be the father. Not important. So she'd contacted them both, along with Lindsay Cronin, and then met Donny . . . at his house. "Nuh-uh," she said to herself as she wound her way through the city streets to Franklin Bell's house. Destiny had gone to the reservoir. So had she met Donny there? Or Kywin? Or both? Had Donny killed her in a fit of rage? Or had Kywin, "her protector" and lover, strangled the life out of the mother of his child?

Alvarez decided to force the truth out of Kywin first. Because he was the only person who had been contacted by both Lindsay Cronin and Destiny Rose Montclaire, the two dead girls. Alvarez had double-checked the phone records, and though Lindsay had conversations with a lot of her classmates, Kywin Bell's number was one of the most frequent. Sometimes their conversations lasted half an hour. Yeah, he knew something, and Alvarez was betting he knew a lot.

"Time to find out," she said, cutting the engine, making sure her sidearm was ready, and tossing off her shades. A feeling of satisfaction stole over her as she strode up the cracked cement walkway to the front porch, where the scraggly gray cat was curled into one of the metal lawn chairs. At the sight of her, it climbed to its feet, took the time to hiss in her direction, then hopped to the worn floorboards and slunk into the near-dead shrubbery.

The door was open, only a screen door in place, and from the dark interior she heard muted conversation—no, more likely a television and maybe the sizzle of something being cooked, bacon frying, she guessed from the smell emanating through the rusted mesh. A bluish glow was visible down a short hallway, a TV at the back of the house.

She pounded on the frame of the screen door, then waited.

Nothing. But Franklin's dusty Suburban, with all of its windows rolled down, was parked in the driveway. Unfortunately, Kywin's jacked-up truck wasn't in sight, which didn't bode well.

She rapped again and this time heard a grunt, then a deep voice yelling, "I'm coming! Hell. What now?" Floorboards creaked as Franklin Bell, all six-four and three-hundred-plus pounds of him, lumbered from the back of the house to the front.

"For shit's sake," he said when he spied Alvarez. He was unshaven, his trucker's cap squarely in place. "You're Pescoli's partner. What the hell do you want?" His gaze swept the porch and dry lawn as if searching for the other detective.

"To talk to Kywin?"

"Again? Didn't you already do that? More'n once."

"New information. I need to speak to him."

"He ain't here. Neither of my boys are."

"Where is he?"

"Don't know," he retorted with satisfaction.

"When do you expect him back?"

He shrugged. "He's a damned adult. Comes and goes as he pleases."

"And he's the father of Destiny Rose Montclaire's unborn baby," she said. "Lab tests confirm it, so I need to talk to him ASAP. If he's involved in her death, he's looking at double homicide."

"You're bullshitting me—"

"DNA doesn't lie." She cut him off. Franklin's usually florid face drained of color. "Your boy's up to his eyeballs in this." She stepped closer to the rusted screens, showing him she wasn't intimidated. "Kywin was in contact with Destiny on the night she died, and again with Lindsay Cronin a little while before she had her 'accident' up on Horsebrier Ridge. So, if you hear from him, let him know that I'm looking for him, and I need to talk to him ASAP."

"Get the fuck off my property!" he growled as the smell of burning meat wafted through the house.

"Just give him the message."

"Didn't you hear me? Leave!" And with that, he grabbed hold of the edge of the open door and slammed it so hard that it rattled the screen as it shut. The cat, watching from the shadows of a near-dead juniper, glowered at Alvarez as she crossed the yard and slid behind the wheel of her Subaru. She didn't start the car immediately. First, she called the station and put in a request for a BOLO, ordering all law enforcement officers to be on the lookout for Kywin Bell's Dodge pickup. No way was Destiny Rose's baby daddy and possible murderer going to slip through her fingers.

CHAPTER 29

"Regan!" Luke banged like crazy on the front door, and the dogs set to barking wildly.

"Hey! Hey! Slow down," Pescoli ordered as she swung the door open and her ex-husband stormed in. In jeans, a gray T-shirt, and boots, he whirled on his ex-wife. His face was flushed, his usually combed hair mussed, as if he'd been running his fingers through it in frustration.

"You have to do something." He pointed an accusatory finger at Pescoli.

"Me?"

"You're the law around here, aren't you?" He punched a fist into the air in frustration. "Son of a bitch!" he said, showing teeth, then strode rapidly toward the family room.

"Wait a damn minute. Why are you acting like a lunatic?" She was on his heels, the dogs barking a cacophony she could do without and trailing behind her. "Quiet," she warned Cisco. "No!"

Luke threw open the refrigerator door, found a beer, and popped the top.

"That's got to stop," she warned him as the door swung closed, and he had the nerve to peer into one of the sacks from Wild Wills. "This is my house. That's my beer, and you can't come striding in here and making demands."

"It's for our kid!" he said, stepping away from the counter and taking a long swig.

"We have rules, you and I. Boundaries." She pulled the can from his hand, took it, and poured the beer down the sink. "You need to respect them, Luke. We've been over this before. You can't come over here, ranting and raving, practically bullying your way inside and then make yourself at home, drinking my damned beer and helping yourself to whatever. No. Get it? We're over, you and I. Been over a long time now!" She crushed the can in her fist, fury coursing through her blood.

"Mom!" Bianca cried from the couch.

"What the hell's wrong with you?" he demanded.

She threw the empty can into the sink, then spun on him. "Something's wrong with *me*? Are you kidding?" He'd been pissing her off for a long time, and she was sick to the back teeth of dealing with him. "You're acting like a maniac."

"I'm just really, really pissed off."

"I get that."

For the first time since roaring in, he actually looked at her . . . and let out a long, low whistle. "What the . . . what happened to you?" he asked, eyeing her cheek while actually taking a step back.

"Hazards of the job."

"Wrestling bobcats? No wonder you're in such a bad mood."

"Leave it alone, and I'm not in any kind of mood whatsoever."

His expression said she was kidding herself, but, slightly calmer, he got to the point. Finally. "You have to call Sphinx and make him honor his damned contract with our daughter."

She made a choking sound.

Spying Bianca, who was starting to get up from the sectional, he waved her back into her seat. "Don't get up. Your mom and I'll handle this."

"Handle what?" Bianca asked.

"I can't believe this, honey, but it's Sphinx! What kind of idiot is he, buying into that Lara's scam? I mean it's so damned obvious. I would think a big Hollywood hotshot like him would see through her little act."

"What act?" Bianca asked warily from her corner of the sectional. She was staring at her parents as if they'd become lunatics, and Pescoli kicked herself for fighting with Luke in front of their daughter. Much as her ex drove her up the wall, he was, after all, Bianca's father, and Regan, fool that she'd been at the time, had made the choice to wed him.

"Come on, honey. You see it, too. Right? I'm talking about Lara Haas's supposed sighting of Big Foot. It's all a big lie. A massive story she cooked up with that O'Hara kid, just so they could get bigger parts in the show."

"Hold on, Luke." Pescoli couldn't let him drag

Bianca into this, not until they knew the truth. "How do you know it's a scam?"

"Because it's fu—freaking obvious, that's how. And there has to be a law against this sort of thing. You can't go faking this stuff—making it up. It has to be *real*. I mean, duh, it's called a *reality* show for God's sake! For the love of Christ, we can't let this happen!"

Pescoli felt another deep pain roll through her, stronger than before. She actually caught her breath.

Not now. This can't be happening now. It's too early for the baby. This is still false labor. It has to be.

"There. Look at that," Luke said, when his eye caught the television screen. On the local news was footage of the most recent Big Foot "sighting" via Carl Jeffe's drone. "This thing is just getting bigger and bigger, and Bianca is being edged out by that lying *bitch*." The television screen changed, and he snagged up the remote, hitting a button to turn on the sound as he flopped onto the couch next to his daughter. On the screen, Lara Haas was being rolled down the sidewalk in a wheelchair, the front facade of Northern General rising behind her, both of her parents hurrying to keep up with the attendant.

"I'm just grateful to be alive," she was saying as a microphone was thrust into her face. The shot widened as the cameraman backed up, and Barclay Sphinx appeared to hand Lara the bouquet of flowers and balloons Pescoli had witnessed firsthand. The producer was smiling and saying how thankful he was that Lara hadn't been hurt in the attack. Then, looking squarely into the camera's eye, he told the audience that "this brave girl" was integral to the filming of *Big Foot Territory: Montana!* and her story would be told in a series of episodes.

"What a two-faced bastard! He has a contract with Bianca and he just nullifies it. Damn it all to hell!" Lucky was livid, his face flushed with color, his gaze fixed on the television, while out of the corner of her eye, through the window, Pescoli noticed headlights flashing through the trees. *Santana! Oh, God, please.*

From the spot he'd claimed on the sectional, Luke was still ranting. "We had a deal and now . . . what the fuck? The man's a lying scumbag, I'm telling ya! A double-crossing son of a bitch."

"Enough!" Pescoli reached over the back of the couch, yanked the remote from his hand, felt another pain start to increase, and clicked the television off. "Why didn't you call Sphinx? Talk to him?"

"You don't think I did? Of course I did. And I told him that Bianca was totally committed to the show and the series, that she would do anything, any damned thing to be a part of it."

"Are you nuts? Isn't that like making a deal with the devil?"

"For the love of God, you are so . . . so suspicious!"

"It's my job."

"Bullshit!" he roared, jabbing an accusatory finger at his ex-wife. "This is her shot, Regan! Her chance of a lifetime. Don't you get it? I'm just supporting her any way possible and you should, too. I told Sphinx that we all were behind her and the project a hundred percent, that we'd all back her."

"Not me," Pescoli said.

"Why not, Mom?" Bianca twisted on the couch to take in the fight, and she glared at her mother.

"It's not you, honey. I'll always have your back, you know that. But I don't like this whole shaky 'reality' show, and I use the term loosely, so for once I agree with your father here: I don't trust Barclay Sphinx. The difference is that I'm not willing to jump in to play ball with him. And I certainly don't like it that you're caught in the middle."

Bianca's eyes began to sheen with unshed tears. "But I want this, Mom. More than anything."

Luke was nodding vigorously. " 'Course you do, honey. And it doesn't matter what Mom says, Sphinx understands what I'm talking about, that you are a thousand-percent committed. And if he doesn't come through . . ." Luke was shaking his head.

"If he doesn't come through, what're you going

to do?" Gritting her teeth against the contraction, she forced out, "Look, Luke, I don't think Barclay Sphinx broke any laws and if you have a problem with the contract Bianca signed, then hire a lawyer!"

"Not good enough," he growled. "Bianca's going to the filming tonight, and that's that. We'll see how things shake out."

"You need to leave. We'll deal with this," she said as she heard the garage door roll open, and the pain increased, intense pressure building. Oh. Jesus. This time, she sucked her breath in through her teeth and grimaced. "Oh, God."

"Mom?" Bianca said, her eyes filled with worry.

"I'm okay." *No, no, I'm definitely not.*

The back door opened.

Santana and Jeremy walked in.

Just as her damned water broke.

Kywin Bell was in the wind.

As if he'd known that Alvarez was onto him, the kid had disappeared, Alvarez thought, as she drove to back to the station. She'd tried to call his phone. No answer. She'd contacted his friends and gotten nowhere. The same had been true with his brother, Kip, who'd answered with, "Leave us the hell alone." Kywin had been fired from his job and the place was closed for the night. None of the road deputies had reported seeing his vehicle.

He had to be in hiding. As if he'd felt the noose tightening and had gone underground. Well, he wouldn't stay hidden forever.

She pulled into the sheriff's office parking lot and headed inside. Pescoli hadn't returned her call, which was odd, but the woman did have a family. Alvarez, on the other hand, lived alone, with her pets. O'Keefe stayed over when he was in town or she visited him, but, for the most part, she was married to her job. That . . . and her inability to get over the death of Dan Grayson. The unrequited feelings she'd had for her former boss had put some strain on their relationship. Grayson's ghost still lingered around these halls, and she was susceptible to it. Especially at night, when the station was quieter and his office was dark.

And Dylan was no fool. He knew she struggled with emotions she couldn't or wouldn't name. Yet, he loved her still. "Idiot!" she admonished herself.

Their relationship was far from an ideal situation, she thought as she parked and stepped into the warm August night. The air was dry and dusty, but there was the promise of thunderstorms on the horizon, a small current of electricity that she felt in the stiff breeze that scattered leaves and debris across the parking lot.

Inside, the offices were quiet, a few detectives working, several road deputies collected in the lunchroom before they headed out for the night. Tonight, however, a light emanated from beneath the sheriff's door, and she paused with her hand on the panels. Maybe she should let Blackwater know of the progress they were making.

What progress? You know the name of the father of the victim's unborn child, and he's missing. Wait until you talk to Kywin Bell and put the screws to him, then discuss it with Pescoli before going to the sheriff with only half-baked theories.

She was about to step into her office when she spied Zoller heading her way. "Glad I caught you," Sage said without preamble. "I was about to leave for the night when I got a call from Carlton Jeffe. The guy with the drone."

"Yeah?"

"Seems as if he's found something with his drone. Possibly another dead body."

"Another? Whose?" she asked, a needle of dread piercing her heart. Kywin Bell was missing. No one was claiming to have heard from him.

"Unknown. Rescuers are on their way."

"Where?"

"Federal land. About a mile south of Reservoir Point."

"Anything else we know about it?"

"Just that it looks like a woman. The drone couldn't get too close because of the foliage, but a leg and arm were visible. The shoe was a woman's sandal. And neither appendage moved. Jeffe sent over a file, so I've got a visual."

"Let's see it."

Zoller led the way into the conference room where they'd met earlier and sure enough, Jeffe had uploaded footage from the drone. As Zoller had stated, the forest was dense, but caught on the drone's camera was a slim, naked leg, and from the toes of the visible foot, a gold sandal dangled. A hand was visible as well, and as Zoller zoomed in, Alvarez saw that the fingernails were tipped with a pearlescent pink color and on her ring finger was a glittering diamond ring.

"Married," Sage said. "Or engaged."

"Has anyone reported a woman missing?"

"Don't know. This just came in."

"Let's find out." Alvarez was already out the door and in the hallway when Zoller caught up with her.

Taj Nyak was working the desk, and upon Alvarez's inquiry about recently filed reports about missing women, she nodded. "We've got a couple that came in. Penelope Jarvis, eighty-six. Went missing from Safe Haven Adult Care."

"Not so safe," Zoller said. "They might want to change their name."

"Someone younger," Alvarez said.

"Got one, just today." Taj pulled the file up on the computer and spun the screen around so Alvarez could view it. "Marjory Tufts," she said. "Her husband was in about three this afternoon." A picture was attached to the file. Alvarez recognized Emmett and Preston Tufts's stepmother.

"He's worried sick about her, said they had a fight and she took off last night. I guess it happens often enough that he wasn't worried, thought she'd spend the night with a friend or in a hotel. It's happened before. But this is the first time she'd taken off, he claims, since she found out she was pregnant. When she didn't show up, he called around. Her friends, the local hotel where she stayed before, even a couple of hospitals, but no one had seen her. So he left work—he owns a car dealership—and came down here to file a report."

Alvarez was nodding, but her eyes were on the photograph attached to the missing persons report. Marjory was young, not yet twenty, with a bright smile, a twinkle in her eye, and a glittery wedding ring that was identical to the one in the image captured by Carlton Jeffe's drone.

No! No! No! Not now. It couldn't be happening now.

The baby had to wait. It had to! She didn't have time to go into labor now, to birth a child, not while this investigation was ongoing.

And what if the case goes on for weeks, for months, even years? Do you expect the baby to wait?

Another hard contraction stole her concentration as Santana drove, pushing the speed limit along the darkened country road. "Hang in there," he advised as she labored in the passenger seat, the baby definitely on its way. The contractions were coming faster now, the forest and fields speeding by, the sun having set and dusk crawling over the land.

"This is such bad timing," she gritted out.

"The department will function without you," Santana assured her. "Trust me, the crime rate won't go up in the next few days just because you're not able to go in."

"Very funny," she said, though neither laughed and for once Pescoli didn't argue. She couldn't. The baby was coming and coming fast. Pains as intense as any she'd ever felt in her life tore through her, with ever decreasing intervals in between.

In flashes of memory, as she clutched the passenger seat, she remembered her previous deliveries. Both Jeremy and Bianca had arrived quickly, her labor lasting less than six hours, but this one, Santana's kid, seemed determined to break their records and race headlong into the world.

Santana floored it on a straightaway.

"Don't kill us," she advised, thinking of the deer and rabbits and whatever that came out at twilight, animals that wandered along the road.

"Before I meet my kid?" he said, slanting a glance in her direction. His grin was an enigmatic and irreverent slash of white. "You hang in

461

there. Concentrate on bringing that baby into the world and leave the driving to me. Deal?"

"Deal," she said, her heart swelling. Damn, but she loved this man. And then another contraction hit with the force of an earthquake and all she could think about was getting through the pain.

She even forgot that life as she'd known it was about to end as he called the hospital and said to the operator who answered: "This is Nate Santana. I'm bringing my wife, Regan Pescoli, to the ER. She's in labor and the baby's just about here! We're preregistered and our Doctor is . . . Peeples . . ." He glanced at Regan.

"Ramona."

"Ramona Peeples. We'll be there in five minutes."

"Hurry," she said through gritted teeth and couldn't believe she had the urge to push. Right here in the Jeep. "It's . . . it's coming!"

"Hold on!" Horn blasting, Santana slowed for a red light and apparently saw no traffic, as he twisted on the steering wheel and the Jeep careened on to the main street leading to the hospital.

Oh. Dear. God.

"I . . . I can't. It's . . . " She let out a wrenching groan as pain ripped through her body. The fingers of her right hand dug into the armrest, while her left gripped the console. "Oh, oh . . ." Northern General came into view. "It's . . .

he's . . . she's . . . almost . . . almost . . . here!" She was fighting the urge to push and failing.

Speeding around a final corner, Santana roared onto the access road, then hit the brakes and slid to a stop in front of the double glass doors of the emergency room. He cut the engine and was out of the Jeep in an instant, rounding the vehicle as Pescoli, deep into a contraction, bit back a scream and clawed at her seat belt, releasing the buckle.

When Santana opened the passenger door, she nearly tumbled out just as two attendants with a gurney arrived and somehow hoisted her onto the stretcher and began wheeling her inside. "Hold on," one of the attendants said, and to Santana: "We're taking her straight to a birthing room. You can do the paperwork later."

They hustled her through the emergency room doors, the lights of the interior of the hospital bright, the walls seeming to gleam, and into an elevator.

The rest of the delivery came fast. They barely got her into the bed and removed her clothes before she could hold back no longer and began to push in earnest. She didn't care that the doctor hadn't arrived or that the staff was scrambling around, not prepared. This baby was being born!

"Okay, Mama," one of the nurses said. "Baby has crowned. Now—"

Regan didn't hear the rest, didn't know if

Santana was in the room or what had happened to her other children, who were supposed to have followed them to the hospital. All she knew was that she had to push this thing out of her, and in a rush, she did.

A nurse caught the baby, she heard a squall and Regan fell back on the raised portion of the bed. She was vaguely aware of a large, warm hand on her head, then Santana's voice in her ear. "Good job, Mama," he whispered as the baby was placed on her abdomen. "We have a son."

Tears filled her eyes as she held the boy, and raw emotion, as deep as the craters in the sea, filled her. "Oh, sweetie," she whispered, all of the worries of her job, her family, the world and universe vanishing with the little gurgling sounds of this tiny, minutes-old infant. "Welcome to our crazy life," she whispered.

Smiling despite the glisten in his eyes, Santana touched his son for the first time, his hand seeming huge as it caressed the back of the dark-haired baby. "Hey, there," he said softly as he looked for the first time at the tiny face of Tucker Grayson Santana.

CHAPTER 30

Richtor Tufts was genuinely upset. He couldn't sit for five seconds without jumping to his feet and pacing in front of the small table separating him from Alvarez in the interview room at the station.

"I just don't understand," he said in a devastated voice for what had to be the fifth or sixth time. "Who would do this? Why?"

"That's what we're trying to find out," she said. "Please, Mr. Tufts, take a seat."

"Oh, right. Right."

At the morgue, he'd ID'd his wife's body, the petite, young woman who had the same dark bruising on her neck as had been evident on Destiny Rose Montclaire.

Alvarez had arrived at the crime scene and seen Marjory's body, tossed carelessly in the brush. Mrs. Tufts had been dressed as if intending to go out, in a short white mini dress, gold bracelet and necklace that matched her expensive shoes. As yet, the ME could give no precise time of death, but it was thought to have occurred sometime the night before. From the condition of her body, the bruises and contusions, Alvarez believed there had been a struggle, the scattering of leaves and pine needles, disturbance of dirt and branches, indicating some kind of fight had occurred. As far as she knew, the only evidence found at the scene was a large footprint discovered about ten feet from the body. A cigarette butt had been found as well and that, too, was being processed, in the hope that there would be DNA found.

The only good news about this killer was that he was careless, a person who didn't watch crime or cop shows, or know about trace evidence.

Finally, a break.

Alvarez had noticed the similarity of bruising on Marjory's body, so close to that of Destiny Rose Montclaire's, but hadn't mentioned it to Richtor, as she'd wanted to witness his reaction. That had been swift. His face had contorted in disbelief, his knees nearly buckling as he'd viewed his wife's corpse. He'd broken into tears and had eagerly agreed to meet Alvarez at the sheriff's department and go over their last conversation, a heated argument that had occurred the night before.

"It was a stupid thing," he said now in the interview room, going over the story again. "Madge had wanted to go out with friends— Madge is what I call her—and I'd argued with her. This was an on-going thing with her. She's pregnant, and her crowd—well, they're young, so they all like to party until the wee hours. Some of them, including my sons, are involved in filming that new reality show, *Big Foot Sightings in Montana,* or something like that."

"Big Foot Territory: Montana!"

"That's it. She didn't say as much, not right off the bat, but Madge, she wanted to be a part of it, and was jealous . . . No, no, that's the wrong word. Not exactly jealous, but envious, maybe, of all the kids who were involved. She would have loved to be a part of that, even knew of that producer guy, Spinks?"

"Sphinx. Barclay Sphinx."

"She was a big fan of a couple of his reality shows, the one about the Hollywood has-beens, *Tarnished Stars,* and she was excited about the new ones, this one about the Big Foot sightings and that one in Oregon about ghosts. . . . She was all over those and when I told her it was stupid, that she was married, going to be a mother, and she should forget all that nonsense, she blew up, said I didn't 'understand.' And that's the truth. I didn't. She has, *had,* a good life and some slick producer wasn't going to change that."

Alvarez was taking notes, watching Richtor's expressions, even though the interview was being recorded on video and audio from a camera mounted high on the cinder-block wall. Others, including Sheriff Blackwater, were observing as well, standing on the other side of the two-way mirror mounted on the wall.

"So what about enemies? Anyone you know might want to harm her?"

"No. Madge is so sweet." He must've caught the

467

skepticism on Alvarez's face because he lifted his hands, palms out. "We had fights. She was a passionate woman. But I can't imagine anyone would want to hurt her. Usually she was the nicest girl you'd want to meet."

"How did your ex-wife feel about her?" Alvarez already knew that Marjory had been the wedge between Richtor and his first wife.

"Oh, Terri." He pulled a face. "They didn't get along. Of course. I mean, that was my fault. I fell in love with Madge before I was divorced. The marriage was dead, mind you—Terri and I hadn't . . . been intimate in years. We'd shared the same bed, but we may as well have been time zones apart. I think we just stayed together because it's what we were used to and we had the boys . . . so . . . ."

"But you met Marjory."

"Yes." He smiled, remembering.

"How?"

"Well." He seemed a bit embarrassed. "You know she's a lot younger than me and . . . well . . ." He was slowly shaking his head, bouncing it a bit, as he tried to find the right words, finally settling on, "She was actually dating my youngest boy, Emmett, at the time it all began."

"The youngest?"

"I know. I'm not proud of that, of course, but hell, there was just such a connection, you know?

And Madge felt it, too. She actually came on to me and I . . . I gave in. She's the most . . . incredible creature I've ever met." His throat tightened and he squeezed his eyes shut. "I just can't believe she's gone."

"What about Emmett?"

"What about him?"

"How did he feel?"

"Oh, well." Another embarrassed grimace . . . or was it something else? Was there a little pride attached to it—the old man besting his son? "He was upset, of course. Fancied himself in love with her, I think. I mean, come on. Who falls in love at that age?"

"Marjory did. That's what you're saying."

"Yes, but she's a woman and mature for her age. Not like boys. They take forever to grow up. I know. I was one." Beneath the fluorescent lights, he looked every one of his years as he leaned back in his chair.

"Did Emmett get over it?"

"Sure. Both boys did. Preston, he didn't like it much, either, but hell, what're ya gonna do when your old man's in love?" He cleared his throat. "Terri and I got divorced quickly and she was angry. No woman wants to lose her husband to a younger, more beautiful woman. Of course she was upset. But I was fair in the divorce, not . . . overly generous, maybe, but more than fair."

Now he was lying. She saw it in the shift of his

gaze, the way he was trying so hard to agree with himself.

"Your sons were okay with your divorce and remarriage?" she asked, just making certain.

"In time, yeah. The next hiccup was her pregnancy. Of course, that took them by surprise."

"So they still haven't accepted it."

"They're coming around and . . . oh, hell . . . now they don't have to." The idea seemed to hit him anew.

"Did she know Kywin Bell?"

"He's . . . a friend of Emmett's. Why?"

"So they hung out?"

"I don't know, but I suppose. They all ran around in the same circle."

"Did you ever see her with him?"

He frowned. "I think . . . yes, of course. He'd visit Emmett, come over to the house. I saw him there a couple of times."

"How well did your wife know him?"

"What does the Bell kid have to do with anything?"

"Just checking."

"I said they were friends." And then he caught her meaning and his jaw tightened. "What're you suggesting, Detective? That Madge and he, that they were intimate?"

"Just asking how close they were."

"Well, you're way off base. Way off. She knew him, but that was it. Okay? There was nothing . . .

you know, nothing going on between them or anyone else for that matter. She . . . she was an angel." He closed his eyes, dropped his face into his hands, and tried to gather himself. It took a few minutes, but he was done, couldn't give her the names of any other ex-lovers or anyone who would want to harm his sweet, precious Marjory.

But, as he left, Alvarez thought he'd offered up three potential suspects. His whole family, his ex-wife and their sons, were definitely persons of interest in this case and potential suspects. Plus, she hadn't written off Richtor himself. After all, through his own admission, they'd had a fight before she'd taken off. How bad had it been? How far had it escalated? She wondered about his temper, if he could actually kill his wife and unborn child. Or had Marjory and Destiny Rose Montclaire been killed by the same person with the same brute force?

Then there were Bianca Pescoli and Lara Haas, both of whom believed they had been attacked by a huge hairy creature, an apparently homicidal Sasquatch. She didn't believe for a second that a Big Foot had chased them, but why would a killer go to all the trouble of dressing up like the mythical beast?

And what about Lindsay Cronin? How did her accident figure in? Or was that just a coincidence?

"No way."

None of it made any sense.

She had to start somewhere, so she decided to begin with locating anyone Marjory Tufts had seen or contacted on the day of the fight with her husband. Alvarez had already called for phone records, and a crime scene team had combed the forest where the body had been found. Her car was missing, but it shouldn't be hard to find: a 1957 T-Bird, pink—or more precisely, "Dusky Rose"—that had once graced the showroom floor of Richtor's Ford dealership. He'd admitted to giving the car to Marjory on their wedding day. "Yeah, we actually drove it into Vegas for our honeymoon," he'd said with a sigh. "God, it looked fabulous on the strip." Then: "You have to locate it. That T-Bird's in mint condition, worth a small fortune." Alvarez had thought the statement odd, considering that he'd just found out his wife was dead and most likely the victim of homicide. There was just something about the man she didn't trust.

For God's sake, she was starting to think like Pescoli, going on hunches and feelings rather than cold hard facts. Mentally berating herself, she found Blackwater's office door ajar and, with a rap on the panels, walked inside.

It still felt strange to find him sitting in Dan Grayson's chair, his elbows on Grayson's desk, his head cocked to the side as he talked into his cell phone.

". . . yeah, I just heard about it," he was saying.

"We're already interviewing the husband. . . . I know. I know. . . . Absolutely." He glanced up at Alvarez and waved her into one of the side chairs. Feeling as if she was wasting time, she dropped into the chair next to the window and tried not to remember how many times she'd sat in this very spot waiting for Grayson to end a conversation. His lab, Sturgis, would be curled on a bed near the desk, his Stetson hung on a peg by the door, which now held a baseball cap. Her heart twisted a little, but the feeling was more nostalgia than grief, and she thought that she might finally be letting him go.

"We're on it," Blackwater said, hanging up. He swung his gaze to Alvarez. "That was the mayor. She wants the Montclaire investigation wrapped up, a killer brought to justice."

"Even if it's her kid?"

"She says her son is innocent." At her expression, he leaned back in his chair to the point that it squeaked in protest. Then he tented his hands and stared at her. Hard. "You obviously disagree."

"He's lying about something, and he's still the last one we know to have seen her alive."

"Hmmm. And now another dead woman. Pregnant. Apparently strangled. Who knew the first victim."

"And there's a third victim, if Lindsay Cronin met with foul play."

"You think that's the case?"

"My badge and a year's salary."

One of his eyebrows cocked. "Tell me you can prove it."

"Not yet. But soon. Here's what we've got." She brought him up to speed on the investigations, then said, "So what I need from you is clout and manpower. I want to talk to the Tufts brothers, the Bell brothers, bring 'em all in. Interview them until someone cracks."

"If they will."

"Someone will. Especially if they think someone else is ratting them out."

"Maybe."

"And I want a rush on Marjory Tufts's autopsy, identify the cause of death, compare her bruising to Destiny Montclaire's. And I want DNA on the fetus. I'd like it yesterday."

One side of his mouth twitched upward. "Let me wave my magic wand."

"Please do. I'll take any help I can get on this."

"Where's Pescoli?"

"Under the radar. I'm waiting for a call back. She is pregnant, you know, and has a family. I'll catch up with her."

"Okay, I'll do what I can. Put pressure on the lab and ME. I bet we can find all the people you want to talk to up at the reservoir at the reality show location. They're shooting again tonight, as I understand it. Most of the kids you want to talk to are part of the crowd scene up there, right? I saw them during the last shoot." His smile was cold as ice. "I'll have a couple of deputies head up there."

"Good. Let's round them up."

She figured she had a long night ahead of her and headed into the lunchroom to find some coffee or tea or cocoa, anything with a jolt of caffeine. Well-read newspapers were scattered on a couple of tables and lined on the shelf were six new Big Foot Daze cups that would send Pescoli through the roof when she saw them.

Pescoli.

Where the hell was she?

It was odd that she hadn't returned Alvarez's calls. As she was about to hit speed dial one more time, her cell vibrated in her hand and she saw her partner's name appear on the screen.

She clicked on to answer, and as she lifted the phone to her ear, she heard Pescoli say, a little breathlessly, "It happened. A little early. The baby came and I'm at Northern General with my new son and he's perfect."

Unexpectedly, Alvarez felt tears sprout in her eyes. She wasn't one to cry, nor ever get very emotional, but this new baby, coming late in life to a woman who'd finally found the right partner, was the first good news she'd heard in a long, long while.

And for that, she could take a break, if only for

an hour or so. Leaving instructions for the lab and Zoller, who was working late as well, to call her with any information, she left the station.

Riding shotgun in Jeremy's truck, Bianca looked in the mirror on the passenger side and saw that her own face was healing, even if her mother's still bore the scars of her recent catfight with Kywin's mother. Jeremy was behind the wheel and, despite her mother's protest, was taking her back to Reservoir Point to continue filming the first episode of "that damned reality show," as her mother called it.

She was running late, the arrival of her new little brother having caused a major time shift in her schedule. But, already, Bianca knew he was worth it. She'd stared at the baby in wonder within an hour of his birth, had been allowed to hold him, which felt a little awkward. He was sooo tiny. Impossibly so, even though the nurses had said a nearly eight-pound baby was a "good size."

As she'd cradled him, afraid he might slip from her arms, she'd looked into his dark eyes, marveled at his thick black hair and long, grabby fingers that were forever trying to work their way out of the swaddling blanket. Given the choice, if she *had* to have a new half-sibling, she would have preferred a sister, but the little guy—Tucker —was kind of cool. Even Jeremy was excited about the baby, and Mom and Santana were absolutely gaga. She'd never seen her mother so serene, so all about this one little baby and seemingly not worried about the world, or her job, or her older kids, or whatever. The things that always kept her a little crazy.

"It's the drugs," Jeremy had advised Bianca when she'd brought it up. "I think they pumped her full of morphine or something."

"They can't," she'd argued. "She's going to be nursing, and they don't want a doped-up baby." God, sometimes he was *such* an idiot.

The truth of the matter was that Bianca was tired and cranky and worried about getting to the shoot late, not that her part was that important. Her big scenes had been shot during the last filming, but there were some others where she was part of the crowd and, according to a text from Mel, they were going to reshoot a couple of the campfire scenes to focus more on Lara, who, despite her trauma of the night before, was already preparing for her expanded role.

Which bugged the hell out of Bianca. Even though Mom didn't understand how important this was to her, at least Dad got it. She was still bothered by her parents' fight in the kitchen earlier. After they'd split up, Mom, with her hothead temper, had tried to keep their arguments behind closed doors, but she just couldn't. When she got mad—boom!—she exploded and Dad knew just how to push her buttons.

Bianca hated their fights and never wanted to pick sides. She knew where her mother was coming from on the issue of *Big Foot Territory: Montana!* and Barclay Sphinx and Hollywood. Bianca understood. She'd already witnessed herself some of the backstabbing and game-playing and, well, out-and-out lying that went on. And yeah, Barclay and his team did seem to pander to the Big Foot Believers and Mayor Justison, and everyone associated with Grizzly Falls, but that was what hype was all about, right? Creating a buzz, getting people interested?

"You're sure you still want to be a part of this?" Jeremy asked as he drove out of the town and into the surrounding hills.

"Why wouldn't I?"

"I don't know. You seem kind of bummed."

"I'm fine," she said as he turned into the entrance to the park and pulled up behind a long row of parked cars, trucks, and SUVs. Ahead, behind the temporary fence, lights were glowing, equipment in place, people moving around the set. "I just hope I'm not fired." She opened the door of his truck.

"You need a ride home? Text me."

"I'll get one. I think Michelle's here, so it shouldn't be that big of a deal."

"I know, but . . . people are going missing and being found dead." From behind the steering wheel, he looked at her.

"You're as bad as Mom." She slammed the door and started toward the camp. Her ankle still hurt, but she kept up a brave face as she reached the gate. She saw Michelle talking to Barclay Sphinx. Upon spying Bianca, Michelle drew away from the producer as if she'd been burned and hurried toward the gate. "Oh, honey," she said with a big frown, "I'm so, so sorry."

"It's okay," Bianca lied. She didn't want anyone making a big deal about it. "Dad says that might change."

"Really?" She frowned, pink lips pouting. "Well . . . maybe." Then she found her smile again. "We'll get through this tonight and see."

"I'm hoping you can give me a ride home. Mom's kind of tied up."

"Right. The baby. Congratulations." Michelle beamed. "How exciting for you. A new little brother, right? Luke called and said it's a boy."

"Tucker Grayson."

"Like that ranching family that lives around here . . . oh, right, because of the sheriff, I get it." She paused and sighed, glanced back at the set, where Barclay was talking to Mel and Lara. "But about that ride," she said, her gaze sliding back to Bianca's. "I'm afraid I can't do it tonight, but don't worry. One of your friends will take you home."

"But I thought—?"

"Is it a problem?" Michelle asked, and the edges

of her beatific smile faltered just a bit. For the first time ever, Bianca saw an edge of steel in her usually effervescent stepmother's expression.

Bianca wanted to argue, to point out that Michelle had promised, but she saw Barclay looking at them and didn't want to make a scene. Besides, she'd rather be with her friends if this was the way Michelle was going to act, and she spied Simone, Maddie, and Teej in the enclosure. "No," she said. "No problem. Jeremy can pick me up if no one can take me home."

"Great!" Back to bubbly Michelle. "Perfect." And then she was off, eager to learn her lines that had been changed and get direction from the great Barclay Sphinx, whom Bianca was starting to think was, as her father had said, "a lying scumbag."

Bianca followed after Michelle and then stopped to look over her shoulder. Out here, beyond the lights, she was alone, everyone else on the other side of the temporary fence.

It almost felt like she was being watched. That beyond the edge of light cast by the lights of the set, there was someone or some*thing* eyeing her every move.

She thought of the night she'd been chased by the monster, about how Destiny Rose Montclaire had been strangled, and she shuddered a little inside. There was nothing out here. Nothing malevolent. Her fear was unfounded.

The rustle she heard was just the flutter of bat wings, or the sigh of the wind rushing through summer-dry branches. The smell that came to her in the dry air was of smoke and musk and sweat, riding on the breeze and coming off of the set.

Yet the hairs on her nape lifted and her throat turned dry as desert sand.

"You're an idiot," she whispered, hobbling to the gate.

Whoever or whatever she thought was observing her from the creeping shadows was just in her overactive mind.

CHAPTER 31

Alvarez stared at the sleeping baby and her heart melted. He was, as Pescoli had said, perfect. Lying on his mother's chest, his tiny lips moving slightly as he breathed, Tucker Grayson appeared at peace with the world. She felt a bit of an intruder in the hospital room with Santana and Regan, but she ignored it and gave in to her fascination with the dozing infant.

"You named him after Dan," she said, and Pescoli nodded.

"We had names picked out for a boy and a girl. Tucker Grayson for this little guy here," she said, stroking the baby's fine hair with a finger, "and Sophia Danielle if he'd been a girl." She glanced at her husband. Santana was sitting in the recliner positioned not far from the hospital bed, in a spot where he could watch and study his newborn son. "I suggested the idea, Santana came up with the names." Regan smiled, looked exhausted but, in Alvarez's opinion, never better. Strange as it sounded, there was a glow to her, despite the circles under her eyes and the scratches visible on her cheek. She'd explained about them, about the attack by Wilda Wyze at Wild Wills hours earlier, about Terri Tufts's remark about her pregnancy, that it was a good thing Pescoli's husband wasn't "shooting blanks." Probably, they thought, in reference to Terri's own ex. Pescoli had heard about the discovery of Marjory's body from Santana, who had seen it online less than an hour earlier, and she had agreed getting DNA on Marjory's fetus was essential.

Though Pescoli had shown some interest in the ongoing cases, it was only peripheral. For now, she was far more wrapped up in this new baby than anything. Alvarez understood, would feel the same if the situations were reversed, but wondered if she'd just lost her partner to this little black-haired human.

"You have to get these guys," Pescoli had said, and Alvarez had agreed. Now, she smiled at the small family but felt a pang on her heartstrings. She'd had a child in her youth, but instead of holding him close and planning a future with him, had given him up for adoption as the circumstances of his conception had been violent. There was no comparison to the making of this little bundle. Though Alvarez had reconnected with her biological son through Dylan, she'd never had this experience, this anticipation and complete and utter joy at the birth. For that, she felt sad, cheated, and yes, even a little guilty. Her son had deserved better and though he was with loving adoptive parents, in some small ways, she'd always felt she'd let him down—or herself down.

Her cell phone indicated a text had come in. From Zoller. Two of the people she wanted to interview had been brought to the station. Good. "Gotta run," she said. "Looks like Kip Bell and Preston Tufts are waiting to answer a few questions."

"Right." Pescoli snorted a disbelieving laugh. "Keep me posted."

"I will. Tomorrow." Alvarez slid a final look at the baby, then said, "Get some rest. My guess is that this guy"—she pointed to the infant—"isn't going to stay this way for long. You'll be busy."

Regan smiled. "Yeah." She touched her child's forehead. "But I'll still want to know."

"You got it," Alvarez said and held up a hand as a silent good-bye to Santana before walking into the hallway and through the main lobby.

Her mind was turning with questions for the

two men who were being brought into the station, the first being: Where's your brother? To each of them. Why had the two older boys been found, but not Emmett Tufts or Kywin Bell, the two she really wanted to grill? If the deputies had gone to the shoot for *Big Foot Territory: Montana!* to round up the potential suspects, as Blackwater promised, why hadn't they come back with the younger brothers?

"Emmett Tufts and Kywin Bell weren't at the location," Watershed explained when she returned to the station. He and Kayan Rule were standing near the doorway to the lunchroom. They were the deputies who'd been charged with the task of finding the "witnesses," as Alvarez was calling them, even though, deep in her heart, she thought them likely suspects. For now, she'd not label them as such—they were just "persons of interest."

Hooking a thumb toward the hall leading to the interview rooms, Watershed said, "We found each of these yahoos at home. The Bell kid tried to convince us he wasn't smoking dope while he was listening to music, plugged into his earphones. Preston Tufts had just gotten out of his car at his father's house after making a run for pizza. So they weren't at the filming."

"They know about Marjory Tufts, right?"

"Yeah." Both nodded.

"They'd heard, one way or another," Rule said.

"But the others—their brothers are definitely MIA. We'd gone up to Reservoir Point looking for all of them, but they weren't there. We asked about them all, talked to the woman in charge of the shoot, Melanie Kline. She was none too happy that we were there, looking for kids who, she insisted, weren't scheduled for filming tonight."

"You accepted that?"

"Nope." Rule had shaken his head. "We double-checked with the producer, Barclay Sphinx, and he confirmed that due to some last-minute changes in the script, those two kids and a couple of others weren't on the roster to show up tonight. He even showed us the casting list. All true."

"So find them," she said, irritated, then went to the lunchroom, grabbed a cup of coffee from the quarter-full pot warming on a hot plate. She drank a couple of swallows of the bitter, over-cooked brew, then mentally steeled herself for the upcoming interviews. She couldn't wait to hear what the older Bell and Tufts kids had to say for themselves, for their brothers. Pausing to check that the audio/video equipment was working and that Blackwater and Zoller were in the viewing area to watch the interviews, she took a look at the "persons of interest" before heading into the rooms.

Through the two-way glass she saw Kip Bell. His face was grizzled from lack of a razor. He sat in his chair, looking around, glaring at the camera he spotted mounted on the wall. His arms were crossed over his massive chest and he glowered, throwing off the vibes that he'd like to tear the next person he saw limb from limb.

In the room next door, viewed through a separate windowed mirror, Preston Tufts was on the move. Nervous. Up on his feet. Back in his chair, knee bouncing uncontrollably as he waited. Chewing on a fingernail. Then standing and pacing again. Ready to crack.

Both of them looked guilty as sin.

And Alvarez, loaded for bear, was hell-bent on finding out why.

"Let's have some fun," she said to Blackwater and Zoller when she left the viewing room and her cell phone beeped with a message from Pete Watershed. He'd heard from another road deputy that Marjory Tufts's dusty rose classic T-Bird had just been located on an abandoned mining road about a mile from the area where the body had been discovered. And it was no longer in pristine shape. Zoller forwarded a picture of the car, vanity license plate MADGE visible, to Alvarez. The bumper was crumpled, huge gouges visible in the pink paint, a large dent over the front driver's side tire.

Alvarez didn't bother with a text, but after giving Zoller and Blackwater the word that these interviews might have to be delayed, Kip and Preston kept "on ice," she rang up Zoller instead. "Tell me where the car is," she said.

"Better yet, I'll show you. I'll meet you in the parking lot."

"I'll drive," Alvarez said.

The crime scene unit was already at the site, flashlights lighting the forest, a larger light focused on Marjory Tufts's once-beautiful car. The T-Bird was destroyed, its body crumpled in spots, the paint gashed, one white wall blown. Obviously, whoever had driven it along an unused mining road and down this near-forgotten spur had bounced the classic vehicle across a creek, over boulders, and through a too-narrow passage that had allowed berry vines and branches to scrape and gouge its once-sleek sides.

Alvarez had parked at the end of the spur. She and Zoller had hiked up the overgrown road. Undergrowth nearly covered the twin ruts of gravel that had been laid half a century earlier and now had eroded into the forest floor.

Two deputies were guarding the area, the crime tech already going over the car that was half in, half out of a dry creek bed, driven as far into the woods as possible, then abandoned.

No one was inside but a tech. Lex Farnsby was carefully combing the interior, which held nothing but a designer overnight bag filled with a woman's change of clothes and toiletries. Marjory's things for her night away from her husband.

"Nothing unusual inside," Farnsby said, "but the

driver's seat is set back to allow a lot of leg room."

"A man," Alvarez said.

"Or very tall woman."

Like Terri Tufts. Ex-wife.

Farnsby went to work on the trunk, unlocking it with a pick and shining the beam of his flashlight over the empty, pristine interior.

"Hey! Got something over here," another tech, a large woman, called as she took a picture of the sparse gravel and dirt of the once-upon-a-time road. "Cigarette butt. Looks like it's fresh." With gloved fingers, she picked it up and held it to her nose. "Yeah. Camel filter." She dropped it into an evidence bag. Alvarez remembered that one of the Bell boys smoked Camels, but he probably wasn't the only one in the crowd of kids who'd know Marjory. Hadn't she seen Preston Tufts slide a pack into his pocket after having a smoke with Donny Justison on the steps of the Sons of Grizzly Falls Building at the end of the Big Foot Believers' meeting?

And wasn't this spur in the forest about half a mile from where the body of Marjory Tufts had been found and less than two miles from the Tuftses' home? For a strong athlete, covering the distance on foot would take little time. Kill the stepmom, dump her body, drive here and sprint home to catch the end of a ball game on ESPN. The gears inside Alvarez's brain began to turn, and for the first time in this investigation, she felt a sizzle of anticipation, the inkling that things were finally falling into place. She was getting close to solving this crime.

Maybe.

"Bingo!" Farnsby said as he slid open a panel in the trunk of the T-Bird. Once the covering was removed, a hidden compartment, meant for more luggage storage, possibly a custom feature, was exposed and it wasn't empty. Haphazardly jammed within that secret space was a very life-like ape suit, mask and foot coverings included.

"The mother lode," Farnsby said under his breath, and Alvarez couldn't agree more.

Size-thirteen tennis shoes were still tucked into the feet of the suit. All a tall person had to do was don the costume, slide into the shoes, adjust the headpiece and voila: Big Foot, alive and well in Grizzly Falls, Montana.

Alvarez and Zoller hung out less than fifteen minutes, then headed back to the station. Once back in the offices, she decided to let the Tufts kid sweat a little longer, let him feel what lock-up was all about. Though he wasn't Marjory Tufts's baby daddy, he probably knew all about it, that his brother had been sleeping with his stepmom. Let him think about it.

So she started with Kip Bell.

He didn't so much as glance her way as she entered the room and introduced herself. Again.

For the record. For the camera and recording. "We need to find your brother," she said, laying a slim file folder on the small table between them.

His eyes barely moved, but he glanced at the folder with its white pages showing a bit. "Don't know where he is."

"I think you do."

Still no eye contact.

"We located an ape suit. Probably the one that was stolen from the Big Foot Believers."

He shrugged.

"You're a member of the club."

Sneering, he said, "Me and like a couple hundred others."

"But you knew Destiny. And Bianca."

Kip sent a bored expression her way. "Your point?"

She tried a different tack. "We know Kywin's the father of Destiny Rose Montclaire's baby. We know he was in contact with both Destiny Rose Montclaire and Lindsay Cronin on the day each girl disappeared. He was one of the last people to communicate with them."

"You don't know shit," he said.

She smiled. "I think we do." She kept calm. Stared at him, and though she wanted to shake the answers from his lying lips, she played it cool. "Both Lindsay and Destiny texted him."

"He never got the texts." He looked up then, his eyes harboring a secret, and she saw that he was silently laughing at her, that he seemed to think he had one up on her, on the police in general.

But she knew better. She slid the file folder in his direction.

"How do you know he didn't get the texts?" she asked.

Again the silent mockery. "Because he said he never got 'em."

"He could have lied. The phone company records say otherwise."

"So what? Kywin says he never saw 'em." A lift of one massive shoulder. "I believe him."

"He's lied about a lot of things. Including being involved with Destiny."

A roll of one big shoulder. Defiance in the set of his jaw, and throughout the rest of the questioning, the attitude that he knew more than she and he wasn't going to tell her a thing.

"So, let's talk about Lindsay Cronin."

He flinched slightly. Not much, but a little twitch near his eye that told Alvarez he was listening. Worried.

"We have phone records," she said, nudging the file folder closer to him. "And the interesting thing, Kip? Not only did Lindsay text Kywin, but she also called you."

"What?"

"On your cell. What appears to be a pocket-dial or butt-dial." She leaned back in her chair and eyed him. "Go ahead, take a look. It's almost as if

Lindsay was warning you. Kind of like Destiny. She did it too. Why? So that you could . . . what? Tell Kywin that she wanted to talk to him, to make certain he got the call?"

He didn't respond. Just froze and stared at the folder.

"I think the short calls were a signal. I'm not talking about the longer conversations she had with you, just those that coincided with the texts to Kywin. I figure the signal told you to pick up your brother's phone, so that no one, not even Kywin, knew how close you and Lindsay were."

"What?" he snarled. "That's crazy."

"I think you knew where Lindsay Cronin was heading that night and you knew exactly when she'd be on Horsebrier Ridge. That somehow, some way, you caused her death."

His eyes, deep in his sockets, glowed with a dark, horrifying rage. "You know nothing," he said through tight lips.

"That's where you're wrong, Kip. I—we— know a lot," she assured him. "And one thing's for sure. You're up to your eyeballs in this. So you have a choice: Come clean, tell us everything you know, and I'll talk to the DA, try to get you a deal. Or you can clam up and it might take a little longer, but we'll get to the truth and when we do?" She paused for effect, arching her eyebrows, then said, "Your ass, my friend, is grass."

"You're no friend of mine!" he bit out.

"That's right. I'm not." She managed an icy smile. "And that is the first time you've ever told me the truth. So think about it." She climbed off her chair and left him alone to stew.

Then, she headed for the next interview room.

At the location of the filming of *Big Foot Territory: Montana!* Bianca watched the action from the sidelines. Her part, after the discovery of the body, and the scene with her "mother," Michelle, was minimal, so she waited around a lot, observing the other actors on the set, seeing how some of the previous scenes were reshot to highlight Lara.

It kinda made her sick.

Maddie grabbed a Diet Coke from the drink cart, and while Teej was in a scene with just boys, she sidled up to Bianca. "Can you believe it?" she said as Lara was positioned on one of the rocks, a guitar at her side, her blouse undone a few buttons, her remarkable cleavage visible. "They're going to make her this orphaned girl with dreams of a singing career or something." She opened her drink, took a swallow, and glanced at Bianca out of the corner of her eye. As she brought the bottle down, she said, "I think she faked it. The attack."

Bianca knew it! Her dad was right. "Did she say so?"

"Nu-uh, she's not that stupid. But Alex did. To

Teej. Just kind of bragging about it. See—" Still holding the plastic bottle, she pointed at TJ's brother. "He's in the scenes, too." Maddie's lips curled in disgust. "It worked out for him."

"I thought that might be because Kywin and Emmett are MIA," Bianca said. "Where are they anyway?"

"Don't know. Don't care. They're both just big bullies." She was eyeing a makeup artist running into the scene to brush some kind of powder on Lara's face. "But trust me, these scenes were changed on purpose because Lara asked them to be. She's kind of in charge now, because of 'the attack.' " Maddie let out a huff of disapproval. Or was it jealousy? "Have you seen how Barclay is around her? As bad as the rest of the boys, practically drooling. Men. All the same."

Somewhere overhead, hidden in the darkness over the lights illuminating the set, an owl hooted softly.

"You heard about Marjory, right?"

"No." Bianca was still watching as the makeup artist backed away from the campsite. "What about her?"

"She's dead."

"Dead?" Bianca said a little too loudly and was rewarded with a warning look from Mel. She lowered her voice to a whisper. "What do you mean 'dead'?"

"What do you think I mean? They found her

body in the forest and I think it was like Destiny's, y'know. She was strangled, I guess. It's all over Facebook and Twitter. My phone's been blowing up. How could you not know?"

"I left my phone at home."

Maddie shot her an are-you-out-of-your-mind look. "What?"

"It was crazy there—when I left. Mom was in labor, Dad was there freaking out about the show, and we all just took off because the baby was coming and fast." Maddie was nodding; she'd heard all the details about Tucker's birth before, when Bianca had first arrived a few hours earlier. Now, it was after midnight, the temperature dropping, the night closing in.

The production crew was wrapping up the final scenes and Bianca couldn't help but wonder why she'd even come in the first place, as she'd been little more than window dressing in a couple of scenes, part of the crowd in the background, her luster, the girl who'd been chased by a Big Foot in real life, dimmed.

Her dad had been right. Her chance at stardom, if there ever had been one, was over. As she watched Lara, the glow from the fake campfire gilding her skin and catching in the blond strands of her hair, Bianca felt something akin to hatred for the girl. Lara had manipulated everything, just as Dad had said. Maddie had confirmed it and it pissed Bianca off.

What was fair about this? Bianca had been scared out of her mind the night the beast had chased her through the woods, scared to death. Of course, now, she wasn't certain a real Sasquatch had been running after her. But *some*thing had been careening down the hillside, crashing after her, breathing hard, smelling fetid, and clawing at her. Her fear had been real. *Real.* Something, she'd been certain, had been hell-bent on killing her.

And Lara fakes it?

She eyed the kids at the shoot. Could it all have been a wild prank, one that had been blown out of proportion? But why? And who would have been behind it? And how did it connect with Destiny Rose's death? That was the really disturbing part, that Destiny had been killed, and now Marjory. Lindsay Cronin, too, if Bianca's mom was right. Regan was convinced that the deaths were some-how connected.

Standing between a crane and the path to the Porta Potties, Bianca stared at her friends with new eyes, her vision changed by the tragedies that had occurred. Despite the warm night, Bianca shivered and rubbed her arms with her hands. As the campfire scene was filmed, then over, the crew switched to the second location in the parking lot, where two pickups and Austin Reece's BMW were parked.

Lara and Austin were to be making out inside

the sports car. According to the script, there was to be a dark shadow looming and moving ever closer behind the back of the BMW. As Barclay had described the scene: "It's going to look like all those ghost stories we all grew up with where the teenagers are really going at it, the girl's blouse is coming off and she's in her bra, but there's a deadly killer outside and we, as the viewers, see it. Know that death is nearby. Bill," he'd called to one of the cameramen, "I'll want the camera to come in from the Big Foot's perspective, at the rear of the car, of course— make sure we don't see the license plate, just the rear window, which will be foggy as things are really heating up inside, okay? Everyone else, back, we want this to look like Lara and Austin are all alone."

How this new scene would fit into the original story line, Bianca wasn't certain, since the scenes were filmed out of order rather than sequentially, then patched together. She didn't know if the make-out scene in the car would be cut in before the guitar scene at the campfire or Bianca's already filmed action scene where she ended up in the creek.

As the actors were moved from one shooting site to the next and the cameras were rearranged, Maddie, the diet soda swinging from her fingers, sought out Teej again. Once more, Bianca was left on her own. She thought about calling Jeremy to come get her, but she wasn't ready to go home yet, and besides, the deal was that everyone was supposed to stay until the shoot was over for the night.

So she hung in the periphery, saw Carlton Jeffe and Ivor Hicks and a few other Big Foot Believers and wondered how she'd fallen out of favor so quickly. Not that long ago Barclay Sphinx had been interviewing her, talking up her story at the Big Foot Believers meeting. And what had happened to all that talk about a trailer and setting up a reward for helping locate Destiny Rose Montclaire's killer? Was that still on the table? She didn't know because she was out of the loop and Lara, now in only a bra and short skirt as she stood near the open door of Austin's BMW, was Barclay's latest discovery.

Bianca couldn't help but feel a little like a girl out in the cold, her nose pressed to the window of a home where a birthday party was in full swing, a celebration from which she'd been excluded or, more likely, recently uninvited.

Wah, wah, she chided. *Get over your bad self.*

"Okay, everyone . . . back up. We need a little more room here," Mel said to the crowd.

The action started up again, and Bianca inched farther into the shadows, her attention focused on Austin's car and Lara overacting all over the place. Bianca couldn't stand it another second. Who cared if she was supposed to stay for the entire shoot? They were never going to ask her to be a part of any of the scenes. She'd been here over three hours, and not once had anyone in production spoken to her, except to tell her to stay out of the way. It was all just a big waste of time. She should just call Jeremy and go home, rest her ankle and figure out what she was going to do with the rest of her life, which, obviously, wasn't going to be a part of *Big Foot Territory: Montana!*

She started for the main gate and reached into her pocket automatically. Of course it wasn't there. Great. Now what? She either had to borrow a phone from someone here or wait for a ride. She started to turn back to the set when she heard the first twig snap.

Craaack!

Glancing over her shoulder, she searched the darkness.

No one.

Nothing.

You're being a moron, she told herself, but felt a movement, a disturbance in the air, an undercurrent that caused her heart to still.

That was crazy, though, right?

She was still inside the gate.

Another sound—the shuffle of stealthy footsteps?

Fear sizzled through her bloodstream, a very primal wariness.

One more look over her shoulder and she saw

only the darkened forest surrounding the lane where cars were parked haphazardly. Nothing to worry about—

She started to look over her shoulder just as something cold and hard was pressed against the side of her neck. A gun? A gun with teeth?

"Don't move," a low male voice ordered, a voice she thought she recognized.

"What?"

Zaaaap!

Pain ripped through her body.

Her scream was a mere gurgle in her throat.

Thousands of volts sizzled through her body. Needles of pain. She jerked. Her legs gave way. She fell, hard, the ground rushing up, her head clunking, dust flying into her mouth, her cheek twitching against the gravel.

What, what, what? She thought around the agony of having no control as her muscles spasmed, her eyes out of focus. Pain ricocheted through her and she tried to think, to see, to scream, but could do nothing.

"I told you not to move, Bianca. Jesus, you're a fuckin' bitch."

She knew that voice. She was sure. But her brain was scrambled, her entire body disconnected. She tried to rise from the ground but couldn't control the violent spasms running through her limbs.

What was happening?

Who was doing this?

Why, oh, God, why?

Her assailant, huge and shadowed, grabbed her with strong, meaty hands and dragged her twitching body along the hard earth.

No, oh, please no! Scraped and battered, pain shrieking through her limbs, agony ripping through her brain, she was hauled into the darkness. Her thoughts were scattered, the world spinning, and suddenly everything went black.

CHAPTER 32

"I need a cigarette," Preston Tufts said when Alvarez slipped into the second interrogation room.

"Sorry." She wasn't going to play nicey-nice. Not tonight. So he was having a few cravings, a need for a hit of nicotine. Fine. Let him itch for a smoke. "No can do. Not in here. But you can have one later, when we're done."

"And when will that be?"

"Depends on you, I guess. When you want to tell me the truth."

"Hey, I haven't lied. And I could really use a smoke."

She acted as if she were considering the request. "What's your brand again?"

"Excuse me?"

"Camels, right?"

He stared at her warily, as if wondering where she was going. "Maybe."

"I'd say, 'for sure,'" she countered. "And you know, that's funny."

"How?"

"Because we found the butt of a Camel cigarette not far from where we found your stepmother's car. The pink classic T-Bird with the vanity plates."

He swallowed hard, his gaze fixed on hers.

"It will be interesting to find out whose DNA is on that butt, a filter-tip by the way, like the kind you smoke. It's with the lab now."

His jaw clenched, but he didn't respond and she noticed a trickle of sweat running from his brow. The room was a couple of degrees too warm by design. She'd wanted him uncomfortable.

She continued, her voice even, "Also, pretty soon we'll find out whose fingerprints are on the steering wheel of her car and if there's any DNA, you know from sweat on the ape suit we found in the trunk."

He froze.

She smiled.

"God, it's got to be hot running in that thing in the middle of summer—and we'll figure out who was wearing the ape suit . . . oh, excuse me, Big Foot costume. Got to be DNA in it."

His Adam's apple bobbed for a second.

"Did you wear it?"

"I didn't even know it was there!"

Another lie. She saw it in his eyes.

"You'd better be straight with me, Preston," she warned him. "Because it will be pretty easy to link the person inside the suit to the murders and whoever chased Bianca Pescoli the night Destiny Rose Montclaire was found."

"Wait a second! What does one thing have to do with the other?" he asked, and his eyes had rounded, a newfound fear evident. "I mean . . . Jesus." His shoulders slumped. He bit his lower lip. "I think I need a lawyer."

Damn!

She'd known it would come down to this, the lawyer request, of course, and she'd gotten more from him than she'd expected, but she'd hoped he'd open up. For now, the interview was over. "Okay, we'll call one for you or if you don't have one—"

He closed his eyes and dropped his face into his hands. "I am so fucked!" he said into his palms. "So damned fucked."

She didn't wait, but there, on the spot, with the cameras rolling, read him his rights, the Miranda warning. "Now, you'll need to stay here until your lawyer arrives. But if there's anything you want to tell me, I promise I'll try to get a deal for you."

He hesitated, then lifted his face. It was wet. Tears shined in his eyes. "I didn't mean to kill her," he said, and she froze in her chair. "I didn't mean to kill Marjory, but she was banging my dad and he would find out, especially with all the DNA samples you took. My mom told me a long time ago that Dad . . . well, his sperm wasn't viable, and that she'd gone to a sperm bank." At her expression, he nodded, his lips pulling into a frown, the dam of silence that he'd built suddenly broken, the flood waters of guilt rushing through.

"Yeah, how do you think that feels, huh?" Preston demanded. "Dad, he doesn't even know. She did it behind his back, only told me because I had to go to the hospital, got in a car wreck and might need a transfusion, and she was afraid it would all come out. That somehow the blood type would show up wrong and . . . But it didn't matter cuz he left her for Marjory. You know the end of that story, that she was originally Emmett's girlfriend and so, once they were married, she and Emmett got back to it. And crap, she gets pregnant?

"How stupid is she?" He was unloading now, still fighting tears but seeming to want to unburden himself. Sniffing, he said, "It was an accident, really. Marjory and Dad had gotten into another one of their fights—rip roarers—and this time Emmett, he thinks he's going to take Dad on. Which is just stupid, so I talk him down, say I'll handle it and you know, talk some sense into Marjory.

"Like that was going to happen. Anyway, I met

up with Marjory in town before she got to the hotel where she was going to stay after her fight with Dad. We drove around and stopped the car, up near Cougar Pass, and you know what? She not only doesn't listen to me, she actually comes on to me. Like kissing me and touching me and . . . and I start to go for it, y'know?" He was staring at Alvarez, hoping she understood.

"Of course," she forced out.

"I mean she's hot and I'm always horny, and we start going at it. I mean, big time."

"You had sex."

"Yeah, yeah, in the car, and then, when it's all over, she kind of freaks out, and not just a little bit, not like she feels a little guilty. Nuh-uh, she fuckin' goes psycho on me and starts to try to kill me and screaming that I took advantage of her, that I raped her when she was all over me—all over me. She was, like, all of a sudden fuckin' nuts!"

"So what did you do?"

"I tried to shut her up. That's all." His hands flew to the side of his head, palms out, as if he were trying, in his mind, to back away from an impossible situation. "When she comes at me, hitting me and trying to bite me, I just try to shut her up, y'know. So I put my hands around her neck and squeezed until she quit attacking me and . . . and I guess . . . I guess I didn't stop. Not when I should have. I was kind of like in a different dimension, you know?"

She didn't.

"It was like almost an out-of-body experience. And when it was over and I knew she was dead and the baby was dead too"—fresh tears erupted from his eyes—"I just panicked and thought, maybe I could leave her in the woods, somewhere close to Reservoir Point and . . . and maybe everyone would think that a Big Foot or whoever killed Destiny Rose had done it." He let out a long, shuddering breath.

"What about Destiny Rose?"

"I don't know. I had nothin' to do with that. Nothin', I swear!" He ran an arm under his nose and sniffed loudly.

"And the ape suit?"

"Shit. How the fuck did that get in there? I have no idea." He looked at her so ingenuously she almost believed him. Almost.

"You didn't kill Destiny Rose Montclaire?"

"No."

"Or Lindsay Cronin?"

"For fuck's sake, didn't you hear me? I said no! I don't know what happened to them." He shoved the fingers of both hands through his hair. "For the love of Christ, Detective, can I please have a cigarette now? And would you call my fuckin' lawyer?"

Where the hell were they taking her? Two men had abducted Bianca. She knew that now. They'd tied her hands quickly, stuffed a rag into her mouth so she couldn't scream, then thrown her into the back of a pickup and driven wildly through the night, the huge truck bouncing and grinding over the old road at Reservoir Point to the country road where the engine had roared smoothly, the tires humming over smooth asphalt, hip-hop music blasting through the open windows.

This she only knew partially, as her rattled brain was trying to make sense of what had happened and regain control of her body again, but it had been impossible and as she'd stared upward, seeing a wide night sky filled with thousands of twinkling stars and feeling the rush of the wind as the truck sped down the road, she could do nothing but wait and see what fate they had in store for her.

Nothing good. She realized that horrifying fact. She'd heard the thrill of excitement in their voices, felt the testosterone thrumming through them, pumping them up, pushing them into the caveman mentality of sheer brutality.

Think, Bianca. You have to get hold of yourself. You have to save yourself. No one knows where you are; no one will be looking for you. Jeremy will think you've gotten a ride with a friend or Michelle. Mom is at the hospital with the new baby. Santana's staying with her. You're on your own. For the rest of the night, these psychos will be able to do whatever they want to you.

Unless you fight back.

She wanted to give up. To fall into a million pieces and cry. To even beg for mercy, but she could tell, even in her current, jangled state, that whoever had taken her was psyched up, adrenaline running fast and hard through their veins, maybe helped along with drugs . . .

At that thought, she knew what she was up against.

She knew who had abducted her, and a cold as icy as the frigid North settled in her gut.

It all came together. In her jolted, jerking state, she mentally ID'd the son of a bitch who had to be behind all of the attacks. She didn't know why he was involved or how, but he was involved.

She hazarded a glance to the back window of the cab and saw the gun rack, in position, the long barrel of some kind of hunting rifle visible. So they were armed with more than a stupid stun gun.

With a jerk, the driver cut a quick corner, and the back tires spun on dust and gravel, throwing Bianca to the far side of the bed before the wheels caught hold again and the pickup nosed upward, gears grinding on some steep backwoods road. She tried to think, to reason things out. Why Tophman, the preacher's son, and drug dealer to the football and baseball teams? Everyone in school knew that if you wanted to get high and needed anything from weed, to meth to 'roids, Tophman could set you up. He himself had bulked up by using steroids, and it was his private joke that his parents and coaches hadn't figured it out. All of the other kids, Bianca included, never ratted him out. In Bianca's case, she was a cop's daughter, already the target of ridicule and suspicion, and besides, she didn't care what the other kids did.

Now it had come full circle, and she was going to pay the ultimate price. Unless she did something and fast. The truck ground upward as she tried to figure out how to save herself. She twisted to her side, raised her head, and through the cab window saw a glow, the headlights spraying light against the trees.

Still she had no idea where she was, just somewhere deep in the wilderness of the Bitterroot Mountains.

Move, Bianca. Get moving. You don't have much time, and if you want to save yourself . . .

Her hands were tied, but in front of her, rather than in back, and she'd already yanked out the filthy rag they'd used as a gag. She worked at the knots at her wrists, but her fingers were still disobeying, unable to loosen the heavy twine. Her legs were free, thank God, and slowly, far too slowly, she was regaining control of her limbs.

The pickup bucked and shook as it hit a big rock.

"Shit! Be careful!" Tophman yelled, his voice reaching Bianca from the open window of the cab.

"It ain't as if this is the damned freeway," another voice said. Kywin Bell. The driver. *Oh, damn!* Her mother's number-one suspect in Destiny Rose's murder. She tried to push herself upright. Her arms gave way and she fell against the floor of the bed, hitting her chin and probably splitting open the wound. *Damn it all to hell.*

She tried again. Her muscles tried to fold in on her, but she gritted her teeth and was able to hold up her weight for a few seconds. Now, if she could just find a weapon, or jump out of the truck without them seeing her.

But she couldn't outrun them.

And she had no source of illumination, while they had flashlights. And the stun gun. And the rifle or shotgun or whatever. And probably more.

No, no, no . . . all she had on her side was the element of surprise.

The truck was slowing—they were reaching their destination, wherever it was. *God help me.* She felt around the bed of the truck. Empty. Except for the toolbox fastened behind the cab, right behind their heads. As they turned a corner, the truck leveling off, she forced her still-shuddering body to her knees and then, as quietly as possible, pushed the lid of the box open just wide enough for her hand to slip through and dig, quietly, across a shelf of flat tools until she felt the handle of what was probably a screwdriver. Just what she needed.

As Kywin braked, she withdrew the small tool and, with shaking fingers, hands still tied together, lifted it to the neck of her T shirt and forced it into her bra. Then, daring another raid in the box, she reached inside again and felt something flat and palm sized and . . . oh Geez, was it one of those all in one tools, like a Swiss Army knife? Could she get that lucky? She slipped it out, saw it was just that and, using her fingers and teeth, pulled several of the deadly little blades from their sheath. Then she went to work on the twine, sawing wildly.

You can do this. You can! At least the feeling was back in her hands and feet, her muscles were beginning to obey her again.

But, she knew, she was fast running out of time.

Kip Bell had finally cracked. Given enough time alone, he'd come to his senses and decided he wanted a deal. But he'd demanded a lawyer and a promise of leniency, both of which had been granted. He'd talked with his lawyer and after an hour of negotiations with the DA, whom Alvarez had called, he finally spilled his guts.

"Just so you know. I didn't kill no one," he said. "Not really."

What kind of confession was that? Alvarez said, "But—?"

He glanced at his lawyer, who sat next to him in the interview room. She was about sixty, with silver hair, no lipstick and tired eyes behind rimless glasses. She'd obviously not wanted to be hauled out of bed in the middle of the night, but now, Diane Moore was giving her all to her client. She nodded.

"It was all supposed to be a joke," he said, and the lawyer winced slightly.

"What was?"

"All of it. The monkey suit. I lifted it from the club, the Big Foot Believers, and yeah, I chased Bianca with it that night. It was kind of a joke, like I said, a prank, a big 'Ha-ha!' but I didn't know anything about . . . Destiny. I swear. That was a total shocker, you know."

Alvarez waited.

Another nod from the lawyer.

"And I got into a little more trouble. You were right, I was, like . . . involved with Lindsay. She was really Kywin's friend. Hell—all the girls are, y'know."

Alvarez didn't.

"But she, Lindsay and I connected. I didn't want Kywin to get wind of it and we share a room at the old man's house—it's really a pain—so Lindsay and me, we worked out this signal system. She'd butt dial me, like a mistake, y'know," he said, trying to look honest when Alvarez knew him to be a liar. "And then she got real upset. Knew that Kywin had something to do with Destiny's death. Destiny had texted her and told her she was going to meet Donny that night, the same as she texted Kywin, so . . . she wanted to go to the cops and tell everyone what she knew." Some of his bravado slipped a little. "I told her to meet me up at Horsebrier Ridge at a park up there, we'd been there before. So she snuck out and I did a stupid thing. I went up ahead of her and left a dummy on the road, so that she'd see it, you know, and swerve. I just wanted to scare her. . . ."

"But she did just what you expected, swerved, overcorrected, and ended up driving her car into the canyon, where she died."

He looked at his hands. "Yeah," he said softly. "I didn't expect her to die."

"You thought she'd survive?" Alvarez didn't bother hiding the skepticism in her voice.

"I didn't know she'd actually drive off the damned cliff. Besides, she was going to rat out Kywin."

"The brother you didn't want to know that you and she were seeing each other."

"That was before everything got so heavy, you know?" He was now searching for reasons to explain his unexplainable behavior.

Alvarez said, "So you thought it would be funny, a prank, to scare the living shit out of her by having her crash her car."

"I already told you: I didn't know that would happen."

"Really?" Alvarez wanted to lean across the

table and throttle the stupid ass, but she controlled herself by holding on to the edges of the table in a death grip.

Diane Moore said, "My client is here giving you information. This is obviously difficult for him."

Difficult, my ass. A girl is dead! She wasn't about to apologize to this jerk-wad. "So what happened to the body you left on the road—the dummy?"

"I picked it up. Still have it. In a shed at my dad's place."

"I'll want to see it."

"Of course," Diane said before Kip could argue. "My client has offered full disclosure for leniency," she said, reminding both Alvarez and Kip Bell of their deal.

"So did Kywin kill Destiny Rose Montclaire?" she asked.

"I don't know," Kip said. "But . . . but Lindsay thought so."

"How did the ape suit get in Marjory Tufts's car?"

"I put it there," he admitted. "I saw it parked in the dealership lot one night—she was out with her husband in his car and had left it there with the keys in it. It was parked out back, no cameras and no one was looking. I wanted it out of my rig, so I took a chance. I figured no one would ever find it."

"Guess you figured wrong." She leaned forward and looked him straight in the eye. "So where's your brother? Where's Kywin? I really need to talk to him."

"I don't know, Detective," he said. "And that's the fuckin' truth!"

The truck shuddered to a stop, engine still thrumming in the darkness. Bianca forced herself to wait, to pretend that the effects of the stun gun hadn't worn off. When her assailants came to do whatever it was they were planning, she'd lay there, still twitching, and act as if she were still tied and not in control of her body. The twine still covered her wrists, she'd retied pieces around each of them and held them tightly together, the little knife in her right palm.

Could she pull this off? she wondered, looking up, through the lacy canopy of branches, to a slice of moon. Thank God for the darkness. She swallowed hard, every muscle tight, her heart trip-hammering wildly.

Stay calm, Bianca. You can do this. Just keep your wits about you. Don't panic. Do not freak.

They were strong and fast and determined. She was lithe and smart and scared out of her mind. She felt a surge of adrenaline as the two doors opened simultaneously. The engine was cut, lights still illuminating the forest in front of the truck, the sudden silence deafening.

The passenger said, "Get her out. I gotta take a piss!" Tophman. She knew it was that loser Tophman! Cowering in the bed, trying to get her courage pulled together, she heard boots drop to the ground, one set of footprints heading away, into the beam of the headlights, the other, from the driver's side, coming around the truck.

Her pulse pounded in her brain.

There was just enough ambient light filtering from the headlights that she could see him, his big body hulking around the side.

Oh, God. Help me.

With a metal squeak, the tailgate fell open.

Could she do it?

Leaning forward, Kywin Bell reached inside to grab her by the legs and pull her out of the truck.

Now!

Before he clamps a hand over your ankle.

Quick as a rattler striking, she kicked. Hard as she could. Hitting him hard in the face with her good foot, jamming the heel of her boot into his nose.

"Yeeeooowww!" Screaming, he fell backward a step. "What the fuck?" he cried, grabbing his head, stumbling to one knee.

Blood gushed out of his nose and ran down his face.

She scooted closer and hauled back.

Bam! She kicked him again. Harder. Aiming directly at his nose and eyes rather than kicking blindly.

Crack!

The cartilage in his nose splintered and he fell onto his butt. Another piercing yell.

"Hey!" Tophman yelled. "What's going on?"

She rolled out of the bed, her feet landing only inches from the half-blind Kywin. Before he could get his brain around the fact that she was escaping, she took off, running into the darkness, fast as she could, branches slapping at her face, cobwebs clinging to her hair, pine needles scratching her skin. Down the hill, faster and faster, her bad ankle screaming, her heart pounding, her brain on fire. At least her body was responding, but how far could she go, how long before he ran her to ground, tracked her like a lion on a wounded gazelle?

Don't think like that!

Don't give up. Do not.

Run, run, run!

She had no idea where she was, but she kept moving down the hillside. The truck had climbed from the main road. She'd felt it heading ever upward so the road had to be downhill. Had it been a mile? More? Less? Oh, God, she had no idea.

Just keep moving!

She couldn't run flat-out. The terrain was too steep, and it was inky dark beneath the branches of the trees. She had to be careful, keeping her balance while her bad ankle began to throb.

Ignore it. Keep running. She hit a root or rock and fell, sliding and tumbling, her fall increasing. She thought of sliding over the rim of a canyon and scrabbled in the dirt and rocks, with her fingers, trying to break her fall, desperate to right herself. Clawing, fingernails breaking, her little knife flying from her hands, she tumbled until she was stopped, her body slamming against the hard trunk of a pine tree.

"Oof!" Her entire body jangled. Dust and dirt filled her nostrils. For a second, she didn't know up from down.

"That little bitch!" Tophman cried, but his voice was more distant now.

She blinked, saw light. The truck. Up the hillside.

"And you, you dumb fuck," Tophman roared. "You let her get away? What's wrong with you? How the hell do you think we'll ever get paid, huh?"

Paid? Someone was going to pay them for abducting her? Killing her? What in the world was that all about?

"Get the shotgun." Bell's voice.

Oh, crap!

"She ain't gettin' away. No way!" Bell again. "She needs to die."

"I should shoot you for being such a dumb ass!" Tophman said.

She started moving, ever downward, her entire

body aching. Surely she'd run into a path or a road or something. Or someone. Please. Oh, God.

"I'd love to kill her, but that wasn't the deal. The old man, he doesn't want her dead."

The old man? What old man?

She heard the click of the shotgun being readied, a shell now in its chamber, and her heart stilled. She couldn't do this. Though she heard Kywin moaning and knew that he was out of commission, Tophman was still coming after her, his footsteps crunching on leaves and debris. He had a flash-light, or the light from his iPhone, was shining it through the forest, the garish white-blue light swinging in a wide arc over the ground.

"You can't get away from me," he yelled. And he was right. God, he was right. Now, her weapon, reduced to a screwdriver, seemed pathetic. "Come out, come out wherever you are, cop kid," he singsonged while Kywin groaned pathetically.

Tophman didn't care about his friend, no way. He was on the hunt. Prowling through the night, searching out his prey, determined to catch her.

Screw that!

As long as he used the flashlight, she could see him and hopefully avoid the swath of light it produced. She was farther down the hill from him, and she moved to the side out of the swinging beam.

When he pointed the flashlight down the hill,

she saw nothing but more forest, and rocks and brush. He paused. Listening. She froze, didn't move a muscle. And then he started turning, rotating, swinging the beam of his flashlight in an arc. She pressed herself up against the bole of a tree and prayed that it was wide enough to hide her body.

Don't let him see me. Don't let him see me, she silently prayed as the light swept over the tree, pausing, the beams stretching out on either side, the tree itself making a shadow in the fake bluish light. She barely breathed.

"Where the hell are you?" Tophman said.

Sweat drizzled down her forehead and neck. Her heart pounded so loudly she was certain he could hear it.

"Bi-AN-ca!" Again the chilling singsong voice.

She licked her lips. Heard him call her name again and then the beam rotated, turned back down the hillside.

"Bitch," he muttered and started down again.

Swallowing back fear, she reached into her shirt and bra, located the screwdriver, and slowly, noiselessly withdrew it. Her palms were slick with sweat and she nearly dropped it, but managed to hold on to it. For now.

Bianca waited. Let him go ahead of her and, once he was twenty yards lower on the hillside, begin to creep up to the truck, her one chance at escape. If she could just get past the wounded

Kywin Bell and Tophman didn't get wise to her plan.

Holding her breath, one eye on the flashlight heading ever downward, she inched upward toward the truck and, she hoped, freedom. Her heart was a jackhammer, her bad leg aching, every nerve end tight. But she was close.

She saw the truck, headlights burning, and kept moving, faster and faster. Twenty yards. Fifteen. Ten.

"Hey!" Tophman's voice. Nearer than she expected. Had he turned around and seen her? Was he even now running up the hill toward her, pointing his gun, ready to blow her to smithereens?

Crap!

Throwing caution to the wind, she began to sprint the last five yards up the hill, through the leaves and sticks, upward, ever upward to the truck—

She let out her breath and kept in the shadows. What if there were no keys in the ignition? If she couldn't get the truck started. If—

Nearly at the truck, she froze.

Kywin!

Where the hell was Kywin Bell?

Frantically she searched the area near the truck. She'd left him writhing on the ground, his face a bloody pulp, but . . .

Every hair on her scalp twitched. Goose pimples crawled up her arms, but she saw the open door to the cab and she flung herself toward it. Just as she heard a low growl and unsteady footsteps.

From the corner of her eye, she saw him. He launched himself through the air, a massive black monster. He hit her hard, his weight propelling her to the ground inches from the pickup.

"You fuckin' bitch!" he growled on top of her, big fists curled, as he worked his legs to straddle her, pinning her arms with his tree-stump legs. "Did you really think you could get away?" He snarled, looming like a monster above her. His nose was mashed, his words nasal, his eyes bright with a need for personal revenge. "You're gonna pay!" He turned his head and yelled into the darkness. "I got her! Up here! At the truck! Alive. For the old man."

Her fingers tightened over the screwdriver. The way he was positioned, his legs spread wide, her arms pinned together beneath his crotch, she had one chance.

Now, she thought, *do it now!*

With all her strength, she reared up. Her clasped hands forced the screwdriver upward, through his shorts and deep into his scrotum.

He roared in pain, tried to jump away. "Aaaaagggh!"

She shoved again.

"Shit! Damn. Fuck. Aaaaah, Geeeeod!" Still he was atop her. And she heard running footsteps fast approaching.

Tophman!

She pulled back on the screwdriver. Heard a sucking sound, then with all her strength, thrust up again driving hard.

With a shriek, he grabbed his crotch as something warm poured from his shorts. He rolled off her, allowing her just enough room to slither away.

Screaming in pain, holding the juncture of his legs, he rolled in the earth and cursed at her.

"What the hell?" Tophman's voice—too close—boomed over the whimpering and swearing of the man curled into a fetal position.

She didn't wait. Clawed her way to her foot. Nearly fell into the cab and forced herself inside.

The keys—the blessed keys—dangled from the ignition.

She turned the switch and the big engine roared to life.

Yanking the door closed, she caught a glimpse of Tophman, running now, not far away, the shotgun at his shoulder.

She found reverse and hit the gas, the truck backing up. Tophman jumped out of the way as the pickup bucked wildly over the rough earth, hitting something solid as it stopped. Bell screamed again.

She'd run over him!

"Hey! Hey!" Tophman was yelling, but she threw the truck into first and, sitting on the edge of the driver's seat, floored it. Gravel and dust sprayed from under the tires.

A horrifying shriek split the night.

Tophman yelled, "No! No! No! You fucking— oh, hell. Fuck her old man!"

She was going to do it! She would make it! If Tophman didn't shoot her first.

What? Fuck her old man? Who were they talking about? Lucky? He was behind this? "No," she whispered. That had to be all wrong. He would never . . . not even for fame or glory or money or . . . "No, no, no!" She pounded on the steering wheel with a fist as the truth hit her. Hard. Understanding, vile as it was, burned through her veins. Her heart thundering, her whole world turned upside down to a dark oblivion, she tried to pull herself together. To save herself. She stared at the break in the trees that had once been a road and now was just dry earth in a narrow swath cutting through the forest. *Good enough!* She nearly stood on the accelerator, the truck bouncing and shimmying as the big tires hit rocks and roots and snags.

Somewhere, not far, she hoped, was the county road. If she could only get there . . .

Blam!

Glass shattered, the back window exploding.

Shards of glass sprayed into the cab.

The truck shuddered. She wondered if the shotgun was capable of hitting the gas line or the tires. Maybe she was lucky that he didn't have a rifle with bullets rather than shells.

Just drive!

Checking the rearview, she saw something on the crest of the hill where the sun was beginning to rise, dawn breaking.

Bryant Tophman, shotgun stock at his shoulder, barrel aimed at the truck, was visible in silhouette. "Try it," she muttered under her breath and shifted down as she started around what had once been a corner.

Blam!

The truck shuddered, but kept moving, and Bianca, determined to make it back to Grizzly Falls, to her mother, to her new baby brother and her bastard of a father who would dare *sell* her, tromped on the gas pedal.

CHAPTER 33

When Lucky Pescoli opened a bleary eye, the sun was streaming through the bedroom windows and his head pounded from a hangover that wouldn't quit. His stomach was queasy and he couldn't remember the last time he'd tied one on like this. It was a mother, a real rager.

He stumbled into the bathroom and peed as if he'd never quit before he really woke up, blinking, shaking off, then seeing himself in the mirror, a middle-aged man who needed to get his act together. Bits and pieces of the night before were starting to tumble through his brain, but in painful shards, scraping and slicing his gray matter. He opened the medicine cabinet, found a bottle of ibuprofen, tried to remember the dosage, and said, screw it, pouring out three or four liquid gels and swallowing them dry.

He closed the cabinet door, saw his reflection again, and recoiled. When had he gotten so old? When had life passed him by? Suddenly he felt as if he were riding a dying pony and everyone else in the world was racing by on thoroughbreds. He knew he'd done something he shouldn't the night before, and he had a vague feeling that whatever it was would come back to haunt him. It was that bad.

Still bleary, his booze-soaked consciousness trying to surface, he nearly fell into the shower, then turned on the spray, the cold needles eventually turning hot. Hands pressed against the plastic stall, he let the water run over his head, clear his mind. Something was wrong. Very, very wrong. Otherwise he wouldn't have passed out . . . oh, man, *how* had he gotten home?

He lathered, smelled the booze still oozing out of his pores, and scrubbed himself and his hair clean. Then he cranked on the handle and the steaming water turned instantly frigid, causing him to suck in his breath and swear a word or two before he turned the damned spray off, grabbed the pink towel hanging by the shower— Michelle's towel, he realized—and dried off.

Michelle.

Crap, that's what had started it all—the fight. He'd found her cell phone and had just been going to recharge it when, because he was suspicious, he'd scrolled through the pictures, texts, and calls. More than a dozen, probably twenty or twenty-five phone calls made to one number, a cell number he recognized as belonging to Barclay Sphinx. Well, that could be explained, right?

Michelle was an actress on his reality show, and though no one other than he and Michelle knew it, she was the reason Barclay Fucking Sphinx had come to Grizzly Falls in the first place. She'd been enamored with the man from the get-go; loved his shows, especially *Tarnished Stars.*

After attending a seminar where he'd spoken, somewhere—Spokane? maybe—and the success of *Big Foot Territory: Oregon!* she'd contacted the producer about a sequel to the show set here, in Grizzly Damned Falls. As it turned out, there was another group of Big Foot enthusiasts north of Missoula and Barclay had been mulling over the idea anyway. Then, lo and behold, Bianca, his very own daughter, had experienced her own Big Foot sighting, one that had ended in the body of a local girl being discovered. What kind of cosmic stroke of luck was that? A gift. From the fates. Not the dead girl, of course, that was a shame, a horrible tragedy, but if anyone was to have found her, it was good fortune that Bianca had stumbled into that creek.

From then on, because of the built-in publicity and hype, Barclay had been interested.

And Luke—Lucky—Pescoli had thought his fortunes were about to change. Through his daughter.

The only trouble was, Luke thought now, as he viewed himself in the mirror and saw his face with its bloodshot eyes, Michelle hadn't just found Barclay an interesting producer or mentor or even stepping-stone to Hollywood, all of which Luke could understand. But oh, no. Michelle, as proven by the pictures on her phone, the late-night calls, and her general disinterest in her husband, had fallen in love and into bed with that loser, scumbag, fucking ass-wipe of a producer!

Michelle!

His Michelle!

The one woman in the world he'd been certain he could trust. She had adored Lucky Pescoli.

Until that son of a douche bag came knocking.

At the thought of it, his blood boiled, and as he shaved off the stubble and eyed his reflection, he hoped that he wasn't seeing just the hint of a jowl beginning on his jawline. He leaned closer to the steamy mirror. And nicked himself.

"Goddamn it!" Luke cried, watching a small dot

of blood bloom just under his lip. He stopped it with a scrap of toilet paper he pinched off from the roll near the toilet. As he did, he remembered the fight with Michelle.

Last night, when he'd returned from Regan's with the news that his ex was in labor, he'd found Michelle dressed for her part in the reality series, that of Regan—how was that for an ironic twist? Then he'd discovered her phone and the incriminating evidence, and that's when the fight had ensued. She'd stormed out and refused to see him when he'd driven up to the set of the reality show.

"It's over," she'd hissed as he'd approached her. She'd been standing near a bank of audio equipment and he'd had to step over cords to get close to her. "I mean it, Luke," she'd warned. "We're through. Got it?" Her eyes had been on fire and her small frame had actually shivered with rage. "Don't you ever come here, to my workplace, again!"

"Your work place? But—"

"Leave. Me. The. Hell. Alone." She'd inched her chin up a fraction. "Don't blow this for me, Luke, and don't blow it for Bianca if she still has any chance here. Just go. I've already talked to a lawyer."

"You've what?" He'd been struck dumb, nearly collapsing. "No! I'm not ready to—"

"Should I call security?" She'd pointed to a burly guy about the size of a mountain, a man who looked like he knew the inside of a cage fight intimately and was watching Luke with eyes buried deep in his skull. With that, she'd turned, leaving Luke physically, possibly permanently.

He'd known that, in part, she was right. He couldn't mess up this opportunity—this gift from heaven—for her or his daughter. Things were already dicey as it was. Bianca was losing out to that lying, fake-faced Lara Haas. A situation that had to be fixed. And quickly.

Rather than risk infuriating Michelle any further or causing a scene, he'd driven into town for the first of several drinks, then bought a bottle and, with a half-hatched plan running through his brain, decided to turn things around.

For all of them.

But now, scraping the last of his beard away around that tiny cut, the memory of what he'd done next rolled through his brain.

Jesus.

He leaned over the sink and immediately puked.

Could anyone ever sleep in a hospital? Between being wokcn up to take vital signs, the noise of other patients and staff, and, of course, a tiny baby in a bassinet right next to her, Regan was certain she hadn't dozed for more than five minutes at a stretch.

Santana had spent the night, rising at dawn from the small couch/ bed built into the wall and dropping a kiss on both her and the baby's heads before he'd left, earlier this morning. She, groggy as hell, had been vaguely aware and had vainly attempted to mumble a quick, "Love you."

That had been over an hour ago. Since then, she'd been woken twice—once by the nursing staff, the other by little Tucker, whom she'd held to her breast and tried to nurse. He was getting the hang of it, and soon, she knew, her milk would come in.

Weird that. Weirder still she'd been offered a lactation nurse to help get him started, a service that hadn't been available at the hospital where Bianca and Jeremy had been born nearly two decades earlier. Through her attempts at slumber, her thoughts, even dreams, had returned to the homicide investigations that had been ongoing, but they seemed almost as if they belonged to another woman as her whole life had shrunken to revolving around the needs of this one tiny baby. Tucker moved in the small bed beside her, made a soft little whimpering noise, then drifted off to sleep again. Regan envied him and was just closing her eyes again when she heard someone enter the room.

"Not now," she said, certain the nurse on the latest shift wanted to take her temperature or blood pressure or God-only-knew-what other vital sign. Whoever it was didn't take the hint. She heard footsteps approach.

She opened one eye and spied her husband, his face drawn, his dark eyes without a hint of his normal sense of humor, staring down at her. "What?" she said, immediately awake, her detective's mind leaping to the worst conclusions possible.

"Bianca didn't come home last night."

"Where did she stay?" She blinked. "Where is she?"

"Don't know."

Don't panic. She's done this before.

"But she went to the shoot, right?"

"Yes. Jeremy left her there, told her to call him if she didn't get a ride home, but she didn't. He assumed she came home, but this morning, after I did the chores at the Long place, I went home, dealt with the dogs, and thought I'd check in on her before I came back here. Her bed hasn't been slept in."

"Then she's with a friend, or went home with Michelle—she was up there, right? Maybe Bianca crashed at Lucky's rather than go home," Regan said, coming up with logical explanations though she was already swinging her feet from the bed.

"I thought so, too. Jeremy and I have already started calling. So far, none of her friends have seen her since a little after midnight last night. What do you think you're doing?"

She was reaching for the handle on the small closet and her clothes. "I'm going to go look for her of course."

"What about the baby?"

The baby! Tucker! For a brief second, she'd been on automatic, had forgotten. She felt a jab of remorse and glanced over at him sleeping so peacefully, unaware of all the dangers in the world, the horrors, the people who would kill innocent girls. "Right. He'll . . . he'll come with me . . ." But as she woke up and her mind cleared, she knew that was impossible.

"Stay, Regan," he said, his face serious. "I'll find her."

"How?"

A nurse hurried into the room. "Is there something I can help with? Mrs. Santana?" She was frowning, sensing trouble.

"No," she said, fear settling deep in her soul. *Bianca is all right. Don't go off the deep end. Just because other girls . . . oh, dear God. She's probably with a friend.*

"I'll start calling. Get Alvarez on it and . . ."

With the nurse still unsure about the situation, standing near the bassinet, Pescoli snagged her phone from the table near her bed and saw movement in the doorway. Her heart did a complete nosedive when she recognized her ex-husband, his face drawn, his eyes red from drink or tears or both. "Luke?" she said, knowing in an instant that the worst had happened. "What—?"

"Forgive me," he whispered, his voice rough.

"For . . . ?" Her heart clutched. *Oh, God.* "Tell

me this doesn't have anything to do with Bianca?" Her voice cracked and she felt as if the earth were shifting on its axis, spiraling to a dark place in space where only evil dwelled.

"It's my fault. It was my idea."

"What?" she nearly screamed, wanting to know, but dreading the worst.

"I set her up. To be kidnapped."

"What? Kidnapped?" She felt as if the world had collapsed. "What the hell are you talking about?"

"Mrs. Santana," the nurse warned, but Luke was talking again.

"It . . . it was to get Barclay Sphinx's attention, to make him want to . . ." His voice faded, his fists balled in frustration. "I was wasted, pissed, upset about . . . a lot of things but I wanted, thought this was her chance—Bianca's—to be something, get a start in Hollywood. So I set it up."

"You bastard! You stupid, idiotic bastard! Girls are dying!" She launched herself then, flying off the bed, landing on the floor in her bare feet, ready to tear him limb from limb. How could he do this? How could he put her daughter, *his* daughter, dammit, *their* daughter at such a risk? "Who? Who has her?" she screamed, taking her first punch as Santana wrapped an arm around her middle and hauled her off her feet.

"Whoa, honey." Santana held her tight. "Slow down."

"I will not! Did you hear what he said? What he did?" Over her husband's shoulder, she yelled, "Who the hell has my daughter and where is she, Luke?"

"That's just it. I don't know."

"Who did you contact?"

"Bryant Tophman."

"Tophman? Why?"

The nurse interjected, "I'm calling security."

"The hell you are," Regan said, "I'm a cop. We *are* security."

"Not here," she said and hurried out as Luke glanced out the window to the morning. His whole face fell. "I knew he'd do it. That Tophman would come through. He . . . sometimes I get weed from him."

"You buy drugs from a kid?" she said, incredulous. "Holy crap and then you, what? Come up with some harebrained scheme to fake kidnap her? Are you insane?"

"No one was supposed to get hurt."

"Was?" she cried, coming unglued. "What do you mean? Is Bianca hurt? For the love of God—"

"No! No! Of course not. I wouldn't put her in danger."

"The hell you didn't."

"Shhh," Santana said, then, still holding his wife, glowered at the man who'd once been her husband. "Slow down and tell us everything you know, you slimy son of a bitch, or I'll kill you myself."

"She'll be all right," Luke said. "She has to be all right."

"Put me down!" Regan demanded, and as Santana dropped her onto the bed, she reached for her phone. With one thumb, she speed-dialed her partner, who answered groggily. "Yeah."

"It's Pescoli."

"I know that."

"Bianca's missing!"

"What?"

"Luke set her up, had her kidnapped by Bryant Tophman." She launched into her story, breaking it down to the bare facts, and when she'd given Alvarez the bullet points, finished with, "I want a BOLO out on Tophman and Bianca. Get a search party. Use those damned Big Foot Believers and Jeffe with his drone. Whatever. Just find my kid," she cried as the baby, finally disturbed, started to whimper and cry. "Oh, honey," she whispered. "You got that, Alvarez?" she said.

"Loud and clear," her partner responded. "There might be one other wrinkle."

"What?"

"Kywin Bell is still MIA. I think he might be with Tophman."

Pescoli's heart turned to stone. The thought of the two muscle-bound thugs, both of whom probably were already involved in the murder of two girls, holding her daughter hostage, curdled her blood with fear. "Get them," she whispered and hung up.

"You bastard," she hissed at her ex-husband. "If anything happens to Bianca!" Her voice broke, and tears of fury and fear stung her eyes. "I swear to you, I will hold you responsible. And I'll kill you."

Santana shook his head. "Nope. I will." To Luke, he said, "That's a promise. Now, get out of here and—"

An obese man in a security uniform strode into the room. "Is there any trouble here?" he asked in a deep voice just as, two steps behind him, Bianca appeared. Her clothes were torn, her face filthy, her eyes round as saucers, and next to the hulking guard, she looked tiny.

Pescoli had never been so glad to see anyone in her life.

"Oh, honey," Pescoli cried, scrambling to get to her daughter, but Bianca wasn't looking at her. Her eyes, narrowed with hatred, were focused on her father.

"Baby," he whispered, tears in his eyes.

"Not anymore," she said, her chin jutting forward, disgust twisting her features. "I'm not your baby anymore." And then she spat on the hospital floor.

EPILOGUE

Two months later

As she stared at her newborn sleeping peacefully in his crib, Pescoli couldn't believe that her maternity leave was nearly over. Soon, within the next few weeks, she would have to decide whether to leave the department, turn in her badge and give up law enforcement, or return to being a homicide detective, which was far more than an eight-to-five job.

As moonlight danced through the open French doors and the hint of autumn rode in on a night breeze, she picked him up and held him close. Her family had expanded and changed. Not only did this little guy need her, but there were other considerations as well.

Bianca.

Ever since she'd returned from her ordeal at the hands of Tophman and Bell, she'd been a changed girl, more like a woman, one who had taken another's life. Kywin Bell had died from his injuries, which were all consistent with Bianca's story of her capture and escape.

Bryant Tophman, who had been found hiding in the forest by Carlton Jeffe's drone that same morning, had been brought to justice by the Big

Foot Believers. Jeffe and Fred Nesmith had delivered him to Alvarez at the station. Tophman was now behind bars, awaiting trial. His story was that Kywin had killed Destiny Montclaire when she'd told him about the baby, but Pescoli wasn't sure that Tophman wasn't involved. Either way, he was facing a long term in jail for his part in covering up the homicide as well as selling all kinds of drugs found in a private stash at his home at the church parsonage. Not to mention the kidnapping and attempted homicide of Bianca. Janie Tophman had quit saying he was a "good boy." Her tune had changed to "Bryant has finally found Jesus." Pescoli wasn't betting on it.

Kip Bell was facing charges for his part of the scheme, in which Lindsay Cronin had died. He'd finally admitted that she'd known about Kywin and Destiny, that Destiny had never considered him her "protector" but had been afraid of him as well as excited by him and wanted to get back at cheating Donny Justison. She hadn't planned it, but she'd ended up getting pregnant.

Lindsay had suspected that Kywin had killed her, and Kip had wanted to make certain his brother didn't go to prison. After Kywin's death, he'd opened up about knowing that his brother had, indeed, killed Destiny and left her in the creek. Kip hadn't known he'd placed her body there and it was just damned bad luck that his prank had gone so bad and he'd chased Bianca straight into the girl's body.

The only true winner in all of this mess was Barclay Sphinx, whose reality show had gained more than its share of ill-gained publicity. The first episode of *Big Foot Territory: Montana!* had aired, and the whole family had watched it together, though Bianca without much interest. The series was still in production, though rumor had it that it might move north of Missoula for the feuding families, and the reward and trailer that Barclay Sphinx had promised never came to fruition. There had been no need. Pescoli had heard that the Big Foot Believers had enjoyed a surge in membership. Mayor Justison, relieved her son wasn't a murderer, was satisfied that she'd put Grizzly Falls on the map and Big Foot Daze had been a roaring success. Pescoli hadn't participated; she'd spent her time here, at their home, with her newborn and other two children.

Tucker was thriving, eating and sleeping and offering up baby smiles, but Bianca was a worry.

Bianca swore she would never forgive Luke despite his repeated attempts at trying to contact her. She didn't want him put in jail, but she refused to deal with him. Though Bianca refused to press charges, the DA and Regan were putting together a case. A strong case. It was only a matter of time. As for Michelle? Who cared? She and Luke were probably divorcing even though her white-hot affair with Barclay Sphinx was rumored to have lost steam.

Pescoli just wished she would disappear.

It was her daughter who concerned her. Bianca had lost interest in school, this, her senior year of high school. Once driven, she now seemed lost. Fortunately, she'd agreed to see a psychologist, but her fun-loving, all-about-me spoiled teenager had disappeared, become a shell of herself, spent her time reading or online. Pescoli couldn't remember the last time Bianca had gone out or even bothered putting on lipstick. Yeah, she was lost.

She needed a mother. Full-time. As did Tucker.

What to do?

Stay home. Be a full-time mother. At least for a while. Until Bianca finds herself. Until Tucker is old enough to enjoy preschool.

Her thoughts drifted back to the Good Feelings Preschool, when Bianca was a toddler. All those innocent babies, all now nearly grown, some now dead, others in prison, still others, like Bianca, forever scarred.

Was that what life was? A series of childhood scars that molded a person into adulthood?

The baby gurgled and opened his eyes to stare up at her with his dark Santana eyes. "You're an angel," she told him as she picked him up and walked him onto the deck. Autumn was in the air, the night crisp, the moon rising. This, living here, was a little slice of heaven. A perfect place to raise a family.

And yet . . . as she gazed across the water, watching the breeze ruffle the surface, she imagined that there was danger lurking in the shadows, a malevolent presence that threatened their peace.

You're being paranoid.

Turning to go inside, she spied her husband walking into the bedroom. Her heart swelled at the sight of him. Yeah, he could still turn her inside out. She slipped through the French doors and walked into his embrace.

"You okay?" he asked.

"Never better."

His smile was familiar, a crooked slash of white against dark skin that caused her heart to skip a beat. He kissed her, then, just a brush of his lips over hers, then did the same to the crown of his son's head.

Yeah, life here was good. Secure. Regan Pescoli had never been happier, but when she turned back to the doors and cast one final glance to the darkness beyond, she felt a tiny chill, like an icy needle pricking the edge of her heart.

Tonight, she locked the door.